Child Abuse

Today's Issues

Child Abuse

Today's Issues

Kimberly A. McCabe

Daniel G. Murphy

CRC Press
Taylor & Francis Group
Boca Raton London New York

CRC Press is an imprint of the
Taylor & Francis Group, an **informa** business

CRC Press
Taylor & Francis Group
6000 Broken Sound Parkway NW, Suite 300
Boca Raton, FL 33487-2742

© 2017 by Taylor & Francis Group, LLC
CRC Press is an imprint of Taylor & Francis Group, an Informa business

No claim to original U.S. Government works

Printed on acid-free paper
Version Date: 20161019

International Standard Book Number-13: 978-1-4987-8041-4 (Paperback)

Visit the Taylor & Francis Web site at
http://www.taylorandfrancis.com

and the CRC Press Web site at
http://www.crcpress.com

For the children who have inspired these stories.
For Whitney, a survivor. KAM
For Susan, my wife and best friend for over 30 years. DGM

CONTENTS

Author   xiii

1   **Introducing Child Abuse**   1

Child Abuse Defined   2
Child Fatalities   3
History of Child Abuse   5
Purpose of This Book   6
References   7

2   **Physical Abuse**   9

Physical Indicators   11
  Bruises   11
  Burns   13
  Fractures   14
  Head/Internal Injuries   15
  Shaken Baby Syndrome   16
  Other Injuries   16
Behavioral Indicators   18
Abusers   21
  Parents or Caretakers   21
    Munchausen Syndrome by Proxy   23
  Siblings   24
  Acquaintances   25
Long-Term Effects   26
Summary   28
Chapter Questions   28
Questions for Further Thought   28
References   29

3 Sexual Abuse 33

Physical Indicators 35
Behavioral Indicators 38
Progression of Sexual Abuse 38
Abusers 41
 Familial Abuse 41
  Father 44
  Mother 45
  Sibling 46
  Other Family Members 47
  Combined Families 48
  Extrafamilial Abuse 48
  Sexual Addicts 49
  Pedophiles 49
  Child Pornography 50
  Sexting 51
  Sex Rings 51
  Child Trafficking 52
Long-Term Consequences 52
Summary 54
Chapter Questions 55
Questions for Further Thought 55
References 55

4 Emotional Abuse 59

Rejection 61
Isolation 63
Terrorizing 64
Ignoring 66
Corruption 68
Property Destruction 70
 Physical and Behavioral Indicators 70
 Abusers 72
 Long-Term Consequences 73
Summary 74
Chapter Questions 75
Questions for Further Thought 75
References 75

5	**Neglect**	**79**
Physical Neglect	82
Medical Neglect	83
Educational Neglect	85
Emotional Neglect	87
Supervision Neglect	88
Indicators of Neglect	89
Physical Indicators	89
Behavioral Indicators	90
Abusers	91
Consequences of Neglect	93
Summary	94
Chapter Questions	95
Questions for Further Thought	95
References	95

6	**Theoretical Explanations for Child Abuse**	**99**
Intraindividual Explanation of Child Abuse	101
Postpartum Psychosis	103
Sociological Theories	104
Feminism	109
Summary	110
Chapter Questions	111
Questions for Further Thought	111
References	111

7	**Child Trafficking**	**113**
Why Children Are Trafficked	117
How Is Trafficking Facilitated?	121
Why Don't Children Leave Their Captors?	122
Why Child Trafficking Continues	123
Legislative Measures	125
Summary	127
Chapter Questions	128
Questions for Further Thought	128
References	128

8   **Child Abuse and Technology**   **131**

Child Pornography   133
   Behavioral Indicators   139
Child Solicitation   139
Cyberbullying   140
   Behavioral Indicators   141
Sexting   142
   Behavioral Indicators   143
Summary   143
Chapter Questions   144
Questions for Further Thought   145
References   145

9   **Criminal Justice Responses to Today's Child Abuse**   **149**

Child Savers Movement   150
Progressive Era   150
The 1974 Juvenile Justice Delinquency Prevention Act   151
Sex Offender Registration   152
Age of Consent   153
HIV/STD Testing   155
Mandatory Reporting Laws   155
   Statute of Limitations   158
Missing and Exploited Children   159
AMBER Alert   160
Courts   161
Juvenile and Adult Court   161
Criminal Court   162
Incarceration   163
Civil Commitment Orders   163
Key Figures in Child Abuse   164
Mental Health   164
Law Enforcement   165
CPS   168
Court Appointed Special Advocates   169
   Guardian ad Litem   169
   Victim Advocate   169
   Forensic Nurse   170
   Foster Care   170

Summary   171
Chapter Questions   171
Questions for Further Thought   172
References   172

**Appendix A: Human Trafficking—Country Demographics
as Related to Tier Classification**   **175**

**Appendix B: Internet Crimes Against Children, 2008 and
2014 (Abridged Report)**   **179**

**Appendix C: Contact Information for Child Abuse
Organizations**   **183**

Index   **191**

AUTHOR

Kimberly A. McCabe, PhD, is a professor of criminology at Lynchburg College in Lynchburg, Virginia. Her research interests include law enforcement, child victimization, and human trafficking. Along with multiple articles and book chapters, she is the author of four books related to child abuse and neglect: *Child Abuse and the Criminal Justice System* (2003), *School Violence, the Media, and Criminal Justice Responses* (2005), *The Trafficking of Persons. National and International Responses* (2008), and *Sex Trafficking. A Global Perspective* (2011).

Daniel G. Murphy, M.J.A., is an instructor of criminology at Lynchburg College in Lynchburg, Virginia. His research interests include child abuse, victimization, and juvenile justice. Prior to teaching, he served as a police officer in New England for 21 years where he specialized in the investigations of child exploitation.

CHAPTER 1

Introducing Child Abuse

Our government has a role in the protection of children. The Child Abuse Prevention and Treatment Act of 2010, originally signed into law on January 31, 1974, is one of the most significant pieces of legislation to guide agencies, both nationally and internationally, in the protection of children.

In 2013, Child Protective Services in the United States received over 3 million referrals of possible cases of child abuse involving over 6 million children (Children's Bureau 2014). International estimates of child abuse include over 500 million known cases of abused or neglected children (UNICEF 2012). Whether the information is national or international, the abuse of children creates consequences not only for the child but also for the society. In the United States, approximately 1600 children die each year as a result of abuse or neglect at a rate of nearly 2 children per 100,000 children in the national population. Internationally, the number of child fatalities due to maltreatment is unknown; however, estimates suggest that the number of incidents is significant. Most child maltreatment deaths result from physical abuse or neglect. Historically, common perpetrators of child maltreatment deaths included fathers, mothers, and mothers' boyfriends. Currently, *friends* met within the online community are now often included as common perpetrators; however, in general, perpetrators of child abuse and neglect still include fathers, mothers, boyfriends, siblings, and other family members with the majority of the cases of child abuse perpetrated by someone known and close to the child. Hence, *stranger danger* is, for the most part, a myth, and although the phrase is simple and rhythmic for ease of memory, it often leaves children with the notion that only strangers will hurt them.

Developed countries such as the United States and the United Kingdom have been active in addressing child abuse. Unfortunately, these proactive approaches have been limited or nonexistent for some parts of the countries and in many countries outside the United States or United Kingdom. In particular, for many individuals within some countries, children are still viewed as property, and, as property, they are often unprotected against their *owners* and without the privilege of government protection. This is the reality for child abuse at the international level.

Examples of child abuse are found and described in many historical texts. In the Old Testament, where children were considered the property of their father, Abraham intended to sacrifice his son Isaac. Again, in the Hebrew Bible, the Pharaoh of Egypt ordered the death of all male infants in an attempt to protect the position and power of his own throne. In addition, after fleeing his biblical home, Lot had sexual relations with both of his daughters. Finally, within Mosaic laws, child sacrifices were prohibited; thus, one must acknowledge that, as laws exist to limit or prohibit an action, the action of child sacrifice was not uncommon within the time period.

In ancient Greek society, pederasty was socially recognized as the sexual relationship between an adult male and a young (usually early teen) male. In these societies, age was not a factor, only consent.

In the Victorian era, sex with a child prostitute was allowed. This child-to-adult sexual activity was often viewed as a necessary evil as it satisfied a man's desire for sex without burdening his wife (Malinowski 1927).

Finally, in early American colonies, girls as young as nine were married to men with parental or, in the absence of parents, community consent. Today, children are abused through a variety of modes to include sex and labor trafficking (McCabe and Manian 2011; McCabe 2008).

☐ Child Abuse Defined

In general, child abuse is the maltreatment of our children. Specifically, the phrase child abuse refers to victimizations that are generally divided into four categories: (1) physical abuse, (2) sexual abuse, (3) emotional abuse, and (4) neglect. Children may be the victims of one type or all four types of abuse; thus, child abuse rarely refers to a mutually exclusive category of abuse. The definitions related to this book are *physical abuse*—the nonaccidental injury of a child by a person or a caretaker (Crosson-Tower 2010); *sexual abuse*—the sexual exploitation of or sexual activities with a child (McCabe 2003); *emotional abuse*—a pattern of psychologically destructive behavior targeted toward a child (Garbarino et al. 1986); *neglect*—the failure by a caretaker to provide for a child's basic needs of survival (Bartollas 2000); *child trafficking*—the recruitment, transfer, harboring, or receipt of a child for sex or labor by threat or use of force (McCabe 2008); and *age of consent*—the age at which a person is considered to be competent to consent to sexual activity.

☐ Child Fatalities

The most rare yet most serious outcome of child abuse and neglect is the death of a child or a child fatality. In the United States, there are approximately four child deaths per day at the hands of their abusers (Children's Bureau 2014). In the majority of those cases, the abuser is a family member. In addition, children who are abused are more likely to later take their own life or commit suicide; hence, child abuse has not only a direct causal relation with child fatalities but also an indirect relationship with child fatalities.

This text is dedicated to the issues of child abuse and neglect. However, for this text to not first address the most tragic of consequences in child abuse—child fatalities—would be a mistake for all who are interested in eliminating child abuse. Thus, child fatalities are discussed briefly. For clarity, a child fatality is defined as the outcome of death for a child caused by an injury to the child or resulting from the physical abuse or neglect of that child and may include injuries by the abuser or the child.

In the United States and other developed countries where attempts to protect and support the rights of children have been in place for decades, a child fatality from abuse seems unlikely. However, child fatalities occur every day. In the United States, as is the case everywhere, younger children are the most vulnerable to death from abuse and neglect. In fact, 70% of child fatalities in the United States are children under the age of three (Children's Bureau 2014). For most of these young victims, neglect is identified as the cause of death.

The abusers of these young victims, in most cases, are the primary caregivers or the mothers. This stands to reason as very young children are rarely outside of the care of their mother or primary caregiver. Thus, child fatalities of the very young are often the result of opportunity, and, by proximity to the child, the opportunity is for the mother.

As the child ages, the cause of death for these child fatality victims often shifts from neglect to physical abuse. In addition, as the child ages, the father or both parents are more likely to be included among the list of the abuser(s). Estimates suggest that at least 80% of the cases of child fatalities involve a parent(s) as the abuser(s) (Children's Bureau 2014). In addition, approximately 60% of the victims of child fatalities are male, leaving one to wonder if socialization has left American society with the notion of interacting more gently with female children.

The majority of child fatalities are classified as a result of either acute maltreatment or chronic maltreatment. Fatalities that result from a specific incident of abuse or neglect are considered cases of acute maltreatment. Fatalities that resulted from injuries or neglect over an extended period of time are considered chronic maltreatment (Brandon et al. 2014). In other words, child fatalities may result from abuse over time or one incident of victimization. In addition, and increasingly more common, a child fatality may be the outcome of a self-inflicted injury or action. In considering the cases of child fatalities, which result from neglect over time, many involve starvation. Battered child syndrome is also a type of chronic maltreatment. Unfortunately, in many cases of child fatalities from chronic child abuse, the abuse did not continue unnoticed. Estimates suggest that approximately 40% of all child fatalities involve chronic maltreatment that was known to either the medical community or Child Protective Services (Walsch 2005).

When considering the cases of child fatalities that occur as a result of one incident of victimization or acute maltreatment, the incident is often a result of physical abuse and is oftentimes categorized as shaken baby syndrome or Munchausen syndrome by proxy. For the younger child fatality victims, the child's brain is injured from violent shaking (shaken baby), or the child dies from apnea/smothering or starvation (Munchausen). Shaken baby, Munchausen, and battered child are all discussed in detail in Chapter 2.

For the older victims of child fatalities, physical abuse often occurs in the form of punches, kicks, and strikes with a weapon by their abuser. However, there are cases of child fatalities that result from specific victimizations such as child trafficking for internal organs (Vinkovic 2010; McCabe 2008), which are also discussed later in this text.

Finally, child fatalities often occur at the hands of the child. Although these statistics are rarely counted in the official child abuse numbers, suicide by a child victim of abuse or neglect is not uncommon (Tischler et al. 2007). Nationally, suicide is the second leading cause of death for children ages 10–18 in the United States. As far as the demographic characteristics of child suicide victims are concerned, the majority is male, and the majority suffers from a mental or addictive disorder. In addition, children who commit suicide are often loners, suffer low self-esteem, have a close relative who also committed suicide, and may identify themselves as a part of the lesbian, gay, bisexual, and transgender community. In fact, rates suggest that 1 out of 100,000 children commit suicide annually. Many reasons for these suicides include child abuse and neglect (McCabe 2003). In fact, over time, children from dysfunctional homes, with a history of child abuse, or negative school experiences such as bullying (also discussed later in this text) are at a higher risk for suicide. Unfortunately, as these young individuals have survived the sexual or physical abuse of their childhood, their decisions to commit suicide are not often identified as an outcome of child abuse. Regardless of when the abuse occurs within the child's life, child fatalities, the most serious of outcomes, are an important aspect of child abuse.

☐ History of Child Abuse

Plato suggested that children with physical or mental handicaps would only weaken the species and urged parents to kill, and dispose of in secret, their defective children (Wallace 1999). In 17th-century Germany, infants were thrown into pools of water to determine their strength or worthiness; infants who did not surface were not rescued (Damme 1978). In England, the bodies of children have been found buried in foundational landmarks such as the London Bridge (Sorel 1984). Today, the remains of children are still being found in landfills and in trash containers across the world, especially in countries such as China, which at one time placed severe tax penalties on families producing multiple children (Crosson-Tower 2010). Hence, child abuse has existed throughout history and continues today.

The history of child abuse in America can be studied in terms of three time periods. The first time period started from early colonial America to a young girl in New York named Mary Ellen Wilson and the 1875 New York Society for the Prevention of Cruelty to Children (NYSPCC). The second time period spans from 1875 to the early 1960s. The third time period began in 1962 and includes today (Myers 2010). Prior to 1875, children were simply the property of their parents without protection under the laws of the country unless there was a case of horrendous abuse. In 1874, horrendous abuse became front stage in America.

Mary Ellen Wilson was an eight-year-old girl in New York City in 1874. She was beaten and starved by her guardians on a regular basis.

This abuse continued, and there were no legal means of protection for Mary Ellen (Riis 1892). When legal authorities finally intervened, they did so, however, without child protective legislation but under the umbrella of Prevention of Cruelty to Animals. In 1875, the NYSPCC and the Prevention of Cruelty to Children Act of 1889 was established to protect children from abuse and neglect. Although legal efforts to end child abuse are discussed later in this text, this was the first attempt from any legal system in any country to protect children from abuse. Over the following years, there were very few cases prosecuted under the Prevention of Cruelty to Children Act; however, this legislative action became the cornerstone for today's actions to end child abuse both nationally and internationally.

The second phase in the history of US child abuse entails not only the first legislative act to reduce child abuse but also the establishment of nongovernmental child-protective societies (Myers 2010) and courts concerned with delinquent children and cases of child abuse and neglect (i.e., juvenile courts). In addition, it was during this time period that a shift occurred from nongovernmental organizations that focused on reducing child abuse to government agencies that focused on child abuse.

Finally, the third time period (1962+) has focused on enacting laws to prevent child abuse, as well as education and awareness efforts to reduce a child's likelihood of victimization. Most recently, those efforts have included a variety of foci to include Internet Crimes Against Children and child trafficking (both discussed in Chapters 7 and 8).

In 1982, Congress resolved that June 6–12 should be designated as the first National Child Abuse Prevention Week. In 1983, President Reagan proclaimed April to be the first National Child Abuse Prevention Month. April continues to be identified as the month dedicated to preventing child abuse.

☐ Purpose of This Book

The purpose of this book is to attempt to explore child abuse from a contemporary perspective in terms of its multiple elements, victims, and criminal justice responses. This text will (1) begin to address the needs of those studying child abuse from a cultural perspective, (2) provide a general profile of today's perpetrators of child abuse, as well as conditions that may facilitate the abuse, (3) provide information on the current modes of child abuse, (4) provide discussions on the long-term consequences for adult victims of child abuse, and (5) provide details in terms of criminal justice responses to child abuse. The examples provided throughout this text are based upon real cases of child abuse; however, the names of the child victims have been changed.

This text is organized to provide straightforward information on each category of abuse: *Chapters 2, 3,* and *4*—physical abuse, sexual abuse, and emotional abuse, respectively, including statistics, physical indicators, behavioral indicators, a discussion on abusers, and long-term consequences on adult victims of child abuse; *Chapter 5*—neglect to include statistics of neglect and the information on the categories of neglect, conditions that facilitate physical and behavioral indicators of child neglect, a discussion on abusers, and long-term consequences on adult victims of childhood neglect; *Chapter 6*—theoretical explanations for child abuse; *Chapter 7*—child trafficking to include statistics on trafficking, the reasons for and factors facilitating child trafficking, and a discussion on traffickers; *Chapter 8*—child abuse and technology to include discussions on individuals who utilize technology to abuse children and the roles of the Internet, cyberbullying, sexting, and child pornography; and *Chapter 9*—criminal justice responses to today's child abuse to include current legislative actions. At the end of Chapters 2 through 9 are questions formulated from the materials presented within the chapter, as well as questions to initiate further discussions on the topics.

In summary, this text not only provides information on child abuse and neglect in today's world but also provides its readers a foundation in child abuse and neglect to further the protection of children.

☐ References

Bartollas, C. 2000. *Juvenile Delinquency* (5th ed.). Boston: Allyn and Bacon.

Brandon, M., Bailey, S., Belderson, P., and Larsson, B. 2014. The role of neglect in child fatalities and serious injury. *Child Abuse Review*, 23(4), 235–245.

Children's Bureau. 2014. *Child Maltreatment 2013*. Washington, D.C.: US Department of Health and Human Services, Administration for Children and Families.

Crosson-Tower, C. 2010. *Understanding Child Abuse and Neglect* (8th ed.). Boston: Allyn and Bacon.

Damme, C. 1978. The worth of an infant under law. *Medical History*, 22(1), 1–24.

Garbarino, J., Guttman, E., and Seeley, J. W. 1986. *The Psychologically Battered Child*. San Francisco: Jossey-Bass.

Malinowski, B. 1927. *Sex and Repression in Savage Society*. London: Routledge and Kegan Paul.

McCabe, K. 2003. *Child Abuse and the Criminal Justice System*. New York: Peter Lang.

McCabe, K. 2008. *The Trafficking of Persons: National and International Responses*. New York: Peter Lang.

McCabe, K. and Manian, S. 2011. *Sex Trafficking: A Global Perspective*. Lanham, MD: Rowman and Littlefield/Lexington Books.

Myers, J. 2010. *The History of Child Protection in America*. Sacramento, CA: University of the Pacific.

Riis, J. 1892. *The Children of the Poor*. London: Sampson Low, Marston & Co.

Sorel, N. 1984. *Ever Since Eve: Personal Reflections on Childbirth*. New York: Oxford University Press.

Tischler, C., Reiss, N. and Rhodes, A. 2007. Suicidal behavior in children younger than 12: A diagnostic challenge for emergency personnel. *Academic Emergency Medicine*, 14(9), 810–818.

UNICEF. 2012. *Children in the Urban World: The State of the World's Children 2012*. New York: United Nations Children's Fund.

Vinkovic, M. 2010. The unbroken marriage—Trafficking and child labor in Europe. *Journal of Money Laundering Control*, 13(2), 87–102.

Wallace, H. 1999. *Family Violence: Legal, Medical, and Social Perspectives* (2nd ed.). Boston: Allyn and Bacon.

Walsch, B. 2005. *Investigating Child Fatalities: Portable Guides to Investigating Child Abuse*. Washington, D.C.: Office of Justice Programs. Office of Juvenile Justice and Delinquency Prevention.

CHAPTER

Physical Abuse

Matthew is a grown man with a 4-centimeter scar at the corner of his mouth. When Matthew was five, his father, upset over something he said, hit him across the face with a beer bottle.

Although the 1974 Child Abuse Prevention and Treatment Act (CAPTA) (42U.S.C.A§5106g), amended by the CAPTA Reauthorization Act of 2010 (hereafter Child Abuse Prevention and Treatment Act of 2010), defines child abuse and neglect, it does not provide a specific definition for child physical abuse. Therefore, for the purpose of this chapter, child physical abuse is defined as a nonaccidental physical injury that results from punching, beating, kicking, slapping, biting, shaking, throwing, stabbing, choking, hitting, burning, or otherwise harming a child by a parent or other person who has the responsibility of the care of that child (Child Welfare Information Gateway 2013). Child physical abuse occurs as both acute maltreatment and chronic maltreatment. It is acknowledged that some of the actions listed under the definition of child physical abuse (e.g., slapping or hitting) are often associated with spanking as forms of corporal punishment in child rearing; however, this chapter is not focused on spanking as a form of discipline, nor is this chapter focused on corporal punishment, but rather this chapter focuses on child physical abuse from a legal perspective. Again, child abuse is defined as the action or failure to act, on the part of a caretaker, which results in an injury to a child.

Controversies continue to be debated on the use of corporal punishment for corrective purposes (Baumrind et al. 2002) as many researchers assert that physical punishment is associated with adverse outcomes such as mental illness, long-term injury, and violence across the lifetime (Afifi et al. 2013). This chapter provides information of physical abuse as a recognized category of child abuse.

In the United States, from 2008 to 2013, the overall rate of child victimization declined from 9.5 to 9.1 per 1000 children in the population (Children's Bureau 2014). This result equates to approximately 30,000 fewer victims of child abuse. Some researchers, attempting to explain this decline, have offered explanations to include better parenting, more resources for parents, and a reduction in the stigma of children as victims of child abuse, thus better awareness by the community. Other researchers have simply referred to demographics and declines in birthrates, thus fewer children to abuse. However, in 2013, there were still approximately 680,000 incidents of child abuse reported in the United States (Children's Bureau 2014). Of those cases, approximately 20% were cases of physical abuse, and, of those cases, approximately 25% were *not* first-time (acute maltreatment) cases.

Child abuse is not exclusively an American problem. When considering countries in the regions of Africa, the Middle East, Asia, and Latin America, reports indicate that at least 80% of the children between the ages of 2 and 14 have experienced violent discipline (UNICEF 2012). In war-torn countries such as Afghanistan, with one of the highest mortality rates in the world, women and children are viewed as the property of the male heads of the households to treat as they see fit (Bush 2010). This social structure results in not only many incidents of child maltreatment in terms of physical abuse but also increases in domestic violence.

In addition, in countries such as India, with approximately 18 million people living in bondage and many of these individuals under the age of 18, child maltreatment is not unusual (Verma 2010). Children are sold for sex, sold for labor, and physically abused throughout their lifetimes. Therefore, child abuse is everyone's problem.

As with many types of victimization, the ages of victims vary by action. However, most often, the child victims of physical abuse are very young. In considering child physical abuse in the United States, approximately 25% of the victims are under the age of 3. In fact, approximately 15% are under the age of 2. In addition, approximately 35% of the victims are between the ages of 3 and 8, approximately 30% of the victims are between the ages of 9 and 14, and approximately 10% of the victims are between the ages of 15 and 17. Therefore, the likelihood of childhood physical abuse decreases with the age of the child. Historically, research has suggested that certain demographic characteristics of a child are risk factors for physical abuse (USDHHS 2008; Friedrick and Boriskin 1976). However, age is just one variable of risk.

Another common demographic characteristic is gender in that more of the child victims of reported cases of severe physical abuse in the United States are male as opposed to female (McCabe 2003). Whether abuse is the result of attempting to *toughen up* the little boy or the gentler treatment of the parent's *baby girl*, boys are more likely the victim of physical abuse.

Another more common characteristic of child victims of physical abuse is a physical or mental disability. In particular, children with multiple disabilities are more likely victims of child abuse than children without disabilities (Ammerman 1991; White et al. 1987). Therefore, in considering age and disabilities, a young child with a severe behavioral or physical impairment is more at risk for physical abuse.

☐ Physical Indicators

As with any crime scene, physical evidence often provides the most attestation of the criminal action. This remains true in documenting cases of child physical abuse as the physical evidence remains on the child. For most children, this physical evidence is in the form of bruises, burns, cuts, and other injuries. This evidence not only documents abuse but, in many cases, also identifies chronic maltreatment and the mode and method of injury.

Bruises

A bruise is defined as evidence of an injury that is caused by a bleeding of capillaries under the skin. In cases of child abuse, this bleeding is the result of some external force that is placed upon the skin of the child. Of course, it is acknowledged that all children acquire bruises; however, the color, the shape, and the location of bruises are indicators of a potential case of child physical abuse (McCabe 2003; McNeese and Hebeler 1977). In other words, a bruise located behind a child's kneecap may be considered suspicious as most children do not receive injuries to the back of the knee from a fall.

In considering the color of a bruise, keep in mind that the color of a bruise varies based upon several conditions to include the type of external force that caused the bruise, the age of the bruise, and (sometimes overlooked) the complexion of the child. Specifically, a blue-colored bruise on a light-skinned individual, assuming a normal nutritional state of the child, is usually between 6 and 12 hours old (Davis 1982). On the same child, a bruise that is black or purple is usually about 12 to 24 hours old. Finally, on the same child, a bruise that is pale green or yellow is usually over five days old (Davis 1982). On a child with darker skin, a bruise may be harder to detect, and, in some cases, a mark that appears to be a bruise may in fact be a birthmark (e.g., Mongolian blue spots). However, a child who has multiple bruises with varying shades of color may be a victim of chronic maltreatment in terms of physical abuse.

Mongolian blue spots are common among children who are of Asian, Native American, Hispanic, or African descent. They are usually blue or blue-gray and are generally located on the buttocks or lower back; however, some have been identified as located on the arms or legs.

The shape of a bruise will often indicate the type of external force (or weapon) used on the skin of the child. Bruises, in some cases, will outline the shape of a hand or the fingers, the space between the fingers of an open hand, a fist or knuckles, or some sort of a paddle. Bruises that occur in a linear pattern often indicate the use of a belt, a whip, or an old-fashioned *switch* (a small tree branch), as made commonly known in the recent child abuse case involving football's Adrian Peterson and his use of a switch on his son as a means of discipline. Bruises in the pattern of a small circle may indicate a ring pattern and abuse by a fist. Bruises that are oval shaped, such as in a loop formation, may indicate the use of a cord such an extension cord or the cord to an iron cord. Multiple bruises of varying shapes and colors are potential indicators of patterns of physical abuse or chronic physical abuse.

Jennifer (age 18) agrees to babysit her neighbor's six-month-old baby. Jennifer is shocked when she discovers that the baby she is caring for has what appears to be severe bruising over the child's buttocks. Jennifer contacts social services who, in turn, notified the family court system that they are placing the child into protective custody and will schedule an emergency custody hearing in court the following morning. The parents are devastated to learn that their child has been taken into protective custody and that they are suspected of physical abuse. A physical examination was conducted at a local hospital where it was determined that the suspected bruising was not caused by abuse but rather a birthmark.

The location of a bruise must be considered. It is expected that children, especially toddlers, will get bruises on the front of their legs, their elbows, and other parts of their body that come in contact with the ground in a fall; however, bruises in other locations, such as the back of the legs, the ears, the neck, and the forearms and/or upper arms, may be worthy of inspection (Crosson-Tower 2010; McCabe 2003). A child who falls, just as is the case with an adult who falls, will attempt to catch himself or herself with his or her hands or knees; therefore, bruises on the thighs or on areas not used in defensive postures are often a cause for concern. In addition, bruises on the backs of the legs may indicate that a child has been hit from behind. A bruise on the earlobe may indicate that the child has been grabbed by the ear. A bruise on the neck may indicate an attempt at strangulation. And a bruise on the upper arm or forearm may indicate that a child has been grabbed or held against his or her will (Crosson-Tower 2010). Again, multiple bruises of varying shapes, colors, and locations on the body may indicate child physical abuse. Individuals who note bruises in unusual locations on a child's body should follow up with questions concerning the injury.

Burns

A burn is the potential result of exposure to heat or fire by intent, accident, or negligence. Burns from intent or negligence are the concern in child abuse. Burns are defined in terms of first degree, second degree, and third degree, depending on how many layers of skin are burned with a first-degree burn the least serious. Burns to children are generally caused by heat or friction. With burns from abuse, there is the concern not only for the initial burn but also for the potential for infection to the untreated burned area(s) as related to child physical abuse.

Burns can result in permanent injury or the death of the child (Pressel 2000). These injuries may be in the shapes of the sources such as irons, curling irons, or range-top burners. Burns that leave centimeter-long diameters may indicate cigarette burns (Pressel 2000), and, those a bit larger, but still round, may indicate the use of a cigarette lighter such as the lighters often found within a vehicle. Scald marks on the hands, feet, or buttocks that have a glove or mitten appearance usually indicate a deliberate immersion of the child in hot water. Additionally, splash burns or burns on areas not usually exposed in accidental spills such as the bottom of the feet or the back may also suggest physical abuse.

In the case of some burns, one must also consider the family background as many cultures and/or religions may practice the burning of certain areas of the body either as a ritual or a component of a cultural medicinal practice (e.g., coining or cupping). In these cases, knowledge of cultural practices can aid in the communications of other medical practices and avoid accusations of child physical abuse. Again, with bruises, one must consider the location of the bruise, the size and color of the bruise, the source of the bruise, and the explanation of the injury before concluding physical abuse.

Cupping is an ancient form of oriental medicine in which cups or glass rods are heated to produce suction to either *draw out* impurities or to mobilize blood flow.

William (age 6) is taken to the hospital by his mother Linda, who states that her son accidently burned himself while stepping into the bathtub without checking the temperature of the water. Linda is crying when she states that she wished she had checked the water before her son entered the tub. She also states that she was in the adjoining room and ran to William's aid once she heard him cry for help. A medical examination of the child revealed that these second-degree burns (although severe) were limited to both feet and ankles. Were these burns accidental or do the facts of this scenario raise suspicion of abuse?

Fractures

For this discussion, a fracture is defined simply as a broken bone. A fracture is treated by aligning the broken bone to allow it to regenerate or heal. The presence of fractures, especially in infants, may be a sign of physical abuse (Crosson-Tower 2010). When investigating these injuries, one must review both the location and extent of the injury. The abused child may be subjected to multiple fractures at one time or single fractures over several time periods. Types of fractures include spiral fractures, greenstick fractures, subperiosteal fractures, and dislocations (Crosson-Tower 2010).

Children break bones in accidents; however, fractures are also very common in cases of physical abuse. In cases where there is a history of child abuse, multiple fractures from different incidents may be present. One type of fracture, the spiral fracture, is very common in child abuse (McCabe 2003). In this type of injury, the abuser most often causes the fracture to the bone by using a twisting motion or a sudden jerk on the child's arm or leg. It is extremely rare for spiral fractures to occur in children under the age of three as their bones are much more limber than those of older children or adults (Wallace 1999). Spiral fractures are often direct indicators of child physical abuse and should be discussed immediately.

Another type of fracture that may occur in a case of physical abuse is a greenstick fracture. In this type of injury, one side of the bone is broken, while the other side is bent (Faller and Ziefert 1981). This type of injury might occur if a child were struck suddenly and with great force on one side of a bone located in an area such as the lower leg. This type of fracture is common in accidents, but it also often present in cases of child physical abuse.

A subperiosteal fracture is a broken bone without a resulting change in its contour and may heal with only calcium deposits remaining around the break as signs of a previous injury (Faller and Ziefert 1981). These injuries are also very common in cases of child abuse. Unfortunately, with a subperiosteal fracture, the injury is usually discovered by accident when treating another physical injury or by a physician attempting to establish a pattern of physical abuse (McCabe 2003).

Finally, a *dislocation* is a fracture in which the bone is separated from its joint. Dislocations may occur by accident (often in sports) or in cases of physical abuse. These cases of abuse are likely to occur when the abuser suddenly grabs the child by the arm while the child is attempting to get away from the abuser (Faller and Ziefert 1981). Investigators examining fractures of any kind for evidence of physical abuse must carefully consider the explanation of the incident by the caregiver before declaring a case of child abuse as not all fractures, even in an unusual location, are caused by abuse. However, a fracture can be an indicator of physical abuse; investigators must consider the possibility that a child's fractures may be the result of a medical condition such as the rare condition of osteogenesis imperfecta, commonly referred to as brittle bone disease. Osteogenesis imperfecta is a genetic disorder creating fragile bones in children and thus increasing the risk of broken bones (Osteogenesis Imperfecta Foundation 2014). Again, with broken bones, one must consider the location, the history, and the explanation for the injury prior to alleging child physical abuse.

Head/Internal Injuries

In head or internal injuries, there are many possible outcomes resulting from abuse. Although head injuries occur in all children, infants are especially vulnerable to this form of child abuse (Crosson-Tower 2010; McCabe 2003). Children with injuries to the top of the head, which would not have occurred in a *typical* fall, are of special concern as, in these cases, an outside force (or person) was involved in the infliction of the injury.

Physically abused children may also experience internal injuries such as a ruptured spleen, a kidney or bladder injury, or an injury to the pancreas, such as would occur in the event of applied force such as a fist to that area of the body (Crosson-Tower 2010; McCabe 2003). In addition to injuries from trauma, abused children may also experience damage to internal organs from intentional dehydration and/or poisoning. Unfortunately, for these most severe types of internal injuries, often, only trained medical professionals can detect the abuse and can prevent these abuses from resulting in death.

Shaken Baby Syndrome

Shaken baby syndrome (SBS) results from violently shaking a child causing the brain to slam against the skull from side to side, which can cause brain damage, blindness, paralysis, seizures, and death (Gosselin 2010). Infants are particularly vulnerable to SBS as their head is large compared to their rest of their body, and their neck muscles are weakened and cannot provide adequate support for the head. Annually, 1000–3000 children are diagnosed with SBS in the United States. Approximately 100 of those SBS children will die. In most cases (80%), the perpetrators of SBS are male and are either related to the child or in a relationship with the child's mother (Seymour et al. 2002). Thus, SBS, an action that causes damage to a child's brain, is more common than many individuals realize.

Other Injuries

Although bruises, burns, and fractures are probably the most common signs of physical abuse, other types of injuries are indicators of child abuse. In particular, lacerations, cuts and stab wounds, human bites, loss of teeth, bald spots on the head, and firearm injuries are also potential indicators of child physical abuse. In fact, cuts, stabs, and human bites are prime indicators of not only physical abuse but also a propensity of some individual toward extreme violence (McCabe 2003). In cases such as these, the child is at high risk for not only injury and further abuse but also death.

> Charlotte is in a relationship with Emmanuel. They currently reside together. Charlotte has a seven-month-old baby (Alyssa). Although Emmanuel is not the biological father, he cares for this child while Charlotte goes to work. Alyssa is teething and is crying throughout the day as the baby's teeth are beginning to erupt. Emmanuel tries to comfort Alyssa but becomes frustrated as she continues to cry. As Emmanuel's frustration grows, he becomes overwhelmed and focuses his anger toward the baby. He aggressively shakes the baby back and forth when he can no longer deal with the crying. He shortly discovers that the baby is no longer crying and appears lethargic. Charlotte and Emmanuel are both concerned with the changes in the baby's demeanor and seek medical attention. Medical personnel report that Alyssa is suffering from intracerebral hemorrhage (bleeding of the brain).

As with the other more common injuries, there are three elements to consider when alleging child physical abuse by documenting other less common indicators. Those elements are (1) the location of the injury, (2) the history of the injury, and (3) the treatment (or nontreatment) of the injury. For example, the location of a cut may provide information on its cause. It is expected that during normal daily play, children will obtain cuts and scratches on their knees, elbows, and hands; however, cuts or lacerations on the palms of their hands, or the undersides of their forearms, may be defensive cuts and may have been acquired in a hands-and-arms-over-the-face position to prevent injury to the face (McCabe 2003).

Today, as many perpetrators of child abuse are now aware of the consequences of being identified, lacerations to the bottom of the feet and other areas of the body normally covered by clothing during the school day are not unusual. A child who has multiple cuts on his or her body, especially those cuts that differ in age and healing, may be a child with a history of physical abuse. A laceration left untreated will most often leave a larger scar than those lacerations that were treated. A child with a history of untreated lacerations may be a victim of physical abuse. In addition, one must consider the fact that the child (especially if a teen or preteen) is injuring themselves through cutting, as is discussed in Chapter 3. However, whether lacerations are self-inflicted or from an abuser, these injuries may indicate abuse.

Determining child physical abuse is probably the easiest form of abuse to document for both medical and criminal justice practitioners; however, it is not a simple task. Children, at many times over their young lives, may experience injuries consistent with physical abuse. Before the assertion of child physical abuse is made, a good investigator considers both the child's and the caretaker's explanations for the injuries and the reasonableness of those explanations.

☐ Behavioral Indicators

In some cases of physical abuse, especially in cases of child self-harm, the physical injuries go undetected. In those cases, the behavioral indicators are the most visible clues of abuse. These behavioral indicators of child physical abuse may be different in each child; however, there are certain common behaviors that are seen more often in children with a history of physical abuse than in children without such a history. Those symptoms vary to include extreme behaviors such as aggressiveness with others or directed at themselves, withdrawn personalities, poor social relations with peers and adults, and difficulties in academic learning (Wallace 1999). Although these symptoms do not always indicate physical abuse, children who display multiple behavioral indicators may be victims of physical abuse.

In addition, aggressive behaviors such as cruelty toward others and self, vandalism of property, stealing or shoplifting, and fire starting may all be behavioral indicators of child physical abuse. These behaviors, which oftentimes are not addressed until the child is cycled into the juvenile justice system, may not be detected in time for an early intervention into the abuse (McCabe and Martin 2005). Actions included under the label of cruelty toward others include pushing, shoving, hitting, and other behaviors such as biting. In many cases, children who are physically abused or dominated by a caretaker feel the need to dominate others (Jennings et al. 2014). Thus, victims of child physical abuse may also be perpetrators of child abuse against peers. If the aggression by an abused child is not toward others, many victims of child physical abuse will turn their need for destruction toward themselves. The most common action of self-destruction, especially for teens, is called *cutting* and involves the child cutting themselves, most often, on their forearms. In many cases, cutting is perceived as a way for the child to gain attention; however, only a very small percentage of children or teens actually cut themselves simply for attention (Lahey 2014). In reality, most victims of abuse cut themselves as a coping mechanism for achieving calmness. As strange as this may seem, children who are victims of child physical abuse state that they often feel that this type of self-inflicted pain actually makes them feel better. In fact, children who cut themselves often report feeling a sense of power and control (McCabe and Martin 2005). Not only are they able to determine the amount of cutting inflicted upon their bodies, but they are also able to control their responses to the pain levels of the self-inflicted injuries.

Destructive behaviors such as vandalism, stealing from others, and shoplifting are all characteristics of conduct disorders and are also often behavioral indicators of child physical abuse. Vandalism, or the destruction of another's property, is often the outlet for an abused child's anger. By destroying the property of an abuser or the property of a peer, who the abused child perceives as having a perfect life, the pain of loss is inflicted upon another. In addition, research suggests that a child who has been abused will often steal or shoplift as a form of self-love (Spaccarelli 1994). Whether stealing provides the child the material objects they feel they deserve as a reward for withstanding the abuse or provides them the material objects they would not otherwise receive, stealing from others and/or shoplifting is more common with victims of child physical abuse than nonabused children. Finally, in most cases of a juvenile starting a fire, the act is simply a result of boredom; however, children who frequently set fires are often victims of family violence to include physical, emotional, and sometimes sexual abuse.

Not all aggressive behaviors in victims of child abuse are destructive. In some cases, child victims of physical abuse will aggressively seek to please adults. In the school setting, these behaviors will sometimes manifest themselves in terms of the child attempting perfection in all that they do (McCabe and Martin 2005). This is the child so starved for positive adult attention that they always volunteer to help the teacher, always help tidy the classroom, and always seek a perfect score on their assignments. When perfection is not achieved, this abused child's reaction is usually extreme emotional distress.

The opposite of extreme aggression is extreme submission. This submissive behavior may also be an indicator of child physical abuse. The image of the abused child who is easily frightened by adults, and who hides in the corner, but is still is eager to please an adult, is not unusual in cases of child physical abuse. In some cases of physical abuse, children are uncomfortable not only around their parents or caretakers but also in the presence of other authority figures such as teachers (McCabe 2003). These children may exhibit an overall fear of an adult's or an older child's presence (Rodeheffer and Martin 1976). They choose to be alone and will often be seen watching others from the edge of the playground and not be involved in games or activities. In addition, these children with very low self-esteem may appear indifferent to life (Martin and Beezley 1976). For example, fire drills at school, a bad grade on a test, or an extra snack at lunchtime will all receive the same low-key response from the child. Finally, it is not uncommon for a child of patterned physical abuse to regress into acting as if he or she is still an infant with *baby talk* when they ask questions or respond to questions from authority figures. These physically abused children, not positively reinforced in their age-appropriate behaviors, may seem displaced in terms of their age and their actions (McCabe 2003).

Children who have been victims of physical abuse, because of their lack of experience with positive adult role models, often lack the capacity to form appropriate social relationships (Jennings et al. 2014; Crosson-Tower 2010). Specifically, in relationships with adults and other children, the children who have been victims of physical abuse often have unstable relationships with behavior ranging from extremely violent interactions to no interactions at all. In addition, the language development of abused children may be inhibited; therefore, the everyday conversations that most individuals take for granted are not always possible for the physically abused child (Rodeheffer and Martin 1976). In time, since language development is delayed, learning problems and even speech problems are not unusual in victims of child abuse and are often dismissed with little or no parental interest.

In general, a child who has been a victim of physical abuse in the home suffers the consequences of an uninvolved parent in their life and often in the school setting (McCabe and Martin 2005). Because of this lack of support, it is not uncommon for abused children to not be ready academically or with school supplies to start school and to perform poorly in school. In summary, with little attention to school work at home, children who are victims of physical abuse rarely do well in the school setting and oftentimes fail to complete their education.

Kevin (age 46) was a child of mixed Vietnamese and American (his birth father) descent. His stepfather, of Vietnamese descent, physically abused him on a regular basis, oftentimes leaving scars on his legs from the beatings. His mother, also of Vietnamese decent, did not intervene and allowed her husband to abuse him. Kevin left his home when he was 13 to live on the streets. He did not finish school. He immigrated to the United States when he was 18. Because of his lack of education, he is unable to pass the citizenship exam for the United States. He has worked as a manicurist for nearly 30 years and has no contact with his family in Vietnam, no family in the United States, and very few friends.

Finally, as mentioned previously in this section, one other consequence of child physical abuse is the potential for delinquency. Much literature exists on the relationship between child abuse and criminal behavior (Bartollas 2000; Siegel 2000). Children who are victims of physical abuse are more likely to run away from home, exhibit disruptive and/or truant behaviors in school, use drugs and alcohol, and become involved in deviant sexual behaviors. With no support at home, these children essentially raise themselves and often turn to the streets for some sort of a family.

☐ Abusers

In today's world of media exposure to child abuse and crime-based television series, one expects a *profile* to exist on every type of criminal. However, there is not one type of individual who abuses children. These abusers vary in physical characteristics, religious backgrounds, and socioeconomic statuses. However, in attempting to profile individuals who physically abuse children, one is tempted to suggest that certain demographic characteristics (e.g., white, males in their early twenties) exist in order that those who abuse children may be clearly identified. This is normal in all societies as we as individuals like to know what our enemies (or abusers) look like. Unfortunately, in crimes against children, there is no *typical* offender. Historically, theories such as the cycle of violence, social bond, and other theories of intergenerational transmission have identified the significant role of child abuse as a critical component for children becoming abusers as adults (Curtis 1963); however, the role of the other qualities of life remains unclear (Rodriguez and Tucker 2011).

Current research supports the importance of other social conditions and not simply childhood abuse given that the majority of parents with histories of abuse do not later become abusers of their children (Scannapieco and Connell-Carrick 2005; Ertem et al. 2000). In addition to the adult abuser who suffered childhood abuse, one must consider the other characteristics related to an adult's propensity to physically abuse a child. In this discussion, abusers are discussed in terms of their relationship to the child victim: (1) parent, (2) sibling, or (3) acquaintance.

Parents or Caretakers

In general, most abusers have a low self-esteem (Crosson-Tower 2010), are young and/or emotionally immature, and possess a low level of self-confidence. Anyone who has children can certainly understand how an emotionally immature parent may be prone to physical abuse when a child's action or reaction is not what they have planned. With new parenting or parenting at a young age, expectations for the child, as well as the understanding of a child's capacity for responsibility and gratification, may be unrealistic or simply wrong. If an immature parent possesses an unrealistic expectation for the child's behavior and that expectation is not met, the reaction from the parent may be of frustration, anger, and/or violence. This anger mismanagement by the parent is significant in predicting the child's risk for physical abuse (Jackson et al. 1999). The immature parent does not understand why the child does not simply defer to them and their rules or why the child is not showing them the gratitude that the parent feels he or she so often deserves. With each stage of the child's life, the parent has an expectation of behavior.

> Abbey (age 17) and Kyle (age 18) are in a relationship when they learn that Abbey is pregnant. They are both excited about becoming parents, and although they don't intend to marry, they are looking forward to raising a child together. They soon discover that their child is constantly in need of care and is always crying or demanding more of their attention. Although they both love their child, they feel the child is becoming spoiled as they feel they can never do enough for her. Kyle becomes disillusioned with fatherhood and breaks off the relationship with Abbey, leaving Abbey alone to care for their child. Abbey's stress level now increases while the emotional bond with her child decreases. Abbey now relies on what she believes is corporal punishment as her primary method of dealing with frustration.

As mentioned, in the first stage of a child's life, a parent may have an expectation of infancy. A parent expects a well-behaved and sleeping (not colic) infant. Again, it is during this life stage of the infant that abuse such as shaken baby may occur. Another stage of childhood development that is especially vulnerable to any emotional manipulation is toilet training (McCabe 2003). The parent knows that toilet training is a process; however, when the process continues for weeks and *accidents* occur, the parent may become angry. From the parent's standpoint, if you need to go to the bathroom, you simply go to the bathroom. From the child's standpoint, they may not understand the urgency of the matter, and often they do not want to interrupt an activity they enjoy for a *bathroom break*. A parent who is emotionally immature may quickly become frustrated with the situation and lash out with physical violence toward the child.

Another stage of childhood development that often causes frustration for the parent is the *why* stage. In this stage of development, children, interested in their environment, consistently ask questions, become quickly agitated and frustrated, and do not understand the notion of delayed gratification. It is during this stage that parents react to their child's temper tantrums or constant questions with physical abuse (McCabe 2003). A later stage of childhood development that is normally difficult for emotionally immature parents is middle and high school. The parents, who have expressed the importance of good grades and doing well in school, may become frustrated with the child who views school as a waste of time or as a purely social event. This frustration from the parent's view, of attempting to provide the best opportunities for a child who does not see the value in those opportunities, may be displayed through violence directed toward the child. On the other hand, the parent who views school as the child's job and not theirs may become frustrated with the child teacher who continually calls them for assistance with the child and may abuse the child as a result of their frustration with the teacher.

Another characteristic related to an adult's propensity to physically abuse a child is substance abuse. Historically, one substance in particular, alcohol, is significantly related to child physical abuse (Freisthler 2011; Berger 2005). Just as alcohol is used by many parents for enjoyment or relaxation, research also suggests that it is used by many adults as a coping mechanism for their day-to-day stresses (McCabe 2003). Specifically, Kelleher et al. (1994) concluded that parents who are alcohol dependent are nearly five times more likely to physically abuse children. In today's world of prescription dependence, home-manufactured drugs, antidepressants, narcotics, and methamphetamines are also playing a crucial role in child physical abuse and child fatalities.

Finally, emotional stresses such as unemployment, poor education, poverty, and marital discourse are often *managed* with alcohol or other substances. Unfortunately, alcohol, which may actually initially create a calming environment, only increases stress with continued abuse; thus, parents lash out in the long term (Gil 1970). Parents who experience these environmental stresses see themselves in a no-win situation and see that the children are the only fuel in their life of frustration. Rather than striking the employer who has failed to recognize his or her value, the parent strikes his or her child.

Munchausen Syndrome by Proxy

Munchausen syndrome by proxy is a type of physical abuse that is now recognized as a special circumstance of child abuse and is increasingly being identified by the medical, police, and social services community. In these cases, the adult perpetrator directly causes a child's illness (APA 2013). In most cases, the abuser is the mother who seeks the attention or praise of others for being such a *strong person* to constantly take care of a sick child. Unfortunately, the child is sick because the mother often gives the child medicines such as ipecac to induce vomiting or phenolphthalein to cause diarrhea. This condition is difficult to diagnose but does draw suspicion when the child does not respond to medical treatment and especially in the cases where the child appears worse in the mother's presence. Unfortunately, in some cases of Munchausen syndrome by proxy, if the action is not discovered, the child is at a high risk for permanent injury or death.

Siblings

One cannot discount the contribution of the siblings when discussing child physical abuse as many victims of child abuse will report abuse at the hands of a brother or sister as well as or instead of the parent(s). Historically, sibling arguments and sibling fights were often recognized as simply a part of the family dynamics. However, as we experience more of a blending of families and more of the recognition of child abuse, more cases of sibling abuse are being reported to teachers, law enforcement, and social services agencies. In fact, many researchers are now recognizing that sibling abuse is one of the most reported and unreported categories of child physical abuse, as abuse by a sibling is oftentimes more violent than child abuse by a parent (McCabe and Martin 2005).

Physical abuse by a sibling is divided into three forms: (1) common, (2) unusual, and (3) injurious (Wiehe 1997). A common sibling abuse is often an angry reaction, which includes hitting, biting, and shoving. In the common form of sibling abuse, the abuser sibling is larger, older, and stronger than the sibling victim (McCabe 2003). The motivating factors for this form of child abuse include jealousy and frustration. For many abusers, the attention and/or gifts given to the smaller or younger sibling from parents and others is the underlying cause of these actions. In these situations, thoughts by the abuser include *look at me* or *I'm important too*. In many cases, once the larger sibling becomes secure with their role and satisfied with their own success, the abuse ends. In other cases, once the younger sibling becomes able to defend himself or herself or removed himself or herself from the household, the abuse ends.

Unusual sibling abuse includes tactics such as tickling or restraining the victim. Although unusual sibling abuse does not leave permanent physical reminders and has historically been identified as play, victims of unusual abuse often report feelings of helplessness and fear, as well as the inability to control their own destinies. For many victims of unusual sibling abuse, the abuse continues until the victim agrees to the demands of abuser. In these cases, often, new incidents of victimization emerge with new demands from the abuser. For adults who report being tickled by a sibling to the point of pain during childhood, the memory of an inability to control the situation is often transferred to adult situations of domestic abuse or discrimination in the workplace in which they feel they have no control.

Finally, injurious abuse includes actions such as smothering, choking, holding someone's head underwater, and shooting the victim with a pellet or BB gun (Wiehe 1997). Although this form of sibling abuse is the rarest, it often leaves permanent physical and emotional scars. For the child who experiences their sibling attempting to seriously injure them, the lack of affection toward the sibling, and sometimes the parent, will probably continue throughout their lifetime. In summary, injurious abuse often results in not only physical pain at the time but also lasting effects such as scars, the fear of small spaces, the fear of water, uneasiness when others attempt to touch a part of their body such as their toes, or the fear of individuals (McCabe 2003).

Acquaintances

Nonfamily members are often provided the opportunity of child care. Unfortunately, in some instances, those friends or acquaintances of the parents are the perpetrators of child physical abuse. Whether these acquaintances abuse a child through ritualistic abuse or bullying, the child is physically abused. Although the definition of ritualistic abuse is still evolving and few cases are confirmed (McCabe and Martin 2005; Bottoms et al. 1996), it begins with the assertion that physical abuse is rarely a single incident, and it is a regular occurrence. The most common forms of ritualistic abuse include cutting and branding; however, it must be acknowledged that some ritualistic actions are culture- or religion-based and are not intended to harm the child.

In the 1980s, the US media devoted much of their attention to cases of satanic child abuse; however, a few, if any, cases of this form of ritualistic abuse were confirmed to exist (Bottoms and Davis 1997). In cases of ritualistic physical abuse (satanic or not), the child is left with a permanent injury or mark that depicts the ownership of the child by another and gains much media attention whether true or not. This ownership of the child (as in a case of child trafficking to be discussed in Chapter 7) leaves the child feeling helpless and without control of their destiny.

Bullying, on the other hand, has become a well-known action that results in child physical abuse and has become quite a popular topic for discussion in today's culture. As bullying was offered as an explanation for the school shooting in Columbine, and cyberbullying is now a common occurrence, bullying is now a conversation in all schools today (McCabe and Johnston 2014; McCabe and Martin 2005). In all cases of bullying, there are four elements: (1) an imbalance of power, (2) the intent to harm, (3) a threat of further aggression, and (4) terror with the final outcome of fear and submission. With child abuse, whether young children or teens, a child is identified, and abuser(s) work to embarrass, shun, or frighten the victim (Coloroso 2003). Reactions from victims of abuse include self-mutilation, starvation, suicide, the bullying of others, and mass murder (McCabe and Martin 2005).

☐ Long-Term Effects

When discussing the long-term effects of childhood abuse, most research-ers focus on adult survivors of child sexual abuse. However, given that there are generations of adults who were victims of child physical abuse, this section focuses on adult survivors of child physical abuse.

Childhood physical abuse is specifically associated with adult depression, disassociation, post-traumatic stress symptoms, and psy-chiatric comorbidity or the overlap of two or more psychiatric disor-ders (Krupnick et al. 2004; Higgins and McCabe 2003). For female survivors of child physical abuse, more is known as females are more likely to seek help or counseling. In general, the female victims of child physical abuse often report feelings of depression and eating disorders and continue to involve themselves in adult relationships that are physically abusive (McCabe 2003). In some cases, the adult female victims of childhood physical abuse will become the abusers themselves. However, in most cases, these females will continue to be the victims of their partner's abuse and perhaps even abuse by their own children and/or grandchildren.

For male survivors of childhood physical abuse, less is known. Whether it is society's suggestion that males should simply *man up* or the fact that male victims are less likely to seek counseling, only the most recent research addresses the male victims of childhood physical abuse (Freisthler 2011). What has been discovered related to adult male victims of childhood physical abuse is that the long-term effects are often differ-ent for males than females.

In general, it is not uncommon for both males and females to con-tinue physically abusive relationships into their adulthood, and it is not uncommon for males to begin the role of abusers to their partner and perhaps their children. However, male victims of childhood physical abuse often begin displaying signs of aggression and abusive behaviors as young children and preteens (McCabe and Martin 2005; Barkan 2001).

John (age 51) was a victim of child physical abuse from both his mother and father. His arms and legs both display the scars of abuse. One day, while observing his son's elementary school football practice, he witnessed his son crying after a larger boy repeatedly tackled him. John, in reaction, began yelling at his son to *stop taking hits from the other boy and to hit him back* with injuries so severe that his teammate could not return to the field. When the coach attempted to intervene, John began a verbal confrontation with the coach and walked out onto the practice field to slap his son. At the end of the season, John's son chose not to continue playing football.

It is not unusual for boys who are victims of physical abuse to physically abuse their siblings and their peers. It is also not unusual for males in their teens and early twenties, and throughout their life span (while physically able), to engage in physical confrontations outside the home on sports teams, in bar fights, and in simple conflicts of opinions with others. In many cases, the adult male victim of childhood physical abuse feels the ever-pressing need to *take care* of his family or friends, and, if he feels that any member of his family is threatened or harassed, he will confront those he sees as responsible for the threats often with a physical attack.

Internally, these male victims of childhood physical abuse are insecure and unsure of themselves (McCabe 2003). Oftentimes, they will attempt to be an overachiever in their jobs or their hobbies; however, when faced with resistance or doubt from others, often, their reaction is anger and hostility. Many of these males have doubts as to their self-worth and will either avoid relationships or remain in a relationship simply to avoid being alone. Finally, when confronted with emotional issues, the adult male victims of childhood physical abuse will often retreat.

Alan (age 44) was a victim of extensive child physical abuse at the hands of his father who was in and out of the household. At age 15, after Alan quit school to help care for his mother and two siblings, his father returned. His mother gave Alan the choice to stay in the home with his father or leave—Alan left and was homeless until his mother allowed him to enter the army at age 17. After being discharged from the army, Alan quickly married a girl from his hometown. Although he and his wife are constantly arguing, they have two children (both with either legal or mental health problems), and he has been told by his wife that she *wished for his death* for her birthday, Alan continues to remain in the relationship for fear of being alone.

☐ Summary

Child physical abuse is defined as a nonaccidental injury of a child by a parent or a caregiver. In the United States, there are over 10,000 reported cases of child physical abuse annually. Of those cases, the majority of the victims are under the age of 10 with approximately 25% of the victims under the age of 3. The victims of child physical abuse are both male and female; however, males are more likely to be victims of severe physical abuse. In addition, the victims of abuse are from various ethnic and racial groups and a variety of economic backgrounds. Child physical abuse is both acute and chronic.

The physical indicators of child physical abuse include bruises, cuts, burns, and bites. Behavioral indicators include violence, aggression, social withdrawal, and self-harm. One final outcome of child physical abuse is death.

Perpetrators of child physical abuse include family members and nonfamily members. Young children are most at risk for abuse by their parents, in particular, their mother. Most recently, the role of siblings and peers as related to child physical abuse has been explored.

Often, adult survivors of child physical abuse report difficulties in social relationships, involvement in domestic violence, and issues related to substance abuse. Finally, adult victims of child physical abuse often report feelings of insecurity, helplessness, and depression that, when left untreated, continues throughout their lifetimes. Hence, child physical abuse is a victimization that occurs at the beginning of one's lifetime and often continues until death.

CHAPTER QUESTIONS

1. Why are infants more at risk for physical abuse by a parent?

2. What are some of the behavioral indicators of a child who is physically abused?

3. What are the three forms of sibling physical abuse? Provide examples of each.

QUESTIONS FOR FURTHER THOUGHT

1. Although some sections in this chapter can clearly be defined as physical abuse, what are some areas discussed that may be more subjective and may be interpreted as corporal punishment?

2. What factors make it increasingly difficult for investigators to discern the difference between accidental injuries and physical abuse?

3. Why are some caretakers more likely than other caretakers to physically abuse children?

☐ References

Afifi, T., Mota, N., MacMillan, H., and Sareen, J. 2013. Harsh physical punishment in childhood and adult physical health. *Pediatrics*, 132(2), 333–340.

American Psychiatric Association. 2013. *Diagnostic and Statistical Manual of Mental Disorders* (5th ed.). Arlington, VA: American Psychiatric Publishers.

Ammerman, R. 1991. The role of the child in physical abuse: A reappraisal. *Violence and Victims*, 6(2), 87–102.

Barkan, S. 2001. *Criminology: A Sociological Understanding* (2nd ed.). Upper Saddle River, NJ: Prentice Hall.

Bartollas, C. 2000. *Juvenile Delinquency* (5th ed.). Boston: Allyn and Bacon.

Baumrind, D., Larzelere, R., and Lowan, P. 2002. Ordinary physical punishment: Is it harmful? *Psychological Bulletin*, 128(4), 580–589.

Berger, L. M. 2005. Income, family characteristics, and physical violence toward children. *Child Abuse & Neglect*, 23, 1225–1238.

Bottoms, B. and Davis, S. 1997. The creation of satanic ritual abuse. *Journal of Social and Clinical Psychology*, 16(2), 112–132.

Bottoms, B., Shaver, P., and Goodman, G. 1996. An analysis of ritualistic and religion-related child abuse allegations. *Law and Human Behavior*, 20(1), 1–34.

Bush, M. 2010. Afghanistan and the sex trade. In McCabe and Manian (eds.) *Sex Trafficking: A Global Perspective*, New York: Lexington Books, pp. 111–117.

Child Welfare Information Gateway. 2013. *What Is Child Abuse? Recognizing the Signs and Symptoms*. Washington, D.C.: US Department of Health and Human Services, Children's Bureau.

Children's Bureau. 2014. *Child Maltreatment 2013*. Washington, D.C.: US Department of Health and Human Services, Administration for Children and Families.

Coloroso, B. 2003. *The Bully, the Bullied, and the Bystander*. New York: Harper Collins Publishing.

Crosson-Tower, C. 2010. *Understanding Child Abuse and Neglect* (8th ed.). Boston: Allyn and Bacon.

Curtis, G. 1963. Violence breeds violence—Perhaps? *The American Journal of Psychiatry*, 120(2), 386–387.

Davis, J. 1982. *Help Me, I'm Hurt*. Dubuque, IA: Kendall Hunt.

Ertem, I., Leventhal, J., and Dobbs, S. 2000. Intergenerational continuity of child physical abuse: How good is the endeavor? *Lancet*, 356(9232), 814–819.

Faller, K. and Ziefert, M. 1981. Causes of child abuse and neglect. In K. Faller (ed.) *Social Work with Abused and Neglected Children*. New York: Free Press.

Freisthler, B. 2011. Alcohol use, drinking venue utilization, and child physical abuse: Results from a pilot study. *Journal of Family Violence*, 26(1), 185–193.

Friedrick, W. and Boriskin, J. 1976. The role of the child in abuse: A review of the literature. *American Journal of Orthopsychiatry*, 46(3), 580–590.

Gil, D. 1970. *Violence Against Children*. Cambridge, MA: Harvard University Press.

Gosselin, D. 2010. *Heavy Hands: An Introduction to the Crimes of Family Violence* (4th ed.). Upper Saddle River, NJ: Prentice Hall.

Higgins, D. and McCabe, M. 2003. Maltreatment and family dysfunction in childhood and the subsequent adjustment of children and adults. *Journal of Family Violence*, 18(1), 107–120.

Jackson, S., Thompson, R., Christiansen, E., Colman, R., Wyatt, J., Buckendahl, C., Wilcox, B. L., and Peterson, R. 1999. Predicting abuse-prone parental attitudes and discipline practices in a nationally representative sample. *Child Abuse*, 23(1), 15–19.

Jennings, W., Park, M., Tomsich, E., Glover, R., and Powers, R. 2014. Exploring the relationship between child physical abuse and adult dating violence using a causal inference approach in an emerging adult population in South Korea. *Child Abuse and Neglect*, 38(12), 1902–1913.

Kelleher, K., Chaffin, M., Hollenberg, J., and Fischer, E. 1994. Alcohol and drug disorders among physically abrasive and neglectful parents in a community-based sample. *American Journal of Public Health*, 184, 1586–1590.

Krupnick, J., Green, B., Stockton, P., Goodman, L., Corcoran, C., and Petty, R. 2004. Mental health effects of adolescent trauma exposure in a female college sample: Exploring different outcomes on experiences of unique trauma types and dimensions. *Psychiatry*, 67(2), 264–279.

Lahey, J. 2014. Why teenagers cut and how to help. *New York Times*, October 30.

Martin, H. and Beezley, P. 1976. Personality of abused children. In H. P. Martin (ed.) *The Abused Child*. Cambridge, MA: Ballinger, pp. 105–111.

McCabe, K. 2003. *Child Abuse and the Criminal Justice System*. New York, Peter Lang.

McCabe, K. and Johnston, O. 2014. Perceptions on the legality of sexting. *Social Science Computer Review*, 32(6), 765–768.

McCabe, K. and Martin, G. 2005. *School Violence, the Media, and Criminal Justice Responses*. New York, Peter Lang.

McNeese, M. and Hebeler, J. 1977. The abused child: A clinical approach to identification and management. *Clinical Symposia*, 29(5), 1–36.

Osteogenesis Imperfecta Foundation. 2014. Facts about osteogenesis imperfecta. Available at http://www.oif.org/site/PageServer?pagename=AOIFacts, April 2015. Accessed November 6, 2014.

Pressel, D. 2000. Evaluation of physical abuse in children. *American Family Physician*, May 15. Available at http://www.aafp.org/afp/20000515/3057.html. Accessed January 17, 2001.

Rodeheffer, M. and Martin, H. 1976. Special problems in the developmental assessment of abused children. In H. P. Martin (ed.) *The Abused Child*. Cambridge, MA: Ballinger, pp. 113–128.

Rodriguez, C. and Tucker, M. 2011. Behind the cycle of violence, beyond abuse history: A brief report on the association of parental attachment to physical child abuse potential. *Violence & Victims*, 26(2), 246–256.

Scannapieco, M. and Connell-Carrick, K. 2005. *Understanding Child Maltreatment: An Ecological and Developmental Perspective*. New York: Oxford University.

Seymour, A., Murray, M., Sigmond, J., Hook, M., Edmunds, C., Gaboury, M., and Coleman, G. 2002. *National Victim Assistance Academy Textbook*. Washington, D.C.: Office for Victims of Crime.

Siegel, L. 2000. *Criminology* (7th ed.). Belmont, CA: Wadsworth.

Spaccarelli, S. 1994. Stress, appraisal, and coping in child sexual abuse: A theoretical and empirical review. *Psychological Bulletin*, 116(2), 340–362.

UNICEF. 2012. *Children in the Urban World: The State of the World's Children 2012*. New York, United Nations Children's Fund.

US Department of Health and Human Services. 2008. *Child Maltreatment 2006*. Washington, D.C.: US Government Printing Office.

Verma, A. 2010. Trafficking in India. In McCabe and Manian (eds.) *Sex Trafficking: A Global Perspective*, New York: Lexington Books, pp. 101–110.

Wallace, H. 1999. *Family Violence: Legal, Medical, and Social Perspectives* (2nd ed.). Boston: Allyn and Bacon.

White, R., Benedict, M., Wulff, L., and Kelley, M. 1987. Physical disabilities as a risk factor for child maltreatment: A selected review. *American Journal of Orthopsychiatry*, 57(1), 93–101.

Wiehe, V. R. 1997. *Sibling Abuse: Hidden Physical, Emotional, and Sexual Trauma* (2nd ed.). Thousand Oaks, CA: Sage.

Sexual Abuse

Sarah is four years old, and Haley is six years old. Their fathers have repeatedly sexually abused these girls since they were toddlers. In 2014, the fathers exchanged text messages that discussed trading their daughters for sexual variety. Only when an Internet service provider identified an exchange of child pornography were these victims discovered.

The sexual abuse of children is among the most horrifying and disturbing category of child abuse. From the media's perspective, the sexual abuse of a child is front-page news. Unfortunately, out of the four categories of child abuse, sexual abuse was the last to receive public attention and a demand for reaction.

Historically, the sexual abuse of anyone was not a subject for discussion. The sexual abuse of children was even less likely to be discussed, and, if the perpetrator was a family member, which was often the case, the subject was taboo. Today, the sexual abuse of children is recognized as a crime of innocence and of public concern, as well as a topic worthy of discussions, prevention, and legislative action.

As referenced, in 2013, over 600,000 children were confirmed victims of child abuse in the United States. Of those cases, approximately 10% were victims of child sexual abuse (Children's Bureau 2014). Loosely translated, there are over 60,000 confirmed victims of child sexual abuse in the United States and on an annual basis. Surveys of child sexual abuse in other countries suggest rates higher than or comparable to rates in the United States (McCabe 2009). This chapter focuses on the sexual abuse of children to include discussions on the physical and behavioral indicators of abuse, the progressional process of child sexual abuse, the abusers, and the long-term consequences of child sexual abuse.

It is being acknowledged that the information presented in this chapter on child victims and their offenders is based upon the known victims of child sexual abuse. However, many incidents of child sexual abuse remain unreported (McCabe 2003; Russell 1983; Hindelang 1976). In fact, when comparing general rates of adult rape reported to law enforcement through the Uniform Crime Reports and those reported on victimization surveys through the National Crime Victimization Survey, it is estimated that only about one-third of the crimes are reported to law enforcement (Barkan 2015).

Given the facts that young children are often unable to report their abuse, that many of their abusers are family members, and that matters of families are still intensely private (Bartollas 2000), it is suggested that child sexual abuse is even more underreported than adult cases of sexual abuse (McCabe 2003). In addition, and as if child sexual abuse is not damaging on its own, current research on the prevalence of child sexual assaults indicates that incidents of child sexual abuse over the last decade have become significantly more violent and, in many cases, end with the death of a child.

The World Health Organization (2008) defines child sexual abuse as the involvement of a child in a sexual activity that he or she does not fully comprehend, and is unable to give informed consent to, or that violates the laws of society. For the purpose of this chapter, child sexual abuse is defined as the inducement or coercion of a child to engage in any unlawful sexual activity to include sexual practices and pornography and does *not* include the restriction of an adult offender.

With the exception of child sexual abuse, most victims of child abuse are under the age of two (Children's Bureau 2014). When considering child sexual abuse, approximately 25% of the reported victims are between the ages of 12 and 14, approximately 35% are between the ages of 6 and 11, and approximately 15% are between the ages of 3 and 5. However, McCabe (2003) suggests that there are more cases of child sexual abuse for victims under the age of three, but, unfortunately, these cases are usually not detected or reported until the child is older.

There are no clear indicators of risk for child sexual abuse. Children from all ages and all backgrounds are victims; however, some research suggests that factors that increase risk do exist. Specifically, Crosson-Tower (2010) suggests that social isolation of the child and/or family is a major contributor. Sedlak et al. (2010) suggest that a child's cultural background is a significant risk factor in their risk for abuse. Kenny and McEachern (2000) suggest that domestic violence is a risk factor for child sexual abuse. Finally, McCabe (2003) suggests that victimization is often simply a result of opportunity. Essentially, a child living in a violent home, without the avenue of outside contact, and without protective supervision, is especially vulnerable to child sexual abuse.

Children who are victims of sexual abuse within the family are, in most reported cases, females. However, in the cases of child sex rings, ritualistic abuse, or abuse by those outside of the family, research suggests that the victims are just as likely to be male (Lanning 1992). One such organization is the North American Man/Boy Love Association, an international organization that has existed for years. This organization advocates for abolishing age of consent laws focusing on prohibiting sexual relationships between adults and minors (McCabe 2003). In addition, research suggests that children with mental or physical disabilities are historically at increased risk for any type of child abuse to include sexual abuse (Daigle 2012; DeYoung 1982). Today, children with disabilities are estimated to be 4–10 times more likely to be sexually abused than the general population (Daigle and Muftic 2016).

As discussed in the cases of child physical abuse, there are physical and behavioral signs or indicators of child sexual abuse. However, different from cases of child physical abuse, in many cases of child sexual abuse, the behavioral indicators are the first signs of abuse with physical indicators later providing the evidence to substantiate the accusation of abuse. This sequence of indicators creates a unique set of circumstances for law enforcement attempting to document cases of child sexual abuse.

☐ Physical Indicators

Unfortunately, for law enforcement, in most cases of child sexual abuse, there are no physical indicators. This is, in part, because the child does not report the abuse immediately; thus, the physical evidence, which may have been present initially, is either washed away or healed as tears through the hymen and anal fissures may heal over a period of two weeks (Johnson 2006). In addition, and contrary to what may be portrayed on television shows, many cases of child sexual abuse do not involve sexual intercourse. Specifically, sexual abuse through fellatio, cunnilingus, and digital penetration is unlikely to leave lasting physical evidence. In addition, with many cases of child sexual abuse, fondling was the abuse, and penetration never occurs.

Therefore, in these cases of child sexual abuse, physical evidence does not exist. For a jury of individuals, who watch police dramas on television, the expectation in any case is deoxyribonucleic acid (DNA), and, for some individuals, the perception of child sexual abuse always includes semen, saliva, and possibly blood. This creates a difficult environment for those attempting to prosecute abusers who do not leave the commonly recognized form of physical evidence.

Today, due to this misperception of sexual abuse cases, forensic experts have been called to testify in certain circumstances as to the lack of physical evidence rather than explaining the evidence discovered. This is especially difficult in the prosecution of cases, similar to prosecuting a murder without a body. As child sexual abuse cases are less likely than adult cases of sexual abuse to have physical evidence such as semen, the relevance of behavioral indicators, testimony, and/or a confession is almost essential. However, in some cases of child sexual abuse, physical indicators do exist and, just as is the case for physical abuse (other than DNA evidence), the physical indicators of child sexual abuse include bruises, burns, cuts, and other injuries. Often more relevant in child cases of sexual abuse is the location of the child's physical injury.

Bruises or injuries on the arms, legs, and neck and in the genital area of a child are a strong indicator of child sexual abuse (Helfer and Kempe 1987). These are injuries that would not normally occur in the daily play of children, and, just as in the cases of physical abuse, one must consider the explanation of the injury before alleging child sexual abuse. Thus, a young boy with bleeding from his rectum or a young girl having difficulty sitting in her desk at school may be a victim of child sexual abuse and may be experiencing pain from an injury or discomfort from an infection that has occurred as a result of the sexual abuse.

Of course, in some cases, there is the presence of bodily fluids such as sperm, saliva, and blood. Again, the explanation for the injury must be considered before concluding child sexual abuse. However, in terms of blood in the genital areas, it is very difficult for a child to injure themselves in these areas to the point of bleeding through normal day-to-day activities. Bleeding within the vaginal and anal areas are common in cases (especially in acute cases) of child sexual assault and most definitely a sign of child abuse. Bodily fluids such as saliva and sperm within or near the genital areas, as well as sperm on the hand or in the mouth of a child, are also an indicator of a sexual assault. Based upon state laws, children are not permitted to provide consent to sexual activity; thus, the presence of sperm is certainly a physical indicator of child sexual abuse. In addition, over-the-counter lubricants, lotions, or petroleum jelly in the vaginal and anal areas are also evidence of child sexual abuse.

As mentioned, other strong physical indicators supporting child sexual abuse are sexually transmitted diseases or the human immuno-deficiency virus. In cases where a child victim tests positive for these types of diseases, law enforcement may apply for a court order or search warrant of the offender's body to link the victim's condition to that of the suspected offender.

In addition to injuries in the genital areas of a child, the piercing of genitals is also an indicator of child sexual abuse. In our society, for both adult males and females, genital piercing is a unique expression of sexuality. For females, the clitoral hood is the most commonly pierced area, and, for males, the most common site for genital piercing is the penis. Currently, approximately 40 states have laws that limit or prohibit the genital piercing of minors; therefore, in a case of a child sexual abuse, not only is the actual piercing evidence of abuse, but the question of why a child's sexuality should be accentuated is also an indicator of concern. A person responsible for the genital piercing of a child is most certainly viewing the child as a sexual object. Thus, a person interested in adorn-ing the sexual regions of a child are of great concern to that intent on ending child sexual abuse.

Finally, female circumcision, an action that may not be viewed as child sexual abuse by the perpetrator, is illegal in the United States, the United Kingdom, and all other developed countries. For clarity, female circumcision or female genital mutilation (FGM) is a procedure that involves the partial or complete removal of the external genitalia of a female and is usually performed prior to puberty (WHO 2008). It is esti-mated that over 100 million females from countries in Africa and the Middle East have been victims of FGM. Some of these females and their families are now residing in the United States and other countries. Just as in the case of genital piercing, FGM victims not only experience the initial pain of the incident but also often suffer multiple infections and chronic pain throughout their lifetime. Although illegal in the United States, some families with a cultural history of FGM may wish to con-tinue the practice while residing within this country.

Although most media reports of child sexual abuse involve physical contact, this is not always true. Sexual abuse may include voyeurism, where the offender watches a child undress, bath, or even urinate for the sole purpose of sexual gratification and pornography. Sexual abuse may also involve masturbation as offenders may become aroused as they instruct the child to touch their own sexual organs, perform sex acts, or masturbate in front of them, or the offender may masturbate themselves (i.e., exhibitionism) in front of the child. Even in cases where sexual intercourse does not occur, sexual abuse is often a traumatic event for the child whether or not there has been physical contact. In cases where there is no presence of physical evidence, behavior indicators may be used to validate a child's disclosure.

☐ Behavioral Indicators

Since child sexual abuse is rarely discovered through physical indicators, and children are oftentimes reluctant to report such abuse, behavioral indicators are, in many cases, often the first sign of child sexual abuse. A child who is sexually abused will often provide hints of that abuse through their actions. In particular, a child who is a victim of sexual abuse may appear depressed, avoid others, become quick to anger, or display a change in appearance (McCabe 2003; Helfer and Kempe 1987). These child victims may appear tired, frightened, or have trouble sitting in the classroom. In addition, the child may experience academic problems at school; start missing school; begin using sexual language; provide descriptions of sexual acts in conversations that are not considered age appropriate (Wallace 1999); fail to bathe or brush their teeth; not comb their hair; wear dirty clothes; or begin to physically, sexually, or emotionally abuse other children (McCabe and Martin 2005).

Finally, some victims of child sexual abuse demonstrate an overwhelming fear of everyday activities or an overestimation of world dangers: begin using drugs, run away from home or school, or attempt suicide (Briere and Elliott 1994; Hibbard et al. 1990). Explanations for these behaviors may not always seem reasonable to an adult; however, these behaviors are reasonable to a child. Specifically, just as in cases of physical abuse, behaviors of depression, social avoidance, and anger are all outcomes of feelings of helplessness and low self-worth. A child who refuses to bathe or perform acts of basic hygiene (even when they are teased by peers) may feel as though by being dirty and smelling bad, they lessen their appeal to the offender; thus, they may avoid further victimization. Unfortunately, the longer the sexual abuse continues, the more likely behavioral indicators will be demonstrated and the more severe and detrimental those behaviors may be to a child.

☐ Progression of Sexual Abuse

In attempting to understand the dynamics behind the sexual abuse of children, one should consider the abuse itself, especially in those cases of continued abuse, as a process and progression of action. To do so, one must first consider the state of the abuser's mind during the seduction of the child. Finkelhor (1984) first described this progression of child sexual abuse. In his identified progression for child sexual abuse, it is suggested that before a sexual assault of a child occurs, there is a progression of stages (or preconditions) that must be completed. These four preconditions to a sexual assault are *Precondition I*: Motivation to sexually abuse, *Precondition II*: Overcoming internal inhibitors, *Precondition III*: Factors predisposing to overcome external inhibitors, and *Precondition IV*: Factors predisposing to overcome a child's resistance (Wallace and Roberson 2010; Finkelhor 1984).

In Precondition I, the perpetrator or abuser attempts to relate to the child on an emotional level. In this stage, the child is seen perhaps not as a person but rather as the source of sexual satisfaction for the abuser. For this abuser, the physical attributes of the child are sexually attractive. It is during this stage that many perpetrators perceive the everyday actions of the child to be seductive (Crosson-Tower 2010). A child who sits on the perpetrator's lap or smiles or hugs the perpetrator is perceived by the abuser to be physically attracted to them. Therefore, the abuser, delighted by the child's interest in them, responds with attention to the child. Many child abusers are uncomfortable in adult interactions; therefore, in this stage, the perpetrator is socially comfortable.

One of the first things to consider during this precondition stage is why the adult places himself or herself in positions to be surrounded by children. For individuals interested in sexually abusing children, their choice of career or hobby is critical to their planned access to children. This is not to suggest that all individuals who choose to work with children are focused on the sexual exploitation of children; however, an individual in search of children to sexually abuse will place themselves in the proximity of children.

In Precondition II, the perpetrator must overcome internal inhibitors or his or her conscious feeling that sex with children is wrong (Wallace and Roberson 2010; Finkelhor 1984). It is during this stage that alcohol, drugs, and perhaps child pornography will be introduced into the perpetrator's life. Just as the use of alcohol and/or drugs to police are associated with most crimes reported to police, they are also often present in cases of child sexual abuse (McCabe 2009). In addition, the majority of individuals arrested on charges of child exploitation are in possession of child pornography (Sheldon 2011). Through the use of alcohol, drugs, or the viewing of child pornography, the abuser's internal inhibitors are reduced and may eventually be overcome. Thus, the perpetrator may now focus on overcoming the child's resistance.

It is during Precondition III that the perpetrator must overcome the external inhibitors of a child (Wallace and Roberson 2010;

Finkelhor 1984). The goal of this stage is to end with a willing or at least a nonresisting child victim. Therefore, from the abuser's perception, the child is a willing participant. When one considers the external inhibitors, one must consider the elements of any crime. Specifically, in crime prevention literature, it is suggested that three elements must always exist for a crime to occur. Specifically, these elements are (1) a target, (2) an offender, and (3) the lack of guardians. In cases of child sexual abuse, a child always exists, and the offender interested in abusing a child always exists. Therefore, guardians or external inhibitors must be eliminated (McCabe 2003). External inhibitors may be the amount of supervision of the child or the child's social support system. A child with little supervision or without an individual to whom they can report abuse is the ideal target for a sexual assault as there exist no external inhibitors.

In addition, for a child who does not have the support or supervision from a parental adult, the attention in terms of time and gifts from another adult is welcomed. Just as research on dating violence suggests that a victim will remain with an abuser as they enjoy most of the time in the relationship, a child will stay with and even try to be around an abuser if no other avenues of enjoyment with an adult exists.

Precondition IV is the final stage prior to the sexual abuse of the child. The factors that eliminate the child's resistance are the focus of the perpetrator (Wallace and Roberson 2010; Finkelhor 1984). Whether creating an environment of powerlessness or a trusting relationship between the perpetrator and the child, the abuser must develop an atmosphere to eliminate the child's resistance to sexual activities with the adult. As the abuser places himself or herself in a pseudo-caretaker role for child, he or she becomes indispensable in that child's eyes. During this stage, the abuser arranges more and more time to be alone with the child. In turn, the child wants to please that adult and, in most cases, will do whatever they must do to stay with the abuser. In these cases, the child does all that is asked by the abuser.

Once this stage has been satisfied, the courting or grooming of the child has concluded, and the child's sexual assault will occur and continue until ended by the child, the perpetrator who is not attracted to the child anymore, or some authority figure. The grooming process is a form of manipulation that will not only convince the child to engage in a sexual act but also persuade the child to maintain their silence. In some circumstances, that silence lasts a lifetime. It should be noted that some child molesters are intelligent and charismatic. Not only do they have the ability to persuade a child to engage in sexual activity and maintain silence, but they also have the ability to convince the parent to provide the abusers complete and private access to their children.

☐ Abusers

In research on the perpetrators of the sexual abuse of children, abuse is divided into two categories: (1) familial and (2) extrafamilial (abuse from someone outside of the family) abuse. In most cases of acute sexual abuse, the perpetrator is outside of the family. Chronic sexual abuse most often involves a family member. Although most offenders who sexual abuse children are male, it is estimated that up to 20% of all child sexual abusers are female (Fergusson and Mullen 1999). In most cases of child sexual abuse, the perpetrator is a family member (Crosson-Tower 2010; McCabe 2003) or a person living within the household. For clarity in the dissemination of this information on the perceptions of child sexual abusers, the perpetrator is discussed relative to his or her relationship to the child.

> Molly (age 9) was in the basement with her grandfather watching television. As she came upstairs, her mother panicked when she saw the expression on Molly's face. She felt that her father (Molly's grandfather) had just molested her daughter. She recognized Molly's expression and behavior immediately as she recalled how she had felt having been a victim of sexual abuse at the hands of her father for years. Molly stated that her grandfather asked her to feel the *roll of coins* he had in his pocket. Molly complied but immediately realized that her grandfather just had her touch his penis. When this disclosure was reported to the police, Molly's mother acknowledged that her father had molested her for several years, and she had never reported it, but was still shocked with this allegation stating that she didn't believe he would molest his own granddaughter. Molly's mother assumed she would be his only victim.

Note: This was the author's first case of child abuse.

Familial Abuse

The sexual abuse of a child by a family member is incest, and, despite the taboo of incest, the activity remains a part of many family households both nationally and internationally (Kamsner and McCabe 2000; Riggs et. al 2007). However, the perpetrator does not necessarily live with the children to abuse them. For example, a grandparent may visit the child's home to *babysit* and use this opportunity to molest their grandchild. Generally speaking, proximity hypothesis suggests that victims do not encourage the activity, but rather they are simply in the wrong place at the wrong time. In cases of incest, children, who are simply members of a family, are in the wrong place (i.e., their homes) at the wrong time.

The term incest most commonly refers to sexual relations between a father and a daughter; however, incest includes other family sexual relations such as between an uncle and a child, a grandfather and a grandchild, a mother and a son, and siblings. In cases of blended families, the lines between blood relations and legal relations are blurred; thus, the social inhibitors that prohibit sex between family members are often not perceived to exist. Adults within the family unit are generally assumed to be the perpetrators of incest; however, some historical researchers suggest that brother–sister sexual relationships are more common than father–daughter incest, and, in these cases, both children are involved—in some cases, both consenting and, in other cases, one consenting and the other abused by the older siblings (McCabe and Martin 2005; Wiehe 1997; Gebhard et al. 1965).

The age of consent is the age at which a person is considered legally able to provide consent to sexual activities. In the United States, the age of consent varies by the state and ranges from 14 to 18 years old.

Literature suggests that incestuous families have similar characteristics (Crosson-Tower 2010). They are often secretive in nearly all of their family activities, the adult is usually overly possessive of the children, the children demonstrate low levels of independence, and an environment exists where the abused child and his or her abuser are often only in the company of each other (McCabe 2003; Sgroi 1982).

Historically, sexual abuse at the hands of a family member is thought of, in many cases, as more damaging in terms of long-term consequences than sexual abuse at the hands of a stranger (Riggs et al. 2007; Gully et al. 1999). Not only does the child suffer the physical and/or emotional damage of the incident(s), but also the level of trust that most individuals would assume to exist between a parent/caretaker and a child is destroyed. The lack of trust between a parent and a child is often revealed in other relationships throughout the child's lifetime. Children who suffer incest must live with not only the sexual victimization but also the fact that the victimization was from someone they thought would protect them. Historically, three categories of incest have been identified to exist. Those categories are (1) molestation, (2) assault, and (3) rape with degree of harm as the deciding measure for classifications into each of the three categories (Mayer 1983).

Molestation cases involve the fondling or sexual petting of the child by the abuser. In this category of incest, intercourse between the child and family member does not occur (Mayer 1983). It is suggested by most law enforcement officials, as well as researchers, that the majority of the cases of incest are molestation and not intercourse. Unfortunately, for most individuals, incest is perceived to only refer to sexual intercourse, not oral sex or fondling. This perception often results in molestation cases not being reported to police. Hence, since the child was not forced into sexual intercourse, from the public's perception, there was no crime nor victimization; thus, the abuse is chronic.

McCabe (2003), in explaining cases of child abuse, suggested that molestation may be one of the most damaging, long-term types of sexual abuse. As the action was not seen as a sexual crime, it was not reported to police. Therefore, the child did not receive the help they may require to end the sexual abuse or to address the emotional damage of the abuse. In these cases of nonrecognized abuse, the molestation continues and sometimes escalates to another category of incest. In summary, the molested child may not suffer physical harm such as vaginal tears or a bleeding rectum; however, with molestation, the child may still be left with the trauma of sexual abuse and betrayal by a loved one and the person who was responsible for their safety.

In the assault category of incest, intercourse may occur. However, the intercourse is generally not what individuals would consider physically forced (Mayer 1983). In fact, in assault incest, the child may *consent* to having sex with the family member. Of course, from a legal perspective, a child cannot provide consent to a sexual activity; therefore, this action is a crime. This is the incestuous assault category that most often occurs as detailed in Finkelhor's (1984) model. The child is led to (or groomed to) perform sexual intercourse with the adult.

When individuals attempt to understand how a child could allow such an action to occur, they must consider that, for most individuals, sexual activity provides pleasure and closeness to another person. Incestuous assaults may also (at the time) provide the child pleasure and intimacy with their loved one. Unfortunately, in incestuous assaults, the child may be left with not only the physical signs of sexual abuse but also the long-term emotional scars of victimization within the family.

Finally, in the category of incestuous rape, the sexual assault is not desired by the child and is forced through violence or the fear of violence. In this category, the child has no control over the action just as in the case in adult rapes and often also experience physical and emotional abuse along with the sexual abuse. In this category of incest, some researchers suggest that the child is most damaged. The more violent the sexual assault, the more harm to the child (Crosson-Tower 2010).

From the child's standpoint, a person entrusted with their care not only has violated their trust and destroyed their sense of security, but they also have physically hurt them in the most intimate of ways. Based upon reports of child sexual abuse, the majority of the family members who sexually abuse their children are fathers, mothers, siblings, and other male family members.

Roy (age 30) was the father to Becky, his sole daughter. Roy did not want to have the responsibility of raising a child, so he made arrangements with his parents to adopt his daughter so that Roy now became her uncle instead of her father. When Becky was in her teenage years, Roy would continuously have vaginal sexual intercourse with his *niece*. Although this abuse went on throughout her teenage years, Becky did not report this abuse until she was in her thirties. Prior to the scheduled trial, it was discovered that Roy had several previous accusations of sexual misconduct. Roy, who had worked as a paramedic, was accused of feeling the breasts of a teenage girl while she was being transported to the hospital. Roy had also been suspected of masturbating outside an elementary school, and most recently had been accused of participating in a parade and raising up his kilt while not wearing undergarments. None of these previous allegations were allowed in at trial as it was considered prejudicial to the jury. Roy was found not guilty of the crime of incest.

Father

When one hears about a case of incest, they generally assume a father–daughter relationship. How one father can comfort his child in their bed after a nightmare, while another father, upon entering the child's bedroom, becomes sexually excited is never fully explained. However, insights into cases of father–child sexual abuse are provided given that many of the cases of incest are father–child. Just as suggested with Finkelhor's (1994) model, there are adult males who are sexually attracted to the physical characteristics of children. The fact that they have a child in their home is extremely convenient.

Other researchers suggest that fathers will often distort the role of their child in order to rationalize the sexual encounter (Crosson-Tower 2010). Specifically, the researchers are referring to a father who, because of a wife's absence (either physically or emotionally), views his daughter as the homemaker and, if there exists other children, the caretaker of his other children. In this view, the daughter occupies the wife's role, and a transference of parental roles is not unusual. Unfortunately, in cases of incest, the husband/wife duties of sexual affection are also within the role assumed by the daughter.

Another explanation for father–child incest is power and control. There are those researchers who suggest that incest is an avenue of control, and those fathers who engage in incest with their children do so in an attempt to maintain a position of power within the household (McCabe 2003). Simply stated, the child is the property of the father. As a property owner, the father has the right to use the child (his property), as he desires.

In the male-dominated family unit such as the one that would exist through power and control, the mother (if available in the home) often remains ignorant of the abuse, ignores the abuse, blames the child, or participates in the abuse. In these scenarios of abuser, ignorer, and victim, the dysfunctional family unit and the dynamics of that unit will continue until the child is removed or removes themselves from the home.

Stephanie (age 10) would have to play what her adopted father, Hank, would call *sex games* just about every day after school while her mother worked. Stephanie would be on a twin bed and have her arms and legs spread apart and tied to the four corner posts of the bed. On some days, he would climb on top of her and engage in anal or vaginal intercourse while she was secured by the ropes. While on other days, no longer secured by ropes, she would lay on top of him and put Hank's penis in her mouth. Stephanie explained that her adopted father would warn to remove her mouth when he was about to ejaculate. Her adopted father liked to play this game and to see how quickly Stephanie could remove his penis from her mouth without getting ejaculate on or in her. When Stephanie turned 13, her biological father, who she had never met, wanted to become a part of her life. It was at this point and to him that Stephanie disclosed the abuse that had occurred over the years. During the criminal investigation, a medical examination was conducted, which revealed various levels of scaring and tearing within the vagina and anus, which supported Stephanie's allegation that the abuse had been going on for years.

Mother

Although not the stereotypical family member to sexually abuse children, mothers are also perpetrators of abuse (McCabe 2003). In cases of mothers who sexually abuse their children, the physical evidence, such as sperm that may be present in father-initiated abuse, does not exist. There are those who suggest that women, especially women with children, would never participate in the sexual exploitation of a child (McCabe and Manian 2011). This is uncommon but not nonexistent in the sexual abuse of children (Russell 2013). However, it may be the case that mothers are simply better at hiding or masking the abuse. A mother may mask the sexual abuse of her child in the daily activities associated with the caretaking of the child. Specifically, bathing the child, changing the clothes, or changing the child's diaper exposes the mother to the genitalia of her child. Exposure to the genitalia of the child leaves the child vulnerable to the individual who is sexually attracted to the physical characteristic of the child. Hence, explanations for mother-inflicted sexual abuse, as with father-inflicted abuse, include pedophilia (the physical attraction to young children).

Money is another explanation or motivation for the action of mother–child incest. A mother (or father) who is in need of money may market her (or his) sexual activities with her (or his) child through child pornography (McCabe 2009). These mothers often have substance abuse and addiction issues. For mothers, the likelihood of participating in incest with their child for profit often comes at the demand of her drug supplier and her need for more drugs.

Finally, the mother who uses her child for a sexual partner may do so in attempt to maintain *closeness* in their relationship (McCabe 2003). As unbelievable as this may seem, these mothers are so closely engaged in the lives of their children that they view their child (usually their son) as their lifelong and romantic partner. These mothers, who do not have an adult companion, place the role of companion on the child. In cases such as these, and especially in cases with other children in the household, the child becomes the second parent, with caretaking and the role of disciplinarian within the household. As the mother views herself as the wife and the son as the husband, neither member sees a reason to separate their lives even as the child becomes an adult. As with father–daughter incest, mother–son (or mother–child) incest will likely continue until the child is removed from the home.

Sibling

Sibling incest is perhaps the most common form of incest; however, it is also one of the least likely to be reported to police (McCabe 2003; Wiehe 1997). Many sex offenders begin offending in their adolescent years (Gosselin 2010). A younger sibling can be an easy target for older juveniles who wish to sexually abuse them. A study revealed that juvenile offenders who were supervising younger children tended to predominately victimize four- and five-year-olds (Moulden et al. 2007). Although most individuals perceive incest as adult–child, sexual relations between siblings are still incest. In some cases, incest between siblings is explained or even excused as part of normal sexual exploration between two young people.

In attempting to explain sibling sexual abuse, Johnson and Feldmeth (1993) provide four group explanations. The first includes young people engaged in incest as a result of curiosity. In this group, the abuse ends when they are told to stop. The second group involves individuals who were sexually abused or overexposed to sexual stimulation by adults. These young people are struggling to integrate their experiences of abuse with other meaningful experiences. The third group who was also abused by an adult, however, now exhibit more age-inappropriate behavior and project a mechanical matter-of-fact attitude in the action of incest. Finally, the fourth group, also sexually abused young people, is aggressive with behaviors that demonstrate the feelings of anger, aggression, and violence. In incestuous families with multiple child victims of incest, sibling incest is also common (McCabe 2003). However, in cases of sibling incest, where there are no other victims of incest, there is generally one older, larger, and aggressive partner and one younger, smaller, and submissive partner. Explanations of these cases of sibling incest include not only an attempt by one sibling to control or humiliate the other (Crosson-Tower 2010; Laviola 1992) but also the perception by the abuser that the younger sibling is in the home to serve them. Just as in the case of adult–child incest, the shame of sibling incest is enough for the victim and the family to remain silent (Tsun 1999). In most cases of sibling incest, the victimization continues until the victim ends the abuse (McCabe 2003).

Other Family Members

Outside of the immediate family, the risk for intrafamilial child abuse still exists. In most of these cases, the perpetrators are boyfriends, uncles, or grandfathers. For individuals who are grandfathers abusing their grandchildren, they are most likely to have abused their own children. Just as with other explanations of abuse by a family member, there exists the motive by the perpetrator to sexually abuse a child, as well as the opportunity for the abuse. In these cases, the decision to report the abuse often depends upon the parent's willingness to acknowledge the abuse, protect the child, and punish the abuser.

> Tara (age 4) was taken by her mother to her pediatrician for vaginal bleeding. While the mother waited in a separate area, the doctor contacted law enforcement reporting they had a four-year-old in their office for vaginal bleeding, and the child tested positive for chlamydia. The police arrived and placed the child in protective custody until an investigation could be conducted. The child was eventually interviewed where she told police that her Uncle Bobby (age 23) would put his *pee pee* inside her *pee pee* (pee pee being a common slang term used by small children to describe genitalia). Her Uncle Bobby has just been released on parole after serving three years for burglary. Part of the parole agreement was that he had to live at a

halfway house for three months, where he had freedom during the day to move about, but was required to return to the halfway house at night. Her Uncle Bobby was interviewed at the halfway house where he adamantly denied the allegation, stating how he loved his niece. The police obtained a search warrant for the interior of his penis in order to obtain a urethral cell sample. The sample was then sent to the state lab for analysis where it was confirmed that he had the same sexually transmitted disease as his niece. Bobby pleads guilty to the rape of a four-year-old, but never served a day in prison as the prosecutors were hesitant to put a four-year-old child on the stand to testify.

Combined Families

Today, the combination of families, which produce stepchildren and stepparents, provides another set of variables in the dynamics of incest. In combined families, especially families with multiple stepparents and children, the taboo of sex among blood relations is diminished, and the opportunity for incest increases (McCabe 2003). These individuals, living under the same roof for extended periods of time, are more likely to experience an increase in sexual attraction to each other; thus, as these individuals are classified as family members, there is an increased risk for incest. Of course, not all child sexual abuse is by a family member.

Extrafamilial Abuse

In extrafamilial abuse, the perpetrator is someone outside of the family. The abusers who target children often do so under the context of a social relationship with the child (Wallace and Roberson 2010; Crosson-Tower 2010). These adults create special circumstances to place themselves in the proximity of children. These offenders include neighbors, teachers, coaches, members of the clergy, and strangers. Surprising to many people and contrary to the notion of *stranger danger* is the fact that less than 50% of the cases of child sexual assaults are extrafamilial (Crosson-Tower 2010). In fact, it is now recognized that many of those who sexually abuse children are actually known personally or virtually to the child and/or his or her family. Often, these cases of extrafamilial abuse involve individuals with sexual addictions (i.e., sex addicts), pedophiles, individuals involved in child pornography, individuals involved in child sex rings, or individuals involved in child trafficking.

John (age 31) was being released from prison on Thanksgiving Eve after a two-year sentence for the sodomy of a young boy. A couple who were friends with John invited him over to their house for Thanksgiving so

John wouldn't be alone for the holidays. After the Thanksgiving meal, this couple walked into the living room where they saw that the lights had been turned off and that the couch had been pulled out away from the wall. As they approached the couch, John said that he was just playing hide-and-seek with their son who was seven years old. The following day, the boy's parents went to the police station to report that their son had been sodomized. John pleads guilty through a plea agreement and served an additional year in prison for the rape of another boy.

Sexual Addicts

The sex addict, similar to drug addicts, adopts a delusional thought process to rationalize their behaviors (Crosson-Tower 2010). These individuals, preoccupied with the thought of sex, plan the abuse and then execute the plan, even though the victim is a child. Sex addicts are dominated by compulsive thoughts of sex and sexual activity. Over time, just as with drug addicts, the sex addict must engage in riskier sexual activities such as with a child to produce the feeling of euphoria they most desire. Although research is conflicted on whether or not true sex addicts actually exist, reports suggest that approximately 70% of child molesters are labeled sex addicts (Shaw et al. 1995).

> Kayla (age 10) waits for the school bus each morning inside her living room as she looks through the window waiting for the bus. She lives alone with her father who waits alongside of her to assure that she makes the bus before he leaves for work. Kayla's father would frequently masturbate in plain sight beside his daughter. Kayla told a friend at school what was happening in her house, and this disclosure was eventually forwarded to law enforcement. Kayla's father was interviewed by the police when he openly admitted to masturbating regularly in front of his daughter. He attempted to justify his actions by explaining to the police that when he felt he was going to ejaculate, he would enter his bedroom so that his daughter *would not see him climax*. Kayla's father was arrested for the sexual abuse of a child, and Kayla was placed in foster care.

Pedophiles

By definition, pedophilia is the sexual attraction to prepubescent children (Feelgood and Hoyer 2008). Numerous studies have been conducted on pedophilia; however, most support the notion that a pedophile is attracted to certain physical characteristics of a child. It is not a crime to be a pedophile as pedophilia only becomes a crime when the offender acts on his or her desire for sexual activity with a child. One particular type of pedophilia is pederasty; this refers to the sexual activity of anal intercourse and is often with a boy (Radbill 1987). It should be noted, however, that juveniles are more likely to commit sodomy compared to adults (Mancini 2014).

Pedophiles who targeted young boys outside of the home committed the greatest number of crimes with each offender reporting an average of over 150 child victims (Abel 1987). This repetitive behavior of pedophiles makes cases involving these individuals far easier to investigate than cases involving situational child molesters or those cases where the child was a victim of opportunity (Lanning 1992).

Much of the research on the subject of pedophiles and situational child molesters suggests that pedophiles molest many more children than the situational molester. The situational pedophile may use force or another tactic to obtain sexual abuse as the current situation has provided the opportunity for abuse. The dependence of children often creates the opportunity for abuse (Pomponio 2004). In the investigation of a sexual assault by a pedophile or a preferential child molester, one must recognize again that just as an adult male (or female) may complete a series of steps or stages in the *courting* of an adult female, a pedophile often completes the same series of steps in the sexually abusing a child.

Child Pornography

Although illegal across the country, the production and distribution of child pornography is another type of sexual abuse (Dretsch and Moore 2014; McCabe 2009). In addition, through improved technology and the increased use of the Internet, the cases of child pornography have multiplied over the years. In these cases, sex offenders use the privacy of the Internet to identify those vulnerable children who use the Internet unsupervised (Medaris and Girouard 2002). Despite federal and state laws prohibiting the transmission of child pornography over the Internet, child pornography is still available.

A registered sex offender is a person who has been convicted of a crime of a sexual nature where the federal, state, or local laws require that they register their name after they may have paid their fine, served their sentence, or been placed on parole.

In some cases of child sexual exploitation, adults coerce and/or manipulate children to pose or perform sexual acts; however, in many instances, physical contact between the child and the perpetrator never occurs. Specifically, in today's advancing technological environment, images of children may be digitally transformed into pornographic materials, and, in fact, many of the children who appear in the electronically distributed pornography never realize that they have been victimized (McCabe and Johnston 2014). In these cases of child pornography, the children are victimized during the production of the pornography and then are repeatedly victimized as the pornography is distributed to the hundreds of viewers with Internet access and in search for child pornography.

Sexting

The use of a cellphone to send sexual graphics or pictures as a form of romantic interaction is considered sexting (McCabe and Johnston 2014). As cellphones are now more popular than landline phones, sexting has become a norm not only in adult relationships but also in teen relationships. A teen sexting a nude picture of themselves to a romantic partner is no different from an adult sending a nude picture of a teen. Legally, in many states, both actions are considered the distribution of child pornography.

Young individuals involved in sexting may not realize that they are producing or distributing child pornography. In fact, some estimates on the transmission of child pornography suggest that approximately 40% of today's child pornography originated with the child sending the picture to a peer (McCabe and Johnston 2014). Unfortunately, once the teen releases the picture on the Web, there is no point of return. The pornography is available for all with access to view, download, and redistribute.

Sex Rings

Finally, another type of extrafamilial sexual abuse involves the use of child sex rings. The term sex ring refers to a situation in which one or more offenders are simultaneously involved in the sexual abuse of several children (Lanning 1992). Therefore, the operation of a sex ring brings a different set of dynamics to child sexual abuse when compared to the *typical* familiar or extrafamiliar case of child sexual abuse.

A sex ring is a business; in particular, it is the business of child prostitution. Just as an adult may pay to have consensual sex with an adult partner in sex rings, adults pay or trade children to satisfy their desire to have sex with a child (McCabe 2009). The difference in these cases lies in the fact that the child does not have the option of participating and is forced into sexual acts with the adult. In child sex rings, there is an interaction among multiple victims and multiple offenders. In fact, today, there is often online communication among the offenders in regard to the demographic characteristics of the child and the sex ringleader's ability to locate the sought-after child (Lanning 1992). Often, children who are victims of child sex rings are passed from abuser to abuser; thus, they are victimized over and over again.

Child Trafficking

Finally, defined by the US Department of State as severe human trafficking, child trafficking is one of the most profitable criminal enterprises around the world today (McCabe and Manian 2011). Children across the globe are trafficked for a variety of reasons including sex. Child sex trafficking involves the involuntary movement of children for the purpose of sexual exploitation. Child sex trafficking, discussed in Chapter 7, involves both men and women as traffickers. The motive for trafficking from the trafficker's perspective, as with child pornography, is money. In cases of child sex trafficking, individuals desiring to participate in sexual intercourse with a child pay human traffickers to supply a child as the property of value for the abuser.

☐ Long-Term Consequences

Although the behavioral indicators mentioned previously in this chapter are indicators of child sexual abuse, some indicators can also be long-term consequences of the sexual abuse. Researchers suggest that some of the long-term behavioral consequences of child sexual abuse demonstrated by adult survivors include low self-esteem, depression, anxiety, substance abuse, somatization (reported physical pains as a result of mental illness or stress), and personality disorders (McCabe 2004; Molnar et al. 2001). These adults often feel the guilt and shame associated with survivors of adult sexual victimization, however, with deep-rooted feelings of worthlessness and self-blame as if they were merely inanimate objects with nothing of value to offer to society (Long et al. 2006).

Victims of child sexual abuse, once they reach adulthood, often find themselves unable to understand and participate in a *normal* adult sexual relationship. Conclusions differ as to whether intrafamiliar child sexual abuse is more traumatic than extrafamiliar child abuse. Allen (2001) suggests that as the evolutionary function of the family is protection, incest is especially damaging to the child and the adult child survivor.

Tyler (2002), in contrast, suggests that the source of the abuse is not as critical; however, the more severe the abuse, the more damaging the effect for the survivor. Adult victims of child sexual abuse report a prevalence of nightmares and flashbacks (King 2009). Just as the victims had difficulty as a child in expressing their want to end the abuse and the need to feel safe and secure, they have difficulties as adults in expressing their want for companionship and need to be loved.

Another long-term consequence of child sexual abuse is domestic violence and spousal prostitution (McCabe 2007; Bynum and Thompson 2002). Whether the adult assumes the role of the victim (as most women do) in the domestic setting or the abuser, the issues of power and control evident in their childhood victimization are again present in their adulthood. In addition and often associated with child victimization and household poverty, spousal prostitution, which involves the husband exchanging money for sexual relations with his wife, is more likely to occur if the wife is an adult survivor of child sexual abuse.

Finally, in terms of long-term behavioral consequences, delinquency and crime have been asserted to be related to child sexual abuse. Running away from home and the area is not unusual for the young adult who is a victim of child sexual abuse (McCabe 2003). Prostitution, drug abuse, sexual assaults, and parricide (the murder of one's parents) are also often not uncommon in the lives of adult survivors of child sexual abuse (Wallace 1999).

Today, the majority of the convicted offenders in prison report a history of child abuse and neglect. In particular, the majority of female offenders report a history of child sexual abuse. In addition, many of the convicted violent male offenders have a history of sexual abuse (Barkan 2015). For prostitutes on the street, selling their body is often better than the sexual abuse they experienced as a child in the home. In these cases, the notion of self-control on the part of the prostitute allows the activity of prostitution to be seen as a better avenue than child victimization that they once suffered.

In addition to long-term behavioral consequences, long-term physical consequences also often result from child sexual abuse. The long-term physical consequences of sexual abuse that have been identified in research include sexual dysfunction or a lack of interest in sex; physical health problems such as chronic pelvic infections and pregnancy complications; injuries related to the abuse; eating disorders (Ratican 1992); and addictions to alcohol, drugs, or prescription medicine (Feinauer et al. 1996).

Adults who have survived child sexual abuse have not only missed a healthy introduction to sexuality; they have also missed a healthy introduction to aging and adult relationships. For many of these individuals, the failure to be able to control their victimization as a child leads to an obsessive control over their adult fate. For those who have lost the desire to maintain some sort of control over their lives (or feel as though they do not deserve control over their lives), the need to stay healthy and safe is absent. For many of these individuals, there exists little quality of life. Finally, for adult survivors of child sexual abuse, suicide is not uncommon (Joiner et al. 2007; Hibbard et al. 1990).

☐ Summary

In 2013, over 600,000 children were confirmed victims of child abuse in the United States with approximately 10% of those children victims of child sexual abuse. Child victims of sexual abuse vary by age, race, gender, and socioeconomic status. Historically, it has been suggested that older females were the more likely victims, although, recently, discussions on the large proportion of male victims and very young victims have emerged. Child sexual abuse is not only intercourse. Child sexual abuse includes fondling a child's genitals, intercourse, incest, rape, sodomy, and the exploitation of children through pornography or prostitution.

Despite recent attempts by state and local authorities to end the sexual abuse of children, it continues and, in cases of child pornography, remains a very profitable business. In fact, it is estimated that thousands of dollars support the commercial sexual exploitation of children and that thousands of incidents of child sexual abuse occur in this county and internationally on an annual basis.

The focus of this chapter was child sexual abuse. Included were discussions on victims and the perpetrators both within the family to include siblings and outside the family. Child sexual abuse is both acute and chronic. Unfortunately, only some of the cases of child sexual abuse are detected through physical indicators. Hence, teachers, law enforcement officials, and social workers often rely upon behavioral indicators of sexual abuse. This chapter also discussed some of the long-term consequences for adult victims of child sexual abuse. As children are sexually victimized across the globe through molestation, incest, pornography, and trafficking, the sexual abuse of children is certainly a topic worthy of discussion. The sexual abuse of children, a topic at one time considered taboo, produces quite severe consequences for the child victim both in the short and long terms. The sexual abuse of children is certainly a victimization worthy of discussion and worthy of elimination.

CHAPTER QUESTIONS

1. What is the role of consent in cases of child sexual abuse, and is consent possible in sexual activity with children?

2. What factors suggest that familial child sexual abuse is more common than extrafamilial child sexual abuse?

3. What are some of behavioral indicators displayed by victims of child sexual abuse?

QUESTIONS FOR FURTHER THOUGHT

1. Why do so many sex offenders of children obtain what are considered *lenient sentences* during plea bargains?

2. How do the long-term consequences of sexual abuse affect the delay in disclosure for victims of child abuse?

3. Why is the *grooming* process such an effective tactic for sexually exploiting a child?

☐ References

Abel, G. 1987. Self-reported sex crimes of non-incarcerated paraphilics. *Journal of Interpersonal Violence*, 2(1), 3–25.

Allen, J. 2001. *Traumatic Relationships and Serious Mental Disorders*. Chichester, England: John Wiley & Sons.

Barkan, S. 2015. *Criminology: A Sociological Understanding* (6th ed.). Upper Saddle River, NJ: Prentice Hall.

Bartollas, C. 2000. *Juvenile Delinquency* (5th ed.). Boston: Allyn and Bacon.

Briere, J. and Elliott, D. 1994. The Future of Children: Sexual Abuse of Children. In R. E. Behrman (ed.), *Immediate and Long-Term Impacts of Child Sexual Abuse*. Los Altos, CA: The David and Lucile Packard Foundation. Vol. 4, No. 2, pp. 70–83.

Bynum, J. and Thompson, W. 2002. *Juvenile Delinquency: A Sociological Approach* (5th ed.). Boston: Allyn and Bacon.

Children's Bureau. 2014. *Child Maltreatment 2013*. Washington, D.C.: US Department of Health and Human Services, Administration for Children and Families.

Crosson-Tower, C. 2010. *Understanding Child Abuse and Neglect* (8th ed.). Boston: Allyn and Bacon.

Daigle, L. 2012. *Victimology*. Thousand Oaks, CA: SAGE.

Daigle, L. and Muftic, L. 2016. *Victimology*. Thousand Oaks, CA: SAGE.

DeYoung, M. 1982. *The Sexual Victimization of Children.* Jefferson, NC: McFarland.

Dretsch, E. and Moore, R. 2014. *Sexual Deviance Online: Research and Readings.* Durham, NC: Carolina Academic Press.

Feelgood, S. and Hoyer, J. 2008. Child molester or pedophile? Sociological versus psychopathological classification of sexual offenders against children. *Journal of Sexual Aggression,* 14(1), 33–43.

Feinauer, L., Callahan, E., and Hilton, H. 1996. Positive intimate relationships decrease depression in sexually abused women. *American Journal of Family Therapy,* 24(2), 99–106.

Finkelhor, D. 1984. *Child Sexual Abuse: New Theories and Research.* New York Free Press.

Finkelhor, D. 1994. The international epidemiology of child sexual abuse. *Child Abuse and Neglect,* 18(5), 409–417.

Fergusson, D. and Mullen, P. 1999. *Childhood Sexual Abuse: An Evidence-Based Perspective.* London: SAGE.

Gebhard, P., Gagnon, J., Pomeroy, W., and Christenson, C. 1965. *Sex Offenders: An Analysis of Types.* New York: Harper & Row.

Gosselin, D. 2010. *Heavy Hands: An Introduction to the Crimes of Family Violence* (4th ed.). Upper Saddle River Prentice Hall.

Gully, K., Britton, H., Hansen, K., Goodwin, K., and Nope, J. 1999. A new measure for distress during child sexual abuse examinations: The Genital Examination Distress Scale. *Child Abuse and Neglect,* 23(1), 61–70.

Helfer, R. and Kempe, R. 1987. *The Battered Child* (4th ed.). Chicago: University of Chicago Press.

Hibbard, R., Ingersoll, G., and Orr, D. 1990. Behavioral roles, emotional roles, and child abuse among adolescents in a nonclinical setting. *Pediatrics,* 86(6), 896–901.

Hindelang, M. 1976. *Criminal Victimization in 8 American Cities.* Cambridge, MA: Ballinger.

Johnson, C. 2006. Sexual abuse in children. *Pediatric Review,* 27(1), 17–27.

Johnson, T. and Feldmeth, J. 1993. Sexual behavior: A continuum. In E. Gil and T. C. Johnson (eds.) *Sexualized Children and Children Who Molest.* Rockville, MD: Launch Press, pp. 41–52.

Joiner, T., Sachs-Ericssson, N., Wingate, L., Brown, J., Anestis, M., and Selby, E. 2007. Childhood physical and sexual abuse and lifetime number of suicide attempts: A persistent and theoretically important relationship. *Behavior Research and Therapy,* 45(3), 539–547.

Kamsner, S. and McCabe, M. 2000. The relationship between adult psychological adjustment and childhood sexual abuse, childhood physical abuse, and family-of-origin characteristics. *Journal of Interpersonal Violence,* 15(5), 1243–1261.

Kenny, M. and McEachern, A. 2000. Racial, ethnic, and cultural factors of childhood sexual abuse. *Clinical Psychological Review,* 20(7), 905–922.

King, B. 2009. *Human Sexuality Today* (6th ed.). Upper Saddle River, NJ; Pearson.

Lanning, K. 1992. *Child Sex Rings: A Behavioral Analysis for Criminal Justice Professionals Handling Cases of Child Sexual Exploitation* (3rd ed.). Quantico, VA: Federal Bureau of Investigation. Behavioral Science Unit.

Laviola, M. 1992. Effects of older brother-younger sister incest: A study of the dynamics in 17 cases. *Child Abuse and Neglect*, 16(3), 409–421.

Long, L., Burnette, J., and Thomas, R. 2006. Sexuality counseling: An integrated approach. *Sexual and Relationship Therapy*, 17(4), 321–327.

Mancini, C. 2014. *Sex Crime Offenders and Society*. Durham, NC: Carolina Academic Press.

Mayer, A. 1983. *Incest: A Treatment Manual for Therapy with Victims, Spouses, and Offenders*. Holmes Beach, FL: Learning Publications.

McCabe, K. 2003. *Child Abuse and the Criminal Justice System*. New York: Peter Lang.

McCabe, K. 2007. Spousal prostitution. In N. Jackson (ed.) *Encyclopedia of Domestic Violence*, New York: Routledge, pp. 673–674.

McCabe, K. 2009. *Human Trafficking: National and International Responses*. New York: Peter Lang.

McCabe, K. and Johnston, O. 2014. Perceptions on the legality of sexting. *Social Science Computer Review*, 32(6), 765–768.

McCabe, K. and Manian, S. 2011. *Sex Trafficking: A Global Perspective*. Lanham, MD: Rowman and Littlefield/Lexington Books.

McCabe, K. and Martin, G. 2005. *School Violence, the Media, and Criminal Justice Responses*. New York: Peter Lang.

Medaris, M. and Girouard, C. 2002. *Protecting Children in Cyberspace: The ICAC Task Force Program*. Washington, D.C.: US Department of Justice, Office of Justice Programs, Office of Juvenile Justice and Delinquency Prevention. (NCJ-191213).

Molnar, B., Buka, S., and Kessler, R. 2001. Child sexual abuse and subsequent psychopathology: Results from the National Comorbidity Survey. *American Journal of Public Health*, 91(6), 753–760.

Moulden, H., Firestone, P., and Wexler, A. 2007. Child care providers who commit sexual offences: A description of offender, offence, and victim characteristics. *International Journal of Offender Therapy and Comparative Criminology*, 51(4), 384–406.

Pomponio, A. 2004. *Investigation and Prosecution of Child Abuse* (3rd ed.). Thousand Oaks, CA: SAGE.

Radbill, S. 1987. A history of child abuse. In R. Helfer and R. Kempe (eds.) *The Battered Child* (4th ed.). Chicago: University of Chicago Press.

Ratican, K. L. 1992. Sexual abuse survivor: Identifying symptoms and treatment considerations. *Journal of Counseling and Development*, 71(1), 33–38.

Riggs, S., Sahl, G., Greenwald, E., Atkison, H., and Paulson, A. 2007. Family environment and adult attachment as predictors of psychopathy and personality dysfunction among inpatient abuse survivors. *Violence and Victims*, 22(5), 577–600.

Russell, B. 2013. *Perceptions of Female Offenders: How Stereotypes and Social Norms Affect Criminal Justice Responses*. New York: Springer.

Russell, D. 1983. The incidence and prevalence of intrafamiliar and extrafamiliar sexual abuse of female children. *Child Abuse and Neglect*, 7(2), 133–146.

Sedlak, A., Mettenburg, Basena, M., Petta, I., McPherson, K., Greene, A., and Li, S. 2010. National Incidence Study of Child Abuse and Neglect (NIS-4): Report to Congress executive summary. Washington, D.C.: US Department of Health and Human Services, Administration for Children and Families.

Sgroi, S. 1982. *Handbook of Clinical Intervention in Child Sexual Abuse.* Lexington, MA: Lexington Books.

Shaw, T., Herkov, M., and Greer, R. 1995. Examination of treatment completion and predicted outcome among incarcerated sex offenders. *Bulletin of the American Academy of Psychiatry and the Law*, 23(1), 35–41.

Sheldon, K. 2011. What we know about men who download child abuse image. *British Journal of Forensic Practice*, 13(4), 221–234.

Tsun, O. K. A. 1999. Sibling incest: A Hong Kong experience. *Child Abuse and Neglect*, 23(1), 71–80.

Tyler, K. 2002. Social and emotional outcomes of childhood sexual abuse: A review of recent literature. *Aggression and Violence Behavior*, 7(4), 567–589.

Wallace, H. 1999. *Family Violence: Legal, Medical, and Social Perspectives* (2nd ed.). Boston: Allyn and Bacon.

Wallace, H. and Roberson, C. 2010. *Family Violence: Legal, Medical, and Social Perspectives* (6th ed.). Boston: Pearson.

Wiehe, V. R. 1997. *Sibling Abuse: Hidden Physical, Emotional, and Sexual Trauma* (2nd ed.). Thousand Oaks, CA: Sage.

World Health Organization. 2008. *Eliminating Female Genital Mutilation.* Geneva, Switzerland: WHO Press.

Emotional Abuse

Jeremy receives an unsatisfactory grade in his college statistics course. During a conversation with his professor, he becomes emotional and refers to himself as dumb and not having the "stuff" to succeed in school. In a follow-up conversation with his professor, she asked who told him he couldn't make it in college. Jeremy's response was—his father. Jeremy is 24 years old.

It has been suggested that emotional abuse is the most common form of child abuse (McCabe 2003). However, since emotional abuse is often accompanied by a more *severe* form of abuse (i.e., physical or sexual), it is often overlooked, and neglect is the most commonly reported type of abuse. Unfortunately, documenting emotional abuse is often difficult or perceived as not abuse; therefore, many cases of emotional abuse go unnoticed, unreported, and unaddressed (Crosson-Tower 2010). Research suggests that emotional abuse is considered the most difficult type of abuse to identify (Burgess et al. 2013). Definitions vary by state, by country, and within disciplines as even clinical psychologists have offered diverging definitions of emotional abuse (Thompson and Kaplan 1996).

To anyone who is uncertain as to whether they have ever witnessed emotional abuse, think about the dinner you attended in a restaurant, and recall the angry verbal reactions of the young couple when their two-year-old child acted tired and cranky. Observe the actions of the parent in a store, when his son has requested a new football, and the father shrugs his shoulders and states that the boy is *not an athlete* as he walks away. Finally, observe a mother as she yells at her child to wipe her *disgusting runny nose again*. All of these scenarios may be considered examples of emotional abuse.

For clarity in this chapter, childhood emotional (or psychological) abuse is defined, based upon a chronic behavior, as the ongoing maltreatment of a child (McCabe 2003). In this chapter, emotional abuse includes not only verbal acts of aggression toward a child but also the destruction of the child's personal property and deliberate attempts to humiliate, scare, ignore, or isolate a child.

In terms of long-term consequences, researchers conclude that emotional abuse is generally the most damaging form of child abuse. Unfortunately, it is most difficult to identify individual perceptions of what is damaging and what constitutes emotional abuse (Chiu et al. 2013). In addition, court cases, based simply upon emotional abuse, are nonexistent. Therefore, when attempting to reduce child abuse, most efforts focus on either physical abuse or sexual abuse and not emotional abuse, although emotional abuse is essentially present in other forms of child abuse. This chapter includes a discussion of the various types of emotional abuse and the indicators of emotional abuse, as well as the perpetrators of emotional abuse and the long-term consequences of childhood emotional abuse.

Just as over the last decade, the number of substantiated reported cases of child physical and sexual abuse has increased, so has the number of reported cases of emotional abuse (McCabe 2003). Unfortunately, physical or sexual abuse is the usual focus of an investigation of child abuse, and, emotional abuse, although always present, is not a deciding factor. There are child victims of physical and emotional abuse, victims of sexual and emotional abuse, and victims of emotional abuse; however, physical and sexual abuses are perceived as the most damaging, even if this is not true. For instance, a parent may strike their child while saying,

"I wish you were never born."

These words may cause more long-term harm than the strike itself. As the saying goes,

"The physical injury goes, the emotional injury may not."

Thus, the negative effects of emotional abuse on self-esteem and the overall mental health of the individual may be more obvious as the child ages (Hart and Brassard 1987).

There are approximately 250,000 child victims of emotional abuse in the United States on an annual basis (Children's Bureau 2014); thus, there are a significant number of children, of varying ages, who are entitled to help. Approximately 40% of the victims of emotional abuse are under the age of 6, approximately 35% of the victims are between the ages of 6 and 11, and approximately 25% are over the age of 12 (Children's Bureau 2014). Hence, victims of emotional abuse, not unlike other forms of abuse, are young, and, as victims of emotional abuse grow older, they often begin to distance themselves from the abuser. Again, most cases of emotional abuse accompany other forms of abuse and are generally at the core of all other types of abuse. Emotional abuse can range from verbal ridicule to isolation and confinement (Kelley et al. 1997). Just as there are varying degrees of emotional abuse, there are also varying consequences to emotional abuse. Essentially, each type and degree of abuse has some negative impact upon the life of a child.

The American Humane Association (AHA) is an organization founded in 1877 and is dedicated to the welfare of animals and children. The AHA defines emotional abuse as a pattern of behavior by a caretaker that can seriously interfere with a child's development. Emotional abuse is also referred to as psychological maltreatment.

This chapter discusses emotional abuse in terms of six categories. The categories of emotional abuse are (1) rejection, (2) isolation, (3) terrorizing (or verbal abuse), (4) ignoring, (5) corrupting, and (6) destroying personal property. Each category is defined through its own set of dynamics, consequences, and perpetrators. However, the majority of the cases of childhood emotional abuse involve the parents or guardians of the child.

☐ Rejection

Rejection involves the refusal of acceptance. Plainly said, some parents reject their children. Whether this parental action is subconsciously or consciously decided, the rejection of a child by a parent is devastating to that child (McCabe 2003). For most individuals, the idea of a parent refusing the love from their children is unimaginable; however, there are many parents who reject their children and many reasons for their rejection. Aside from mental illness in the parent, reasons for the rejection of a child by the parent include disappointed expectations, family dynamics, family physical resemblance, and secrecy.

For many women in particular, being pregnant and having a child are a childhood fantasy, and they have expectations of a wonderful experience. In this fantasy, the pregnancy goes well, the mother glows, her hair is beautiful, and she thrives within an environment of euphoria for nine months. The fantasy continues with the pregnancy resulting in an adorable healthy baby to be brought home to a lovely house by a beautiful mother and handsome father. Unfortunately, for these mothers, fantasy is not reality.

In reality, the mother's pregnancy was difficult; the mother was ill throughout the nine months, and she was exhausted and worried not only about the expenses related to the pregnancy but also regarding the expenses related to raising a child. When the child is born, the labor was long and difficult and resulted in a cesarean birth. The child was not adorable; the child was small and underdeveloped. When the baby comes home, the mother has not recuperated from her surgery, she still carries the pregnancy weight, she has no help at home, and the baby has colic. In a nutshell, the expectations of a wonderful experience are shattered, and the mother is miserable. From the mother's perspective, the child is to blame for her unhappiness, and the result is the rejection of the child by the mother. If the child has a physical disability, then rejection is even more of a risk (Crosson-Tower 2010).

Another explanation for the rejection of a child is related to the dynamics of the family. In some of these cases, the child may be forced upon the first parent by the second as the second is not interested in parenting or not interested in parenting with this particular partner. Whether the child is a result of a pregnancy not mutually desired or the blending of already existing families, the child (or children) may not be accepted by the other adult. This nonacceptance may be obvious or subtle; however, the rejection of the child still occurs.

In other situations, within a family, one child may be rejected by one adult and another child rejected by another adult (McCabe 2003). These cases of rejection, often in reaction to the child labeled as the *favorite* of one of the adults, are an attempt to *balance* the love within a family unit. Oftentimes, these cases involve the father choosing to spend more time with one child (often the older) and the mother attempting to compensate with extra time focused on the younger. Hence in these cases, the older child feels the rejection of the mother, while the younger child feels the rejection of the father.

Children need a sense of belonging and attachment to all of the adults in their family. Abusive treatment toward children (even in the form of rejection) may impair attachment and increase the likelihood that the child will engage in aggressive behavior (Gosselin 2010). Children who come from abusive or neglectful homes are more likely to seek out a pseudo-family such as a criminal street gang or a delinquent middle-school clique to fulfil their emotional needs (Hanser and Mire 2011; Valdez 2005). In these cases, the gang becomes the child's family. As Hirschi (1969) concluded in some of the earliest works on delinquency, the weaker the tie between parent and child, the greater probability of delinquency.

In some cases of rejection, a child is rejected by a parent because they simply resemble the physical characteristics of the other biological parent. These cases most often involve the mother who was abandoned or hurt by the father of the child, and now she rejects the child. The child who looks like the man who hurt her is a constant reminder of the pain she felt with the father. As a result, she rejects the child.

Finally, a child may be rejected by a parent if the child is a reminder of a painful or shameful incident that occurred in the parent's life. These incidents include rape, incest, teen pregnancy, or extramarital affair. The child was not wanted, and the presence of the child is now a reminder of a shameful and painful event that the parent wished had never occurred.

☐ Isolation

Isolation involves the state of being placed in a situation alone or that is separate from others. The isolation of a child, in terms of emotional abuse, involves an adult refusing a child the opportunity for social interactions with others (Crosson-Tower 2010). This is one of the most common categories of emotional abuse not only for children but also for adult victims of domestic violence.

In cases of emotional abuse through isolation, the perpetrator eliminates the potential for all social interactions for the child. In some cases of isolation, the abuse of the child is not through a malicious effort by the abuser, but rather it is an extension of the abuser's need to be socially isolated. In these cases, the parent who becomes anxious and uncomfortable in social settings will isolate their child as an indirect consequence of their direct efforts to isolate themselves (Crosson-Tower 2002). Hence, the child suffers continued isolation because the parent is unable to function within social settings.

In other cases of child isolation by a parent, the parent, as in cases of domestic violence, controls the child's life by controlling the social interactions of the child. These parents, either afraid that the child will leave them, or fearful that the child may betray the confidentiality of events within the home, will isolate the child from others.

In these cases, the child is confined to the home and is not allowed to visit the homes of peers or other family members. They are not allowed to participate in sports or after-school activities; in a nutshell, they are not allowed to attend events without the parent. Unfortunately, in many cases, the willful and consistent isolation of a child by a parent is accompanied by another type of child abuse such as sexual abuse or physical abuse.

Finally, nonfamily members involved in other types of criminal victimizations often isolate their child victims. In cases of abduction, sexual abuse, child pornography, and sex trafficking, children are isolated by their abusers to avoid the detection of their victimization (McCabe 2008). In these cases, the children not only suffer the victimization by their abuser(s) but also the victimization of isolation and the inability to seek help.

> Coleen, age 27, lived alone with her five-year-old son Thomas. Coleen and Thomas very rarely went out of the house, as Coleen thought there was a conspiracy with organized crime to have her son and herself killed. This delusion consumed her, which had a detrimental effect on Thomas, as she refused to leave the house, causing Thomas to be fearful of the world. Coleen had her front door double-locked at all times and had her house secured as if she lived in a fortress. Her ex-husband Dennis contacted the police with concerns of the welfare of his son, as Coleen shared her fears with Dennis and would not allow him to take Thomas for his time, as they had shared custody. Social services was contacted for a welfare check of the child, but Coleen refused to allow entry. Social services reported this to law enforcement, and they were unable to make contact with Coleen or her son as well. Due to the concern of Coleen's mental health, a court order was attained to place Thomas into protective custody. When the police arrived at her residence, there was no response, which caused law enforcement to forcibly gain entry. The child was placed in protective custody by law enforcement, and an emergency hearing was held the next day to determine whether Coleen was emotionally abusing Thomas due to her paranoia. The court gave temporary custody of Thomas to his father pending an investigation by social services. The following day, Coleen drove to a busy highway pulling over into the breakdown lane and, in front of heavy traffic, ended her life by shooting herself in the chest.

☐ Terrorizing

Terrorizing produces widespread fear. Another type of emotional abuse is terrorizing, in which the abuser verbally assaults the child on a continuous basis to create a climate of fear (Crosson-Tower 2010). Many children are terrorized within the family by not only parents but also, more commonly, siblings (Wiehe 1997). For a young child, this terrorizing may include the use of loud noises or quick and random movements intended to startle the child and produce fears. In addition, the use of the dark, confined places and animals such as dogs only helps to increase the child's terror.

Terrorizing, although a category of emotional abuse, is often disguised as play or fun among family members. Siblings hide from each other, jump out from closets, hide under each other's beds, and scare each other in the dark—all under the umbrella of practical jokes. Unfortunately, this family environment often enforces fear, nervousness, and insecurities among its child victims.

For older child victims, terrorizing often includes verbal threats of injury, abandonment, and public humiliation. In addition, terrorizing may include displays of knives and other potential weapons to create stifling and hostile environments. Unfortunately, for older children, the child may perceive themselves as too old to be afraid, yet, because of the chronic terrorizing they have experienced over the years, they are fearful and often embarrassed to report their victimization.

Finally, terrorizing often occurs in conjunction with other categories of abuse. Specifically, children are terrorized by abusers in an attempt to maintain the silence of the child or to coerce the child into participating in activities that are embarrassing, humiliating, and painful for the child such as sexual abuse. For these abusers, the terrorizing of the child will ensure that the child will continue to participate in the activity and/or will not report the abuse. Just as with child abuse by isolation, children are often terrorized to support the criminal actions of child sexual exploitation and child trafficking (McCabe 2008).

Abe, age 34, had two children: Grant, his first, and a younger daughter. Grant, the older son, could never seem to do anything right. At the same time, the daughter, in Abe's eyes, could never seem to do anything wrong. Abe bragged how he could control his teenage son with strict discipline and was never afraid to be too harsh. Abe would administer extreme punishments for minor infractions to his son but showed compassion and understanding to the younger one's behavior. Abe seemed to enjoy ridiculing and belittling Grant in front of family, friends, or anyone whom Abe considered an audience. In Grant's eyes, there was no bond with his father, as Abe was never willing to display any love toward him. Grant began acting out at middle school and continued this behavior into his high school years. This behavior drew even more consequences from his father, where Grant did not have any of the freedom or privileges most teenagers had at his age. Grant joined a street gang, which, in his eyes, was the family he never had. He continued to get involved with criminal behavior into his young adulthood and eventually was convicted on crimes and incarcerated.

In summary, the intimidation of an adult is a crime; the intimidation of a child, even at the hands of his or her parent or caretaker, is also a crime (McCabe and Gregory 1997). Often, in these cases, the child views the world as hostile and rejects any initiatives from others outside of the home. These victims live in fear of their abusers—a fear of victimization and the fear of failing to please that abuser. In addition, these children are often fearful of everyday activities and often choose to be alone.

☐ Ignoring

To ignore someone is to fail to notice them. For clarity, ignoring a child, when applied to the child's basic needs of food and shelter, may be referred to as neglect (Wallace 1999); however, when a child is deprived of social stimulation and responsiveness from his or her caretaker, this action of ignoring is classified as emotional abuse (Crosson-Tower 2010). Ignoring a child often results in a child with a self-perception of worthlessness.

In many of today's parenting magazines, it is advised that if you ignore inappropriate behaviors by a child (e.g., crying for a toy in a store or demonstrating a temper tantrum when asked to leave the pool), then the child will most likely end those behaviors. However, the chronic ignoring of a child is considered a form of emotional abuse (McCabe 2003).

Children learn through relationships with others. Parents who ignore their children fail to provide these children the social interactions required for healthy mental and physical development. In the overwhelming majority of cases of ignoring a child, the abuser is the parent or the caretaker. As a result, it is not uncommon for an ignored child to lose interest in not only social interactions but also eating, bathing, and school. In many circumstances, the ignored child, similar to an adult grieving the loss of a loved one, also exhibits behaviors of grief. Without someone to ensure proper nutrition and care, it is not unusual for ignored children to experience health problems to include malnutrition, delayed physical development, and substance abuse.

Parents may either intentionally or unintentionally ignore their children. Reasons for unintentionally ignoring their children include mental illnesses such a depression on the part of the parent, the focus of the parent on another child in the family (often a child with special needs such as a learning disability or a special talent such as athletics), or the focus of the parent on another adult in the family. Researchers are now acknowledging the problems of mental illness as related to the ignoring of a child by a caregiver (Smith et al. 2014). Parents with problems such as depression are often unable to function within any setting (to include the family). Hence, the child of a depressed parent is often ignored as an indirect result of their parent's mental illness (O'Hagan 1993). The parent, often unaware of the effect of their mental illness on the family, fails to recognize their need for treatment. Thus, the noncomplaining child, as they see the behavior as normal, continues their life course as being ignored.

In cases other than the mental illness of the parent, in many instances, a parent with a disabled child will focus all of their efforts on the care of that child. Unfortunately, this results in the other child (or children) in the family being ignored (Crosson-Tower 2010). The parent, who feels that the nondisabled children are able to provide their own care, is more likely to fail to interact with them on a regular basis. In other instances, a parent with one child displaying specific talents such as athletics may ignore the other children in the family to continue to provide the time, support, and resources required for their *talented* child to hone their talents. This is not uncommon in cases with multiple male children and one with a special talent for sports such as soccer. The parent will provide the time for practices, transportation, and tournaments for their athlete; however, the non-soccer-playing son is ignored or labeled as a nonathletic.

Finally, the parent, who focuses their attentions on pleasing another adult either for care or to maintain a violence-free relationship, may not provide their child the attention they require. Of course, this scenario of ignoring is often the case in homes that experience domestic violence. One adult dedicates their life to pleasing the other adult in the family; hence, the child or children are ignored.

Parents also intentionally ignore their children. Reasons for intentionally ignoring a child include the choice of work (not due to economic pressures), the choice of interacting with another person, and the personalities of both the parent and the child. Unfortunately, many adults perceive that work and a successful career are the most important aspects of their lives. These individuals, often also ignored as children and sometimes raised in poverty, perceive their identity as an extension of their career position (McCabe 2008). For these individuals, love is equated with money. As researchers of adult relationships may indicate, these adults equate the giving and receiving of material gifts as expressions of their love rather than words of affirmation or quality time (Chapman 2004). If these parents are providing for their children, then they are expressing their love for their children and fulfilling their parental obligations.

Unfortunately, in many of these cases, and especially in cases with two-parent career families, the children are ignored as words of affirmation or time together are not perceived by the parents as important.

Parents also ignore their children when they choose to devote their attention toward another individual. In some cases, the other individual is also an adult, and the two individuals are in an intimate relationship. In other cases, the individual is a child, and, as one parent focuses on one child, the other parent focuses on the other child or children. In these cases, one child is often labeled as one parent's *favorite*, and the remaining child or children are considered the favorite(s) of the other parent. This also occurs in situations where a problem emerges with one child such as a problem in school or substance abuse issues; thus, the parent may feel that it is better to provide the *problem child* their undivided attention to *get them through the rough spot*. Unfortunately, for the child without the issue, he or she becomes the ignored child.

Finally, parents may choose to ignore a child either as a punishment for a behavior or because of an incompatibility between the parent and the child. Just as adults in conflict around differences of opinion ignore each other, a parent may ignore a child if they are unhappy with or disagree with the child. In these cases, parents will choose to ignore the child as displayed in the silent treatment as an attempt to control the child by not interacting with the child until the child's actions are pleasing to them. In addition, and not always acceptable to acknowledge, just as some adults do not care for the company of each other, some parents do not care for the company of their children. In these cases, the individuals vary on opinions, taste in clothes, choices of peers, etc. Although this type of parent–child ignoring usually occurs when the child is older, it is still considered a form of emotional abuse.

Unfortunately, the ignoring of a child creates consequences for that child. Just as adults seek and desire social relationships, children also seek and desire such relationships. If a child is ignored in the home, eventually, the child will seek a satisfactory relationship of acknowledgment outside of the home.

☐ Corruption

Corruption is an action that destroys the trust among parties. The corruption of a child involves engaging the child in self-destructive and sometimes criminal behaviors and is also a type of emotional abuse (Crosson-Tower 2010). Corruption includes providing the child alcohol or drugs and enticing the child into participating in criminal activity.

Generally, adults corrupt children for one of two reasons: (1) individual pleasure or (2) economic gain (McCabe 2000). For clarity, perpetrators of corruption are not limited to adults; however, generally, perpetrators of child corruption are of adult age. As the child is corrupted, the adult–child bond of trust is destroyed.

An adult or older child who uses a child for the completion of a criminal activity such as a burglary, smuggling drugs, or selling drugs engages the child into the activity for financial gain. These criminals know that the penalties for a child engaged in criminal activity are often less severe than for a convicted adult. However, these adults are subject to the lesser criminal charge of contributing to the delinquency of a child.

The child who wishes for that attention of an adult and to please the adult will do whatever is asked. In addition, if the child receives a monetary award for participating in the criminal activity, then they are more likely to continue the illegal activity.

Finally, an adult who engages a child in sexual activities with them, in prostitution, or pornography corrupts the child. If the child perceives the activity to be worthwhile, in terms of either attention by the abuser or being profitable, the activity may continue (McCabe 2003). Unlike most aspects of emotional abuse, law enforcement will intervene when a child is a victim of corruption as the act is usually classified as illegal under a criminal statute, thus allowing a law enforcement officer to arrest an offender. Unfortunately, children who have been corrupted by an adult often display antisocial and violent behaviors (Bynum and Thompson 2002; Bartollas 2000). In addition, these child victims of corruption often become the perpetrators of adult criminal actions (Jensen 2009; Barkan 2001).

An adult who provides a child alcohol or drugs does so to gain the favor of that child; that favor obliges the child to act as the adult desires (McCabe 2003). Whether the adult desires to be seen as a leader by the child, desires the sexual attention of the child, or wishes to exploit the child, the action of corruption is illegal as is a form of emotional abuse. However, it is a form of emotional abuse that benefits the adult.

Cassandra, age 33, a school bus mechanic for a local school district, had a son, Adam, who told friends at school that his Mom had been having him take photographs of her partially nude, and he brought the digital camera to school to show his friends. This eventually came to the attention of law enforcement, and they seized the camera as evidence. The photographs revealed Cassandra, partially nude and posing in what appeared to be provocative positions. The police confronted Cassandra, who openly admitted to having her son take these pictures, but defended her actions, stating she did not feel that she did anything inappropriate. She explained that these photographs were being sent to her new boyfriend and that Adam was not harmed in any way. Cassandra was arrested for endangering the welfare of a child, and the school district terminated her employment, since they were concerned with her working around children.

☐ Property Destruction

From a legal definition, property destruction occurs as a result of either negligence or willful damage. Emotional abuse may also be manifested in the destruction of a child's property or pets by an abuser (Wiehe 1997). Although more commonly seen in abuse by a sibling and not originally recognized as a form of emotional abuse, the destruction of a child's possessions can be devastating to the child, especially when this destruction occurs in view of the child (McCabe 2003).

For the abuser, the destruction of the child's property is an indicator of their power and control over the child and the child's belongings. In addition, if the property destroyed was purchased by another person, the abuser has demonstrated his control over property that he does not own. If the property destroyed was purchased by the abuser, then the ability to introduce and remove items from the child's life, without the consent of the child, has been demonstrated.

From the child's perspective, the abuser may provide items for the pleasure of the child and remove items for the punishment of the child. The killing of an animal or pet demonstrates the power over life and death held by the abuser. From the child's standpoint, if the abuser would kill their pet, then the abuser would kill them. If this type of destruction occurs, the child not only is fearful of the abuser but also now feels the guilt of responsibility over the destruction and the guilt of not being able to stop the destruction.

In cases of emotional abuse by property destruction, the child is powerless against their abuser. Property destruction is a tactic that allows the offender to manipulate the child into compliance. Just the threat of harming a child's pet, or taking away or destroying a child's favorite toy, can be an effective facilitator in the exploitation of a child.

Physical and Behavioral Indicators

As a supportive parent–child relationship is the basis for developing self-confidence, emotional abuse disrupts that development. In many cases, this developmental disruption affects the child both physically and behaviorally. These physical indicators include low weight, limited growth, and stress-related ailments. As with many symptoms of abuse, these behaviors often change with the growth of the child; however, children of all ages may be victims of all categories of emotional abuse.

Specifically, for many young children, terrorizing is a part of the emotional abuse. These children are dependent upon the interactions of parents. In addition, these children, who react to loud sounds and sudden movements with surprise and fear, are often anxious toward new experiences, especially sensitive and fearful to loud noises (such as the ocean), and often appear confused by the actions of others (McCabe 2003).

School-aged children are often the victims of isolation, ignoring, and the destruction of property. School-aged victims often express feelings of guilt at the thought of disappointing their teacher, avoid eye contact, and are often emotional to the point of frequent crying and the inability to trust other adults (Hibbard et al. 1990). In addition, these children may experience sleep disorders, speech disorders, problems in school, and a disinterest in eating and proclaim negative statements about themselves and their undesirability (Crosson-Tower 2010).

For many older child victims of emotional abuse such as corruption, their behaviors display the variation of either extremely happy or manically depressed (Crosson-Tower 2002). This is especially the case for the preteen females in their attempts to conform to their environment and attempt to place the needs of others ahead of their own needs. This altruistic attempt, when met with unexpected resistance, often results in an emotional reaction by the child (Kashani and Shepperd 1990). Preteen male victims of emotional abuse, on the other hand, do not generally display the emotional extremes; instead, their behaviors are often aggressive and violent (McHale and Rasmussen 1998).

Finally, older child victims of emotional abuse, because of low feelings of self-worth, depression, and powerlessness, attempt to feel better about themselves (McCabe 2003). In females, these attempts often include sexual activity at an early age, bullying or cyberbullying, anorexia or bulimia, tobacco use, cutting themselves, and attempts at suicide by taking sleeping pills (Bynum and Thompson 2002). In males, these indicators include the use of alcohol, tobacco use, poor school performance, a propensity toward aggression and violence, bullying, and suicide (Jensen 2009; Bartollas 2000). Hence, indicators of emotional abuse, most often the only outward signs of abuse, vary by the demographic of the child and the category of emotional abuse.

Abusers

With the exception of corruption and destruction of personal property, most cases of child emotional abuse involve a parent or caretaker, and most involve a mother between the ages of 20 and 35 (Children's Bureau 2014). Emotional abuse among siblings is rarely recognized as parents usually perceive this behavior as *normal* sibling rivalry (Wiehe 1997). However, there are significant long-term effects due to sibling abuse. Specifically, siblings have an increased risk of acquiring neurotic traits and are at risk of attempted suicide from prolonged abuse (Kiselica and Morrill-Richards 2007). In fact, research suggests that emotional abuse by a sibling results in greater mental distress by the child victims as compared to emotional abuse by a peer (Tucker et al. 2014). Although sibling emotional abuse may continue through adulthood, the majority of abuse occurs when both the abuser and the victim are still children and still living in the same home (Wallace and Roberson 2015).

Explanations for the motives of these abusers include mental illness, personality, family upbringing, and the current family environment. Unfortunately, parents with mental illness are often unable to understand their actions toward their child. With their mental illness often comes depression and social withdrawal; hence, the child, because of their parent's inability to interact within the social boundaries, is often rejected, isolated, or ignored.

The personality of the abuser is also an explanation of emotional abuse. Many abusers are self-absorbed, egocentric, and narcissistic. These individuals often treat others (especially children) as inferior. These individuals have difficulties apologizing, are extremely sensitive to comments toward them, and often blame others for their unhappiness (McCabe 2003). The child who wishes to avoid the abuse will remain silent to avoid issues that may distress or anger the abuser (Bar-On 1995).

Some abusers, because of internal emotional battles, often the result of child abuse, continue the abuse. These abusers, who were often victims of physical abuse as a child, perceive emotional abuse as very mild discipline (O'Hagan 1993). For the abuser, as a child, they experienced physical pain at the hands of their parents, and their children do not experience that pain of physical abuse by their hands. If the emotional abuse by the abuser is questioned, they will often respond with a minimization that compares their actions with those of their parents or the actions of other more abusive parents.

In addition, one cannot discount the fact that many abusers, although they entered into parenthood with the best intensions, do not enjoy being a parent. These individuals have often had little experience with young children and are uncomfortable in adult–child relationships. Therefore, they view parenting in a negative light, with the interactions with their children founded in the authority of their parents and their positions in the family (McCabe 2003).

The current structure of the family may affect the actions of the abuser. Stress, unemployment, marital problems, and long work hours may all contribute to the abuser's emotional abuse of the child. Their child, induced to feel guilty about the abuser's unhappiness, suffers in silence (Yehuda et al. 2001). Over time, abusers who suffer from substance abuse are more likely to escalate from an emotionally abusive state to a physically abusive state. In addition, an abuser who has a child who is mentally or physically handicapped is more likely to emotionally abuse that child on a continuous basis (Crosson-Tower 2010).

Finally, when discussing emotional abuse at the hands of a family member, one cannot discount the fact that the abuser is a sibling. Siblings, just as they may be the perpetrators of sexual and physical abuse, can emotionally abuse each other (Hardy 2001). In most cases, the emotional abuse among siblings is from the older sibling to the younger; however, there are incidents of younger siblings terrorizing older siblings; this is especially the case in a mentally or physically disabled older sibling (McCabe 2003). Abusers who corrupt a child or destroy a child's property are often engaged in the behavior in an attempt to control the child. These abusers, with professions based on the criminal activities of child pornography or child trafficking, use threat and intimidation to ensure the child's continued participation in their criminal enterprise.

Long-Term Consequences

Both male and female adult survivors of childhood emotional abuse often report a variety of long-term physical and mental consequences. Many of these mental consequences include depression, high levels of anxiety, and suicidal thoughts (Delga et al. 1990). These diminished feelings of self-worth continue to develop as the child continues into adulthood and are demonstrated in underachievement, an inability to trust, and emotional instability (Scharf 2007). These adult survivors often choose partners who are emotionally abusive to them (Chiu et al. 2013).

In addition, many adult victims of childhood emotional abuse are more likely to continue the behavior with their own children (Smith et al. 2014). These individuals are also likely to remain in these abusive relationships for fear of being alone or for the feeling of them not deserving a better life.

The adult physical consequences of childhood emotional abuse include health problems, substance abuse, sleep disturbances, and suicide. These adults are less likely to participate in preventive health or dental care and less likely to seek medical attention for minimal discomforts. In addition, adult survivors of emotional abuse are more likely to participate in HIV-risky behaviors (Black 2011), practice poor prenatal care during pregnancy (Leserman 2005), and have a variety of health problems (Chiu et al. 2013). In particular, adult survivors of childhood emotional abuse are more likely to report problems with obesity and diabetes (Smith and Breiding 2011). They are also more likely to commit suicide (Sar et al. 2007), experience a premature death (Black 2011), or report post-traumatic stress disorder. Hence, emotional abuse, which does not leave permanent physical scars, leaves emotional scars throughout the victim's life and, for some individuals, begins their path to self-destruction.

Post-traumatic stress disorder is a mental health condition that has resulted from exposure to experiencing a terrifying event.

☐ Summary

Research suggests that, although not reported, emotional abuse is one of the most common categories of child abuse. In this chapter, emotional abuse was discussed in terms of chronic child maltreatment. In addition, emotional abuse is often viewed as the most damaging type of child abuse.

Categories of emotional abuse include rejection, isolation, terrorizing, ignoring, corrupting, and the destroying of personal property. Emotional abuse, as with the other categories of child abuse, is most often perpetrated by a parent or a caretaker. Whether emotional abuse was a part of the child's sexual or physical abuse, or whether it was the single form of abuse, children who have experienced emotional abuse are often withdrawn, depressed, and continue other antisocial behaviors as adults.

Unfortunately, emotional abuse is viewed as not leaving permanent injuries; therefore, it often goes unnoticed by the victims and society (Crosson-Tower 2010). Most abusers of emotional abuse are parents; some are siblings. In many cases, the child victims of emotional abuse continue the pattern of abuse as an adult. Unfortunately, despite efforts to end child abuse, emotional abuse often continues without notice. Few efforts have been initiated to end the emotional abuse of children. As with any cycle of abuse, unless proactive efforts are implemented to address victimization, the emotional abuse of children continues.

CHAPTER QUESTIONS

1. Emotional abuse includes six general categories. What are those categories, and what are the real-world examples of each category?

2. What are some of the physical and behavioral signs displayed by an emotionally abused child, and are these signs age specific?

3. Why is emotional abuse so difficult to identify and less likely to be reported to law enforcement than any other category of child abuse?

QUESTIONS FOR FURTHER THOUGHT

1. Why does sibling abuse subside as siblings enter adulthood, and why is sibling abuse considered so damaging in the long term?

2. Why are so many aspects of emotional abuse difficult to define and thus difficult to identify?

3. If emotional abuse is thought to be the most damaging in the long term, then why does the public perceive it to be only a minor form of abuse?

☐ References

Bar-On, D. 1995. *Fear and Hope: Three Generations of Five Israeli Families of Holocaust Survivors*. Cambridge, MA: Harvard University Press.

Barkan, S. E. 2001. *Criminology: A Sociological Understanding* (2nd ed.). Upper Saddle River, NJ: Prentice Hall.

Bartollas, C. 2000. *Juvenile Delinquency* (5th ed.). Boston: Allyn and Bacon.

Black, M. 2011. Inmate partner violence and adverse health consequences: Implications for clinicians. *American Journal of Lifestyle Medicine*, 5, 428–439.

Burgess, A, Regehr, C., and Roberts, A. 2013. *Victimology: Theories and Applications* (2nd ed.). Burlington Jones & Bartlett Learning.

Bynum, J. E. and Thompson, W. E. 2002. *Juvenile Delinquency: A Sociological Approach* (5th ed.). Boston: Allyn and Bacon.

Chapman, G. 2004. *The Five Love Languages*. Chicago: Northfield.

Children's Bureau. 2014. *Child Maltreatment 2013*. Washington, D.C.: US Department of Health and Human Services, Administration for Children and Families.

Chiu, G., Lutfey, K., Litman, H., Link, C., Hall, S., and McKinlay, J. 2013. Prevalence and overlap of childhood and adult physical, sexual, and emotional abuse: A descriptive analysis of results from the Boston Area Community Health Survey. *Violence and Victims*, 28(3), 381–401.

Crosson-Tower, C. 2002. *When Children Are Abused: An Educator's Guide to Intervention*. Boston: Allyn and Bacon.

Crosson-Tower, C. 2010. *Understanding Child Abuse and Neglect* (8th ed.). Boston: Allyn and Bacon.

Delga, I., Heinssen, R., Fritsch, R., Goodrich, W., and Yates, B. 1990. Psychosis, aggression and self-destructive behaviors in hospitalized adolescents. *American Journal of Psychiatry*, 146(3), 521–525.

Gosselin, D. 2010. *Heavy Hands: An Introduction to the Crimes of Family Violence* (4th ed.). Upper Saddle River, NJ: Prentice Hall.

Hanser, R. and Mire, S. 2011. *Correctional Counseling*. Upper Saddle River, NY: Prentice Hall.

Hardy, M. S. 2001. Physical aggression and sexual behavior among siblings: A retrospective study. *Journal of Family Violence*, 16(3), 255–268.

Hart, S. and Brassard, M. 1987. A major threat to children's mental health: Psychological maltreatment. *American Psychologist*, 42, 161–165.

Hibbard, R., Ingersoll, G., and Orr, D. 1990. Behavioral risk, emotional risk, and child abuse among adolescents in a nonclinical setting. *Pediatrics*, 86(6), 896–901.

Hirschi, T. 1969. *Causes of Delinquency*. California: University of California.

Jensen, G. 2009. *Delinquency and Youth Crime* (4th ed.). Prospect Heights, IL: Waveland.

Kashani, J. and Shepperd, J. 1990. Aggression in adolescents: The role of social support and personality. *Canadian Journal of Psychiatry*, 35(2), 311–315.

Kelley, B. T., Thornberry, T. P., and Smith, C. A. 1997. *In the Wake of Childhood Maltreatment*. Washington, D.C.: US Department of Justice. Office of Justice Programs. Office of Juvenile Justice and Delinquency Prevention, (NCJ-165257).

Kiselica, M. and Morrill-Richards, B. 2007. Sibling maltreatment: The forgotten abuse. *Journal of Counseling and Development*, 85(2), 148–162.

Leserman, J. 2005. Sexual abuse history: Prevalence, health effects, mediators, and psychological treatment. *Psychosomatic Medicine* 67(6), 906–915.

McCabe, K. 2003. *Child Abuse and the Criminal Justice System*. New York: Peter Lang.

McCabe, K. 2008. *The Trafficking of Persons: National and International Response*. New York: Peter Lang.

McCabe, K. A. 2000. Child pornography and the Internet. *Social Science Computer Review*, 18(1), 73–76.

McCabe, K. A. and Gregory, S. S. 1997. *The Nature of South Carolina Violent Crime*. Columbia, SC: SC Department of Public Safety, Office of Safety and Grants.

McHale, J. and Rasmussen, J. 1998. Copa rental and family group-level dynamics during infancy: Early family precursors of child and family functioning during preschool. *Developmental Psychopathy*, 19(1), 39–59.

O' Hagan, K. 1993. *Emotional and Psychological Abuse of Children*. Toronto, Canada: University of Toronto Press.

Sar, V., Akyuz, G., and Dogan, O. 2007. Prevalence of dissociative disorders among women in the general population. *Psychiatry Research*, 149(1–3), 169–176.

Scharf, M. 2007. Long-term effects of trauma: Psychosocial functioning of the second and third generation of holocaust survivors. *Development of Psychopathology*, 19(2), 603–622.

Smith, S. and Breiding, M. 2011. Chronic disease and health behaviors linked to experience of non-consensual sex among men and women. *Public Health*, 125(9), 653–659.

Smith, A., Cross, D., Winkler, J., Jovanovic, T., and Bradley, B. 2014. Emotional deregulation and negative affect mediate the relationship between maternal history of child maltreatment and maternal child abuse potential. *Journal of Family Violence*, 29(5), 483–494.

Thompson, A. and Kaplan, C. 1996. Childhood emotional abuse. *The British Journal of Psychiatry*, 168(2), 143–148.

Tucker, C., Finkelhor, D., Turner, H., and Shattuck, A. 2014. Sibling and peer victimization in childhood and adolescence. *Child Abuse and Neglect*, 38, 1599–1606.

Valdez, A. 2005. *Gangs: A Guide to Understanding Street Gangs*. San Clemente, CA: Law/Tech.

Wallace, H. 1999. *Family Violence: Legal, Medical, and Social Perspectives* (2nd ed.). Boston: Allyn and Bacon.

Wallace, H. and Roberson, J. 2015. *Victimology: Legal, Psychological, and Social Perspectives* (4th ed.). Upper Saddle River, NJ: Pearson.

Wiehe, V. R. 1997. *Sibling Abuse: Hidden Physical, Emotional, and Sexual Trauma* (2nd ed.). Thousand Oaks, CA: Sage.

Yehuda, R., Halligan, S., and Grossman, R. 2001. Childhood trauma and the risk for PTSD: Relationship to intergenerational effects of trauma, parental PTSD, and cortisol excretion. *Development and Psychopathology*, 13, 733–753.

5

Neglect

An accusation of child neglect is reported to a local law enforcement agency. An officer responds to a small home to find the backdoor unlocked and two children, both under the age of three, unsupervised and confined to a large playpen with two cups of juice and two bowls of dry cereal. The mother is at work.

Legislative and social actions exist worldwide in attempts to end child abuse and neglect; however, when considering child abuse (physical, sexual, and emotional), the foundation of intent is critical; this is not the case with child neglect. In fact, neglect may occur by intent, by accident, or through ignorance. However, it is no less an issue in discussions of child maltreatment. In general, neglect is defined as a failure to provide attention to certain areas or circumstances.

For the purpose of this chapter, neglect is defined generally as a type of maltreatment related to the failure to provide age-appropriate care (Sanders 2014). Of course, one of the major problems in addressing neglect is that of subjectivity, in that a variety of opinions exists as to what is considered providing appropriate care. Thus, a variety of opinions exists as to what is considered neglect. For this text, neglect jeopardizes a child's welfare.

Brooke (age 7) was in the first grade when she would wait at a designated bus stop every morning with her mother Carol. It did not take long before the other parents began noticing that Carol almost always appeared to be under the influence of alcohol or had a strong odor of alcohol on her breath. Parents of the other children either expressed their disgust or concern when Carol was not around and wondered about the type of care Brooke was receiving. These parental discussions continued for months; however, no one ever called social services or law enforcement. One morning, Brooke, who slept in the same bed with Carol, was unable to wake her mother. Carol had died from alcohol poisoning.

Many researchers believe that childhood neglect is one of the most common forms of child abuse (Quinn and Brightman 2015; McCabe 2003). In fact, childhood neglect is consistently the most common type of abuse reported to social services agencies and law enforcement officials. Although society has advanced in many ways in addressing the abuse of children, efforts to reduce neglect, which is related to the care of our children, has not kept pace with those advances (McCabe and Martin 2005).

Parents still fail to seek medical assistance for their children, fail to provide nutritional meals for their children, fail to supervise their children, and fail to ensure that their children are safe and attend school. Whether it is explained as ignorance or callousness, multiple cases of neglect occur every day. As Americans, we feel that there is a responsibility on the part of society to protect all children from neglect, even when the neglect is at the hands of the caretakers (Horan and Widom 2015).

Unfortunately, of all the categories of child abuse, neglect has probably received the least amount of attention from researchers. One reason for this lack of attention is the fact that neglect is not seen to be as detrimental to the child's well-being as abuse. Another reason is that neglect is less dramatic and fails in the *shock factor* that is often required by the public to act (Gabarino and Collins 1999), although children left unattended in vehicles during extreme weather conditions certainly gain significant media attention. In addition, neglect does not lend itself to a quick solution or short-term evaluations of success as many cases of neglect are never reported (McCabe 2003). Finally, addressing neglect often involves a long process of educating parents on the basic needs of a child and the ways in which they may satisfy those basic needs (Crosson-Tower 2010).

Therefore, most researchers in the area of child maltreatment opt for another category of abuse in lieu of neglect. However, neglect, which is present in over 80% of reported cases of child abuse in the United States, is a significant problem in the victimization of children.

It has been estimated that approximately 60% of all child victims of physical, sexual, and emotional abuse are also victims of neglect (Children's Bureau 2014). In addition, many child deaths from maltreatment or abuse are associated with neglect (Brandon et al. 2014). It is estimated that approximately 80% of the child abuse cases reported to law enforcement agencies within the United States are cases of neglect (Children's Bureau 2014). Thus, in the United States and other developed countries, neglect is not only prevalent but also significant in the abuse of children.

This chapter discusses five general categories of neglect: (1) physical, (2) medical, (3) educational, (4) emotional, and (5) supervision, as well as some of the behavioral and physical indicators of child neglect. Also discussed in this chapter are the perpetrators of neglect and the long-term consequences for adults with a history of childhood neglect.

Within each category of neglect, the degree of severity is considered in responses by the criminal justice system and social services agencies. Specifically, *mild neglect* is mostly likely acute neglect and is least likely to be perceived by the child or guardian, but provides the potential for harm to the child. An example of mild neglect may include a parent allowing their child to walk on railroad tracks. *Moderate neglect* is also most likely acute and is identified when some harm comes to the child. An example of moderate neglect may include a parent failing to take their child to a doctor after they burn themselves and should receive medical treatment. Finally, *severe neglect* is chronic as it occurs over time and results in significant harm to the child. An example of severe neglect might include the failure of a parent to provide sufficient milk or formula to their newborn baby.

At some point in their lives, all children may feel that they are neglected by the parent who misses their ball game, the parent who failed to purchase a particular birthday gift, or the parent who asked a 10-year-old child to prepare his own sandwich for lunch; however, these examples are not identified as cases of neglect. Hence, neglect is often difficult to identify by the public, as well as legal authorities. In fact, due to the necessity of evidence, not all categories of neglect receive the same amount of attention from law enforcement officials and social services agencies. In particular, physical neglect is the most commonly investigated type of neglect (Crosson-Tower 2010).

All children are potential victims of neglect; however, based upon the over 500,000 cases of neglect reported in the United States annually, approximately 50% of the cases involved children under the age of 6, and approximately 30% of the cases involved children between the ages of 6 and 11 (Children's Bureau 2014). Research suggests that some demographic characteristics of the family are related to not only the categories of neglect but also the severity of neglect.

☐ Physical Neglect

An example of physical neglect may be dressing an infant in sandals and shorts to take them outside when the temperature is below freezing. By definition, physical neglect refers to the caretaker's inability to reduce or prevent the child's likelihood of physical harm (Crosson-Tower 2010).

Again, physical neglect is the category of neglect most likely to be investigated by law enforcement or social services. This form of neglect includes failure to provide adequate nutrition for the child, a disregard for the child's personal hygiene, failure to provide a sanitary home for the child, failure to prohibit the use of alcohol by the child within the home, a disregard for the child's safety, and the risk to an unborn child due to the use of drugs and/or alcohol by the mother during pregnancy (McCabe 2003). Hence, physical neglect includes a failure to provide the necessary requirements to reduce a child's risk of injury or illness.

Historically, it was suggested that physical neglect was a result of low socioeconomic conditions (Helfer and Kempe 1987). Today, we know that physical neglect does not mean poverty (McCabe 2003). Physical neglect occurs across all social classes. However, many cases of physical neglect may be explained (not excused) from the perspective of parental choices and limited resources.

In some cases of physical neglect, a parent is provided a resource to obtain food and clothing for their child; however, the parent chooses other items such as alcohol or tobacco products for their own use. In other cases, parents may abandon their child or children to begin a new life for themselves often with individuals who do not want to include the child or children (McCabe 2003). This problem of abandonment occurs more often than most individuals believe and is especially common in cases of female-headed homes. In fact, research suggests that children of single-parent homes have nearly a 90% higher risk for physical neglect than children from two-parent homes (Sedlak and Broadhurst 1996).

In addition, failure to provide adequate nutrition and personal hygiene is an example of physical neglect and is common in cases reported to law enforcement officials and social services agencies. David Pelzer's (1995) best-selling *A Child Called It* is a popular memoir focused on physical neglect and is an account of his starvation at the hands of his mother. Pelzer's book brought to the public consciousness the reality of child neglect in the family and the importance of agency intervention. In addition, to single-parent homes, research on families with cases of physical neglect also suggests that families with multiple children are at a higher risk for physical neglect than families with few children (Sedlak and Broadhurst 1996).

Finally, the failure to maintain a safe home or to ensure that a child utilizes a car safety seat may also constitute physical neglect. Children may ingest common poisons in the home, fall from the top of staircases, or drown in inches of bath water. The caretakers who choose not to take the proper precautions to protect their children may face prosecution in family court, and lawsuits can be filed in civil court even if the neglect was not intentional.

Finally, children with disabilities are often victims of physical neglect (Gosselin 2010; Higham and Horwitz 2001). Caretakers who are not emotionally attached to a child or suffer from mental illnesses may become frustrated with the disabled child (Daigle 2012) and may not be willing to provide the extra attention required to meet the needs of these children.

According to the US Department of Health and Human Services, approximately 13% of the reported cases of child maltreatment involve children with disabilities.

☐ Medical Neglect

Medical neglect is defined as the refusal or delay of medical treatment to the detriment of the child. Although many researchers combine medical and physical neglect, for the purpose of this text, and as medical neglect is often captured separately from child neglect, this text will discuss medical neglect and physical neglect separately (Children's Bureau 2014).

From a legal perspective, one of the most common examples of medical neglect is a caretaker's choice to not seek medical treatment for an injured child (Wallace 1999). Established in 1880, the Heinemann's Appeal and the Supreme Court of Pennsylvania supported the principle that states may intervene in the best interest of the child when parents fail to provide medical care (Wallace 1999). Through this ruling, a child does not have to suffer without relief from illness or injury if the parents refuse medical treatment. In cases of medical neglect, the state may order the treatment of the child (McCabe 2003). Some states, however, recognize that some parents will not seek medical care due to their religious beliefs, and, unless a life or death situation emerges, state or county officials will generally not intervene (Doerner and Lab 2015). However, if the child is older (older as defined by the state), the state may intervene and provide medical treatment if the child requests medical attention.

Unfortunately, for some children too young to request treatment, medical neglect may result in significant negative outcomes. In particular, the medical community has identified a childhood condition called nonorganic failure to thrive syndrome in which a caregiver not knowing how to properly feed a baby or a caregiver failing to provide an adequate amount of milk/formula for the baby results in the delayed development of the child and, in some cases, the death of the child (English 1978). Failure to thrive recognizes that all neglect is not intentional; however, with or without intent, the outcome for these neglected children may be death.

Caylee, age 22, is the primary caretaker of her three-week-old baby. This is Caylee's first child, and she has no family support to help guide her as she cares for her child. Caylee, in her mind, is very conscientious as she tries to meet the needs of her child whom she truly loves. She bathes him regularly and changes his diaper when needed. Caylee chose not to breast-feed her child and began feeding him formula from the very beginning. She purchased (brand name) canned formula on a regular basis as she wanted her baby to have the best that she could provide. It didn't take long before the baby was appearing sick and died a few weeks later. The cause of the death was dehydration. Caylee was devastated and confused as to how her baby died of dehydration. Law enforcement officials opened an investigation to determine how the baby died. The investigation revealed that the canned formula Caylee was feeding her baby was condensed formula that required mixing with water. No charges were brought against Caylee.

Any time a child dies, states require that a determination as to the cause of death be identified. Some explanations may be as simple as the result of a car accident, the result of a birth defect, or the result of a long-term illness such as cancer. Other states may require experts to determine if the child's demise was a result of homicide, child abuse, or neglect. These experts are generally called medical examiners.

Various jurisdictions have established Child Fatality Review Boards, to determine the cause of a child's death. The primary purpose of these boards is to reduce the number of preventable child deaths; thus, research into the causes of child fatalities is critical (Burgess et al. 2013). Board members usually include, but are not limited to, a medical examiner, a pediatrician, a social services agent, a law enforcement officer, and the District Attorney's Office within that jurisdiction (Wallace and Roberson 2015).

It is the cases of medical neglect that most often result in the death or permanent injury of a child. The parent who fails to take the child to the emergency room with a broken arm, who fails to take the child to the doctor when they contract the flu, or who fails to ensure that the proper vaccines are administered to their child may be deemed guilty of medical neglect.

Medical neglect is not limited to only born children. One of the most recent concerns under the umbrella of medical neglect is prenatal care. In particular, the failure of a mother to seek prenatal care for her unborn baby and the use of drugs and alcohol by the mother while pregnant may also be reasons for the criminal charge of medical neglect. For example, the condition of fetal alcohol syndrome, which results from significant alcohol consumption during pregnancy, can permanently affect the health of a child. This is a topic of liability in the criminal courts, and, in many states, the definition of a child has been rewritten to include an unborn child (McCabe 2003).

According to the US Department of Health and Human Services, approximately 10% of the reported cases of child maltreatment involve a caregiver and the abuse of alcohol. In addition, approximately 20% of the reported cases of child maltreatment involve a caregiver and the abuse of drugs.

☐ Educational Neglect

Educational neglect refers to the caretaker's failure to provide an education or a means to obtain an education for the child (Crosson-Tower 2010). Included in this category of neglect are chronic school truancy, a failure to enroll the child in school, and inattention by the parents or caretakers to a child's special education programs. Each of these examples of educational neglect is a reason for prosecution in the US court systems.

> Sam (age 43) failed to complete high school. When he was in the ninth grade, his mother sent him to live with his father in another state. His father neglected to enroll him in school; instead, Sam began working. To this day, he has failed to complete high school and continues to work 70+ hours per week to help support his family.

All children in the United States are required to attend school until age 16 (Quinn and Brightman 2015). In turn, parents are required to register their children for school. In some cases of educational neglect, parents fail to register their children or fail to send their children to school.

Researchers have suggested that, in some cases, educational neglect is a result of poverty as parents allow their children to work instead of attending school (McCabe 2008).

In other more controversial cases of educational neglect, parents are not involved in the education of their child to the extent that they do not attend school functions or return calls from their teachers. From this perspective, the parent ensures that the child is enrolled and attends school; however, the child is often late to school, dismissed early from school, or is absent from school due to *family events* (McCabe 2003).

From an educational standpoint, a child who does not perceive attending school as a priority for their parent will not perceive attending school as a priority for them. These children will place little effort in their assignments and simply be passed from grade to grade until the time that they can decide themselves if they would like to continue their education. Without parental support, many children will not choose to be successful in school.

From a legal standpoint, it is important to investigate the reasons why a child is not attending school before labeling the parent neglectful. Many parents live with the frustration of having an incorrigible child who refuses to attend school or often skips school without the parent's knowledge. This situation is especially overwhelming for a single parent who is trying to ensure that their teenage child receives an education but must leave for work before the child leaves for school.

In some cases, the parent may reluctantly allow the child to stay at home to avoid a conflict and for fear of facing the consequences from their employer if they are late to work. When a child is incorrigible and refuses to attend school, that child can face consequences from authorities and be charged as a *status offender* for truancy. However, if a parent has an incorrigible child who refuses to attend school, and the parents do not seek assistance from the proper authorities, then the parent(s) can be held accountable for educational neglect.

With more and more students receiving their education through homeschool programs, one would assume that truancy would not be an issue; however, this is not always the case. Children who are enrolled in homeschool programs may still be victims of educational neglect (McCabe 2003). Although the majority of homeschool programs have credentialed teachers and curricula, states determine the standards for programs, and not all programs meet regularly as required. For the majority of children, homeschool is an excellent avenue for educational achievement. However, for a few children, it is the avenue to avoid attending school on a regular basis. Thus, even children enrolled in homeschool programs may be victims of educational neglect.

Finally, educational neglect may involve the education of a mentally challenged child or a child with a learning disability and a parent or caretaker who makes little or no effort in an attempt to assure that child an education or educational progress (Crosson-Tower 2010). The rights as US citizens afford all children the opportunity of education; however, some children may require extra assistance to be successful in education. Parents are the responsible parties for ensuring that their children seize that opportunity. Unfortunately, in many cases of educational neglect, the educationally challenged children are the victims (McCabe and Martin 2005).

☐ **Emotional Neglect**

The emotional or psychological neglect of children may be, in the case of threats or intimidation, classified as emotional abuse (McCabe 2003). However, for the purpose of this discussion, emotional neglect includes a lack of or inadequate nurturance and affection, the abuse of another person in the presence of the child or domestic violence, and a refusal to provide the child psychological care by the parent or the caretaker.

Just as emotional abuse is nearly impossible to document, emotional neglect is even more difficult as, by definition, it involves a behavior or support system not applied to the life of the child. In other words, how do you measure the number of cases of neglect that do not occur? Child development consists of a series of stages, and each stage provides a new or additional set of circumstances for the emotionally neglected child. The child who is not nurtured and shown affection but simply ignored has an unstable foundation for a *normal* relationship. The child, who never experiences positive contact between a parent and a child, is unaware of these types of relationships and, in many cases, is unable to initiate the process of bonding with other individuals even as they grow into adults. In some cases of emotional neglect, an older sibling who did not receive the love and attention from his or her parents attempts to fulfill that role for the younger siblings.

In other families where emotional neglect exists, the roles of parent and child are often undefined, confused, and traded. In these cases, it is not unusual for the child to become the nurturer to the parent.

Finally, in other cases of emotional neglect, the child, because of some mental illness, requires psychological intervention; however, the parent, either because of limited knowledge or a failure to recognize the mental illness within their own child, does not seek help from the psychological community. Unfortunately, in cases of emotional neglect, the consequences to the child may be severe to include self-injury, violence toward others, and suicide (McCabe 2003).

☐ Supervision Neglect

Supervision neglect is the failure to adequately supervise a child by leaving them alone, in the care of inadequate guardian, or ejecting them from the home. Supervision neglect includes abandonment. Also included under this category of neglect is the parents' acceptance of the child's absence in the home either overnight or for extended periods of time without the caretaker's knowledge of the child's location.

In many of these cases, the child leaves home, and, as the parents are not in the habit of knowing the whereabouts of the child, when the parent eventually realizes that the child is missing, the runaway is not reported to law enforcement officials (Crosson-Tower 2010). Other types of supervisory neglect include *throwaway children*. Cases of throwaway children occur often when parents evict (abandonment) their own children from the household due to the child's lifestyle despite still being legally responsible for them. Other scenarios of supervisory neglect can include when a child runs away from home and the parents do not report the child missing or make an attempt to learn of their whereabouts and who they are with.

Unfortunately, in today's world of single parents, long-distance work commuting, and parents who travel extensively, child supervision is one of the most common categories of neglect (McCabe and Martin 2005). The issue, which creates even more controversy around the notion of inadequate supervision, is the maturity level of the child. In some instances, an 11-year-old staying at home during the day while the parent works is fine; in others, it is not. In some instances, a 15-year-old staying alone over the weekend is fine; in others, it is not. Unfortunately, without supervision, many children are at risk for injury, delinquency, victimization, and death (Bartollas 2000).

Finally, the allegation of supervisory neglect at times is used as a tactic during custody battles. A parent may use a social services agency or a law enforcement agency as pawns for allegations of neglect against the other parent claiming inappropriate supervision, for the sole purpose of building support for their custody. In these cases, law enforcement officials are often required to respond to a residence with a complaint that young children are alone without supervision. Despite the allegation being unfounded at times, documentation will still exist stating that the police responded to the house on a neglect complaint and that documentation (whether valid or not) is used as evidence of a reported incident during custody hearings.

☐ Indicators of Neglect

Just as there are physical and behavioral indicators of child physical, sexual, and emotional abuse, there are also indicators of neglect. School officials, because of their proximity to the child, are often most likely to be involved in identifying a neglected child (McCabe 2003). In fact, educators, because of their legally identified positions of mandated reporters of child abuse and neglect, must accept that responsibility in reporting all possible cases.

As with other types of child abuse, neglect often manifests itself either physically or through behavioral indicators. However, it must be acknowledged that, after child physical abuse, neglect is the most often investigated by law enforcement officials and social services agencies. Also acknowledged is that although the following behaviors are indicators of neglect, they are not always the result of neglect, and, just as with any type of child abuse, those alleging neglect should consider all the facts prior to proclaiming child neglect.

☐ Physical Indicators

One of the most common physical indicators of neglect is poor physical development. Research has revealed that neglected children are often smaller than their peers (Crosson-Tower 2010; Wallace 1999). In fact, a neglected child will often be below the fifteenth percentile of their growth range for their age and sex. In many cases, a neglected child may appear to be constantly hungry or even to suffer from malnutrition. These children may steal food or hoard food and eat quickly.

The child's hygiene is also a good indicator of neglect (DeMuth 2004). In particular, a child with poor hygiene, dirty clothes, the smell of urine, or head lice may be a victim of neglect (Crosson-Tower 2002). In addition, a child who always appears ill; has bad breath and cuts and scars of varying ages and without medical treatment; and has limited flexibility and mobility of arms, legs, feet, neck, and hands may be a victim of neglect. These children, with multiple or unusual injuries, may be victims of neglect and physical abuse. Finally, a child who often appears tired or fatigued may be a victim of neglect. Therefore, the individuals who are in the positions to recognize the physical signs of neglect are the child's teachers, family members, and neighbors.

☐ Behavioral Indicators

In many cases of abuse, behavioral indicators of abuse emerge along with the physical indicators. Therefore, an individual who may not be able to visit the home of a child or observe the children alone at home may see signs of neglect in their behaviors. A child who lacks self-confidence or self-worth and is withdrawn or depressed may be a victim of neglect (Chapple et al. 2005; Bolger and Patterson 2001). Other behavioral indicators of neglect include begging for food, being socially withdrawn, being destructive, and eliciting negative responses to gain attention (Crosson-Tower 2002).

Other behavioral indicators related to the education of the child include being developmentally behind other children in the same age group in the understanding of concepts or the advancement of motor skills, difficulties with language comprehension, and an overall lower intelligence. Finally, neglected children are often self-destructive, destructive to others, and have poor or negative relationships with peers (McCabe 2003; Wallace 1999).

In many cases, neglected children are expected to assume the role of caretaker for their younger siblings. In these cases, a child who appears to be mature for his or her age in actions or who acknowledges responsibilities in the home, such as cooking dinner for the family or the bathing of siblings, may be a victim of neglect. In fact, families with a large number of charges are often reported with cases of neglect (Perry et al. 2002).

Children who are neglected rarely see school as a necessary part of their lives; therefore, a child who is often tardy or absent from school may also be a victim of neglect. These children are often rejected by their peers and have the inability to regulate their emotions (Hildyard and Wolfe 2002). Female victims of neglect often begin participating in sexual activity at an early age, while male victims of neglect often begin participating in criminal activity at an early age (Horan and Widom 2015). Most of these neglected children fail to complete high school.

Finally, it is not unusual for child victims of neglect to attempt to be the *perfect child* for another adult (McCabe 2003). These children, desperate for adult attention and support, will attempt to excel in school, push themselves in sports, and even allow themselves to be abused simply to please an adult (Rodriguez and Tucker 2011; Scannapieco and

Connell-Carrick 2005). Unfortunately, many of these children, when they discover that they cannot always do the best or be the best, become frustrated with themselves and others around them. Neglected girls will often be very affectionate in terms of hugs and hand-holding with the adult they choose, and neglected boys will attempt to be seen as the rescuer by carrying heavy objects or opening doors for the adult. These children are often without their parent; therefore, they plan their activities around the opportunity to be in the company of another adult. Unfortunately, this type of neglect can provide abusers interested in sexually abusing a child the opportunity and access to the child.

☐ Abusers

Just as parents are responsible for the care of their children, they are also the most likely perpetrator of neglect in approximately 80% of the reported cases (Children's Bureau 2014). However, one cannot discuss neglect by parents or caretakers without discussing the dynamics behind the caretaker's inability to care for the child. From that perspective, most research would assert that child neglect is a result of three different types of parental and family characteristics: (1) the parent's/caretaker's developmental history and personality, (2) the characteristics of the family and child, and (3) environmental influences (Crosson-Tower 2010).

The first attempt to explain the abusers of neglect is from the perspective of the caretaker's own developmental history and personality (Gaudin 1993). Caretakers themselves who have grown up in an environment of neglect are likely to neglect their children. Just as with other forms of abuse, neglect is often a generational outcome. Many of today's abusers were raised in an environment of neglect. Therefore, this characteristic of the uninvolved parent seems normal. In most cases of neglect, the parent was raised in an environment where they quickly became self-sufficient or they were the caretaker of another sibling. As child care is generally considered a female responsibility, it is not surprising that over 50% of the perpetrators of child neglect are female (Children's Bureau 2014).

One must also consider the personality or physical condition of the caretaker in the discussions on abusers of neglect. Caretakers, in particular, mothers, again, who are the more likely perpetrators of neglect, may suffer from depression or have an impulsive personality in which their actions, such as sleeping for days, or their lack of actions, such as providing meals for the child, may result in child neglect (McCabe 2003). Some abusers are apathetic, and some are psychotic (Crosson-Tower 2002).

Substance abuse or a mentally disadvantaged caretaker may also promote neglect of the child by the abuser in the household (Perry et al. 2002; Gaudin 1993). Finally, abusers who are physically ill themselves or perceive themselves to be physically ill may not be able to provide for the child's basic needs; in turn, the child is neglected (Crosson-Tower 2010; Helfer and Kempe 1987).

The second attempt to explain neglect focuses on the characteristics of the abuser's family and the child (Gaudin 1993). As the personality traits of the caretaker may be used to explain child neglect, so may the personality of the child and the characteristics of the abuser's family structure. Just as two adults may have a personality conflict, the child and his or her abuser may also clash (McCabe 2003). In addition, children who are introverts or children who do not have the ability, because of some physical or mental handicap, to request help from an abuser may become neglected.

Deanna, age 34, was divorced and lived in a large townhouse community with her seven-year-old son, Ryan. Deanna had a reputation among the townhouse community and the city for having parties and sex with teenage boys. There were several complaints from neighbors claiming that there was a smell of marijuana emanating from her residence while teenage boys came in and out of her place at all hours of the night. A teenager was arrested for possession of marijuana and became a confidential informant with the police reporting on the activities of Deanna. The informant reported that Deanna would sexually please several teenage boys as they stood in line. These allegations were reported as happening while her son, Ryan, was still at the residence. It was also reported that there were illicit drugs always left around her residence where Ryan had easy access. Information was also released that Ryan would drink beer in front of his mother alongside the teenagers. Despite this information, there was insufficient information for the police to apply for a search warrant. In lieu of this, law enforcement contacted social services complaining the Deanna was not properly supervising her child and that the child was in potential danger. Social services responded to the residence and counseled Deanna about appropriate parenting and took no further action. Approximately 30 days later, in a neighboring city, a man stabbed a homeless man several times and fled to Deanna's residence (where Ryan was present) to hide. The police located and arrested the fugitive from justice while filing separate charges against Deanna for supervisory neglect. The court ruled that Deanna was neglectful, and the custody of Ryan was turned over to his father. The facts of this case were so outrageous that Deanna obtained dubious national attention where Sally Jesse Raphael, a talk show host, contacted Deanna requesting that she appear on television to explain her actions.

It is not unusual for child neglect to be present in families with abusers who fail to provide emotional support. In fact, research suggests that children whose parents provide weak discipline and poor super-vision are likely to be victims of neglect (Hope et al. 2003). In these families, especially among male victims of neglect, adolescent violence is common (Chapple et al. 2005).

In addition, within the dynamics of the dysfunctional family and the abuser, the neglected child often associates himself with individuals outside of the family in order to establish some sort of emotional connec-tion. Finally, children who are members of a family in which domestic violence is present may also be victims of child neglect (DeMuth 2004). In these cases, to avoid physical and emotional abuse, many of the child victims of neglect will choose to be absent from the home much of the time. By not focusing the family's attention on themselves, they avoid the family violence.

The third explanation of neglect is related to environmental influ-ences or sources of stress from outside of the family of the abuser. In addition, abusers who isolate their families from others within the com-munity often lack outside resources when it comes to child care. In these families, the risk for neglect of the children is high. Economics is another source of stress on the family (Crosson-Tower 2010; Avakame 1998; Gaudin 1993). With both parents working or, in the case of a single-parent household, with the one parent working perhaps multiple jobs, there is little time for the child or children. These children, sometimes referred to in literature as latchkey children, are often victims of neglect (McCabe 2003). As suggested by some researchers, children who are vic-tims of neglect often suffer from poor self-control, low self-esteem, and poor peer relations (Chapple et al. 2005).

☐ Consequences of Neglect

It is unfortunate that neglect may result in children feeling hungry, in pain, or afraid to be alone; however, there are other consequences of neglect. One of those consequences is poor academic performance (Scannapieco and Connell-Carrick 2005). Other than disruptive school behavior or withdrawn personalities, children who are neglected may suffer from sleep problems, weight loss or weight gain, and poor social relations (Chapple et al. 2005; Bartollas 2000). These children may suffer from frequent illnesses or be labeled hypochondriacs (Helfer and Kempe 1987).

Finally, the neglected child may turn to drugs or alcohol as an escape from their situation or to promiscuous sexual behavior to gain attention. In addition, neglected children may become runaways or throwaways if their parents decide that their presence in the home is no longer acceptable (Bynum and Thompson 2002; Perry et al. 2002). In some cases, these children then become available for other types of victimization such as human trafficking (McCabe 2008). Later in life, it is not uncommon for neglected children to become adults who neglect their children or adult partners.

Other long-term consequences of neglect include poor self-control and the inability to regulate emotions or curb impulsivity (McCabe 2003). For the adult survivor of childhood neglect, the memories of being hungry, of being cold in a house without heat, or the memory of others teasing them about the way they dress or speak or smell never ends. In response, the adults often either turn to alcohol and/or drugs, or they dedicate their lives to work and earning money to assure that they will never be without the things they need or the things they want (Kotch et al. 2014). These are the adults that lack the ability or desire to depend on others for everyday assistance or support. They generally isolate themselves socially, have few friends, and often view violence and verbal aggression as a means to an end (McCabe 2003).

In addition, adult survivors of child neglect often have higher expectations of responsibilities and behaviors for their own children and often become irritated when those expectations are not met. Finally, it is not unusual for adult survivors of neglect to be involved in domestic violence and other criminal behaviors (Horan and Widom 2015).

☐ Summary

Child neglect, generally defined as the failure to provide age-appropriate care for a child, is not a new problem for those persons who are in daily contact with children. Although neglect may not be as obvious as abuse, the long-term effects can be just as detrimental (Brown et al. 1998). However, child neglect is a problem of serious concern. Effects on a neglected child can include emotional, behavioral, and developmental delays, which can lead to frustration resulting in behaviors such as dropping out of school and entering the criminal justice system as a juvenile delinquent (Cox et al. 2014).

Categories of child neglect include physical, medical, educational, emotional, and supervision. Neglect, due to its underlying dynamics within the family structure and personalities, does not lend itself to a simple fix (McCabe 2003).

In the United States, many child fatalities are associated with neglect. For law enforcement officials and social services agents, child neglect, after child physical abuse, is one of the easiest forms of child abuse to document as most agencies simply make photographs of the scene and the conditions. Most efforts by law enforcement and the departments of social services are focused upon physical or medical neglect; however, all forms of neglect may produce long-term consequences. Only through education and intervention may the problem of child neglect be addressed. Only through interested parties will the problem of child neglect be solved.

CHAPTER QUESTIONS

1. There are a number of categories of neglect. What are these categories of neglect and what are the examples of each?

2. What are the different types of parental and family characteristics of abusers?

3. How is neglect different from other forms of child abuse?

QUESTIONS FOR FURTHER THOUGHT

1. Why is it so difficult to define neglect?

2. Why does it appear that, in general, neglect does not generate the same media attention, outrage, or concern as the other types of child abuse?

3. Is neglect related to poverty? Is neglect a parental choice?

☐ References

Avakame, E. 1998. Intergenerational transmission of violence, self-control, and conjugal violence: A comparative analysis of physical violence and psychological aggression. *Violence and Victims*, 75(2), 301–316.

Bartollas, C. 2000. *Juvenile Delinquency* (5th ed.). Boston: Allyn and Bacon.

Bolger, K. and Patterson, C. 2001. Development pathways from child maltreatment to peer rejection. *Child Development*, 72(2), 549–568.

Brandon, M., Bailey, S., Belderson, P., and Larsson, B. 2014. The role of neglect in child fatality and serious injury. *Child Abuse Review*, 23(4), 235–245.

Brown, J., Cohen, P., Johnson, J., and Salzinger, S. 1998. A longitudinal analysis of risk factors for child maltreatment: Findings of a 17-year prospective study of officially recorded and self-reported child abuse and neglect. *Child Abuse and Neglect*, 22, 1065–1078.

Burgess, A., Regehr, C., and Roberts, A. 2013. *Victimology: Theories and Applications* (2nd ed.). Burlington, MA: Jones & Bartlett Learning.

Bynum, J. and Thompson, W. 2002. *Juvenile Delinquency: A Sociological Approach* (5th ed.). Boston: Allyn and Bacon.

Chapple, C., Tyler, K., and Bersani, B. 2005. Child neglect and adolescent violence: Examining the effects of self-control and peer rejection. *Violence and Victims*, 20(1), 39–53.

Children's Bureau. 2014. *Child Maltreatment 2013*. Washington, D.C.: US Department of Health and Human Services, Administration for Children and Families.

Cox, S., Allen, J., Hanser, R., and Conrad, J. 2014. *Juvenile Justice: A Guide to Theory, Policy, and Practice*. Thousand Oaks, CA: SAGE.

Crosson-Tower, C. 2002. *When Children Are Abused: An Educator's Guide to Intervention*. Boston: Allyn and Bacon.

Crosson-Tower, C. 2010. *Understanding Child Abuse and Neglect* (8th ed.). Boston: Allyn and Bacon.

Daigle, L. 2012. *Victimology*. Thousand Oaks, CA: SAGE.

DeMuth, M. 2004. Understanding the delinquency and social relationships of loners. *Youth and Society*, 35(2), 366–392.

Doerner, W. and Lab, S. 2015. *Victimology* (7th ed.). Waltham, MA: Anderson.

English, P. C. 1978. Failure to thrive without organic reason. *Pediatric Annals*, 7, 774–780.

Gabarino, J. and Collins, C. C. 1999. Child neglect: The family with the hole in the middle. In H. Dubowitz (ed.) *Neglected Children: Research, Practice, and Policy*. Thousand Oaks, CA: SAGE, pp. 1–23.

Gaudin, J. 1993. *Child Neglect: A Guide for Intervention*. Washington, D.C.: US Department of Health and Human Services. Administration for Children and Families. (HHS-105891730).

Gosselin, D. 2010. *Heavy Hands: An Introduction to the Crimes of Family Violence* (4th ed.). Upper Saddle River, NJ: Pearson.

Helfer, R. and Kempe, R. 1987. *The Battered Child* (4th ed.). Chicago: University of Chicago Press.

Higham, S. and Horwitz, S. 2001. Family sues over foster child's death: $120 million case alleges negligence and abusing by D.C., Delaware Nursing Home. *The Washington Post*, B2, November 28.

Hildyard, K. and Wolfe, D. 2002. Child neglect: Development issues and outcomes. *Child Abuse and Neglect*, 26(4), 679–695.

Hope, T., Grasmick, H., and Pointon, L. 2003. The family in Gottfredson and Hirschi's general theory of crime: Structure, parenting and self-control. *Sociological Forces*, 36(4), 291–311.

Horan, J. and Widom, C. 2015. Does age on onset of risk behaviors mediate the relationship between child abuse and neglect and outcomes in middle adulthood? *Journal of Youth and Adolescence*, 44(3), 670–682.

Kotch, J., Smith, J., Margolis, B., Black, M., and English, D. 2014. Does social capital protect against adverse behavioral outcomes of child neglect? *Child Abuse Review*, 23(4), 246–261.

McCabe, K. 2003. *Child Abuse and the Criminal Justice System*. New York: Peter Lang.

McCabe, K. 2008. *The Trafficking of Persons: National and International Responses*. New York: Peter Lang.

McCabe, K. and Martin, G. 2005. *School Violence, the Media, and Criminal Justice Responses*. New York: Peter Lang.

Pelzer, D. 1995. *A Child Called It*. Deerfield, FL: Health Communications, Inc.

Perry, B., Colwell, K., and Schick, S. 2002. Child neglect. *Encyclopedia of Crime and Punishment*. Thousand Oaks, CA: SAGE, pp. 192–196.

Quinn, E. and Brightman, S. 2015. *Crime Victimization: A Comprehensive Overview*. Durham, NC: Carolina Academic Press.

Rodriguez, C. and Tucker, M. 2011. Behind the cycle of violence, beyond abuse history: A brief report on the association of parental attachment to physical child abuse potential. *Violence and Victims*, 26(2), 246–256.

Sanders, C. 2014. Child neglect. *Psychology Today*, New York: Sussex, November.

Scannapieco, M. and Connell-Carrick, K. 2005. *Understanding Child Maltreatment: An Ecological and Developmental Perspective*. New York: Oxford University.

Sedlak, A. and Broadhurst, D. 1996. *Executive Summary of the Third National Incidence Study of Child Abuse and Neglect: National Clearinghouse on Child Abuse and Neglect Information*. Washington, D.C.: US Department of Health and Human Services. The Administration for Children and Families. National Center on Child Abuse and Neglect (ACF-1059418).

Wallace, H. 1999. *Family Violence: Legal, Medical, and Social Perspectives* (2nd ed.). Boston: Allyn and Bacon.

Wallace, H. and Roberson, J. 2015. *Victimology: Legal, Psychological, and Social Perspectives* (4th ed.). Upper Saddle River, NJ: Pearson Education Inc.

6
CHAPTER

Theoretical Explanations for Child Abuse

Researchers in the area of child abuse and neglect have attempted to explain (not excuse) why anyone would harm a child. In Chapters 2 through 5 of this text, information is provided on the four categories of abuse, the typologies of abusers, and victim outcomes. However, child abuse remains a complex series of conditions, interacting dynamics, and events that may not ever be fully explained.

This chapter is designed to provide a brief introduction and discussion on the classical and contemporary theories as related to child abuse. By providing some sort of theoretical foundation, it is the goal of this chapter not only to assist in explaining the actions of child abuse but also to provide readers the background to understand further readings of empirical research, which focuses on specific aspects of child abuse. Research has suggested that insufficient attention has been provided to the theoretical explanations for child abuse (Crosson-Tower 2010; McCabe 2003); this chapter will attempt to address that gap in the research and the discussions that attempt to explain child abuse.

In early attempts to explain deviant behaviors, the notion of evil spirits or *the devil made me do it* was the cornerstone for such acts. This perspective, known as demonology, was first identified around 80 BCE and suggested that people committed evil deeds because of the influence of mysterious and evil supernatural power (Moyer 2001). Hence, these actions were committed not by individual free will but because of forces beyond the individual's control (Cox et al. 2014). Specifically, demonology is the study of demons, evil spirits, and evil actions. From this perspective, child abuse may be explained in terms of the abusers, who torture or kill children because of inability to control their own actions.

The demonological explanations of deviant behavior were based upon a blend of cultural superstitions and religious rules.

An abuser kills or hurts a child because he or she is possessed. In addition, to rid the community of an evil child, the child may be killed to protect the community from evil spirits perceived to be within the victim. In other words, the child is a *bad seed* or a person predisposed to committing evil and wrongful acts.

Although demonology, as a perspective to explain evil actions, was prevalent up until the 18th century, classical theory or choice perspective gave way to a process of considering and explaining evil behaviors as a result of the individual's choice. The time period of the Classical School of Criminology Era, which began during the Age of Enlightenment (or Age of Reason), produced a shift from the-devil-made-me-do-it mentality to a *crime-is-a-choice* rationale. Hence, the victimization of a child was not from circumstances beyond the abuser's control. However, it should be noted that some individuals still perceive other individuals as evil and capable of only criminal actions (McCabe 2003).

Under the Classical School of Criminology, political philosopher Cesare Beccaria (1738–1794), who has been regarded as one of the fathers of modern criminology, suggested that individuals acted of their own free will and that these actions were decided based upon careful considerations of which action would create more pleasure or more pain (Barkan 2015). As is reasonable, the premise for this line of thought was that an individual would choose to optimize his or her pleasure and minimize his or her pain. As applied to child maltreatment, if an individual decided to harm a child, then it was because the action would result in much pleasure for the abuser and little chance of pain.

Although the Classical School began over two centuries ago, it is still applied to criminal behaviors today in its contemporary form of rational choice theory. For example, in the criminal action of child trafficking (discussed later in Chapter 7), a reasonable or rational offender would decide, based upon the potential for reward and punishment (pleasure and pain), whether or not they should traffic a child. If one considers that a child is a product, and the economic gain from the sale (or trafficking) of that child is enormous, and that law enforcement has demonstrated limited efforts in arresting traffickers or even identifying the victims of human trafficking, then the rationale choice perspective suggests that the abuser will make the decision to traffic a child. Specifically, from the choice perspective, the traffickers received much financial gain (pleasure) from the trafficking of a child with little chance of detection and an endless supply of children (pain); hence, child trafficking is a rational crime.

☐ Intraindividual Explanation of Child Abuse

In discussions on problem-solving and choices, both interindividual and intraindividual perspectives are applied to explain actions (Bialystok and Craik 2006). From the interindividual perspective, actions based upon interactions with others are explained. However, intraindividual decisions (those based upon variables within a given person) may also explain actions and, in particular, the actions that lead to the abuse of a child. In a nutshell, intraindividual theories suggest that child abuse is the result of the offender having some abnormality, a type of mental defect, or a flaw in their genetic makeup. These abnormalities include mental illness and chemical imbalances. As explained by these abnormalities, these individuals are predisposed to committing violence, and child abuse is simply one aspect of that violent behavior.

Cesare Lombroso (1835–1909) suggested that individuals were born criminals, and they could be recognized by physical features thought to exist within that current criminal population. Lombroso suggested that criminals were atavists or throwbacks to a more primitive nature and thus had not yet obtained the personal control necessary to reduce egoistic actions. From this perspective, an individual who would harm another would do so because of a basic predisposition to harm. Unfortunately, children, because of their small and often fragile physical state, are prime victims for an individual with a predisposition to do harm.

Later, Earnest Hooton (1887–1954) suggested that the primary cause of crime was biological and advocated that the government sterilize criminals. From this perspective, criminals were simply biologically inferior. A person who would kill an innocent child would do so because of some mental defect, which altered that person's sense of reality. Even later, psychological explanations were used in an attempt to understand child abuse; thus, the human mind has long been considered a source of abnormal behavior and, therefore, the cause of criminal behavior.

Sigmund Freud's (1856–1939) psychoanalytical approach suggested that mental disorders arose from conflicts within society and the instinctive needs of the individual (Freud 1920). According to Freud, the individual's personality was based upon three distinct parts (or regions)—(1) the id, (2) the ego, and (3) the superego. The id is the natural drive with the demand for immediate gratification. The ego is the rationale part. The superego is the mediator and acts as the individual's consciousness, determining the incidents in which someone might feel guilt or shame for their actions. This approach can be applied to pedophilia as a pedophile, by definition, is someone who is sexually attracted to prepubescent children, whereas a *child molester* acts on those sexual desires (Lanier and Henry 1998). Some pedophiles who have the sexual attraction (id) may never act on their desires as their ego and superego are governing their desires.

Criminal justice practitioners argue that many sex offenders do not have control over their desires and suggest this lack of superego explains why convicted sex offenders are rarely rehabilitated, and are the only convicted persons in the United States who are required to register as sex offenders for disclosure to the public as a means to public safety. Again, it is because of this individual-level (intraindividual) perspective that many criminal justice proponents support sex offender registries for individuals convicted of sex crimes. Unfortunately, although the perspectives may help to explain why individuals abuse children, it is still unclear why some adults are sexually attracted to children (McCabe 2003).

Jimmy, age 29, is being sentenced to 20 years in state prison for the sexual molestation of two boys ages 8 and 10. Jimmy had already served a two-year sentence for the sexual assault of another eight-year-old boy and was only out of prison for two weeks when these most recent allegations came forward. At the sentencing hearing, Jimmy acknowledged his guilt but stated he was not a criminal but rather a *sick man* who needed treatment. Jimmy elaborated on his remarks by stating that, although he knows it is wrong to have sex with children, he cannot stop himself and will reoffend if he does not receive treatment. Jimmy stated that he cannot help but be sexually aroused around young boys and was willing to be sterilized as part of a treatment plan in lieu of a prison sentence.

Psychological explanations have been used often to rationalize or explain horrendous acts of criminal behavior. The criminal justice system has attempted to use *insanity* as a defense. However, in most of these cases, the insanity defense is not successful, and juries find the defendant criminally responsible (guilty) for their actions.

The cycle of violence is one of the most common theoretical explanations for domestic violence as it suggests a pattern of abuse in partner relationships that increase in levels of violence over time. This theory may also be used to explain chronic child maltreatment.

Postpartum Psychosis

On June 20, 2001, Andrea Yates was accused of drowning all five of her children in the bathtub. She plead not guilty by reason of insanity (NGRI) stating that she was suffering from postpartum psychosis. A Texas jury found Andrea guilty of first-degree murder, but the Texas Court of Appeals reversed the decision and found her NGRI. Postpartum psychosis is a condition where a woman suffers from a severe case of mental illness and may be unaware of her actions or be unable to appreciate the wrongfulness of her behavior (Bienstock 2003). This is one example of a mental illness that can lead to the abuse and even the death of a child or children.

The physical abuse of children is unfortunately still a common problem in many households. When parents or caretakers develop anger toward their children, they can exhibit rage as they inflict what in their mind is *corporal punishment*. As we know, administering discipline without control of emotions can lead to serious bodily injury to the child. In cases such as these, some psychological explanations are attributed to brain abnormalities. Brain impairment, especially in the frontal lobe, has been associated with violence and antisocial behavior as this impairment can lower an abuser's ability to control impulses (Raine et al. 2013).

Glandular and hormonal imbalances, adrenaline sensitivity, substance abuse, and even diet deficiencies have also been associated with many different types of criminal behaviors (Burke 2005). There exists much controversy with the application of biological theory, as it focuses on medical procedures to control the sexual impulses of convicted offenders, which many individuals label as inhumane (Gosselin 2010). Specifically, medroxyprogesterone is a synthetic hormone that lowers the blood serum testosterone levels in men, thus reducing the sexual interest, which is believed to reduce sex offender recidivism (Bund 1997). Although there is some disagreement about the application for treatment with this condition, there are some aspects of biochemical imbalance that have been widely accepted as the causation for criminal behavior. Alcohol or other types of substance abuse are a significant factor attributing to neglect, sexual, physical, and emotional abuse. Due to the impact of alcohol and substance abuse in child abuse cases, some courts have mandated offenders to seek treatment for substance abuse in lieu of incarceration.

Finally, many children with disabilities are encouraged to live with their families who become their primary caretaker. Unfortunately, children with disabilities are often targets for those who chose to prey on these vulnerable victims. A molester may seek a child who is disabled as he or she may be easier to manipulate into engaging in sexual activity and may not comprehend that the behavior is inappropriate for them. For those children who do understand the sexual abuse, they may not have the knowledge, awareness, or communication skills to report their victimization. Mentally challenged children may also be subjected to physical abuse as their caretakers become frustrated with the responsibility and demands of a disabled child. Children with disabilities can have responses that are uniquely difficult because they are not always adequately prepared to decipher and manage what they are feeling or what is happening to them (Burgess et al. 2013). When comparing persons with severe mental illness to those in the general population, those with mental illness are nearly three times more likely to be violently victimized (Hiday et al. 1999).

Sharmaneke, age 33, has a 12-year-old boy (Kershon) who is severely mentally challenged and requires 24-hour care, which Sharmaneke provides. Sharmaneke just graduated from college, and was starting a new career, when she had to leave her job to care for Kershon while her husband continued to excel in his career. She loved her son and was happy for her husband, although she was envious that he was able to pursue his dreams.

Every day, Sharmaneke would take care of her son including assisting him in keeping up with his hygiene. Sharmaneke was becoming overwhelmed and tired of the day-to-day caring for her son. Although Kershon had soiled himself in the past and that was just part of the daily routine, Kershon soiled himself yet again minutes after his mother had helped bathe him. Out of frustration and anger, Sharmaneke strikes her son across the face with such force that he receives multiple facial fractures requiring hospitalization.

☐ Sociological Theories

Just as there are individual-level (intraindividual) theoretical explanations for child abuse and neglect, there are also interindividual (macro-level or structural) explanations for the abuse. Many of the earliest sociological theories approach child abuse from this macro perspective.

As suggested throughout this text, both males and females are victims of child abuse and neglect. Emile Durkheim (1858–1917), considered the father of sociology, stressed that social forces and conditions influence attitudes and behaviors (Durkheim 1895). From this perspective, child abuse may be explained by examining the events that were external to the individual as influences on the action(s). This perspective has especially gained prominence in providing viable explanations for child maltreatment (Doerner and Lab 2012). For the purpose of this chapter, a selection of sociological theories is presented in an attempt to explain child abuse.

Edwin Sutherland (1883–1950) developed the theory of differential association when he discussed his principles of behaviorism with the notion that learning takes place through interactions with small social groups with the primary group being family or gangs (Sutherland 1939). Deviant behavior is a learned behavior that occurs through a process of interaction with intimate groups. The level of learning is based on the duration and intensity of those interactions.

Differential association has been used in an attempt to explain child abuse and neglect, as well as delinquency. Abusive parents learn abusive behavior; thus, child abuse becomes an intergenerational phenomenon (Cox et al. 2014). Research has also revealed that there is a correlation between child abuse and delinquency. Children who were abused at a young age are at a higher risk for delinquent behavior than children who were not abused (Siegel and Williams 2003). Children who associate with older children may learn delinquent behavior and may also be subjected to sexual abuse.

In later research to explain child abuse from a sociological perspective, Bandura (1973) argued that aggressive tendencies are learned rather than inborn in that children become hostile after witnessing aggressive behavior. These observations can result from the violence they view on television or other sources, which may later lead to the development of criminal behavior. Although controversial in terms of violence and the media's influence, these sources suggest in a child's mind that violence is acceptable; they model aggression, which they may observe on television and within their own family. Older children can be physically abusive to their siblings and may eventually be abusers to their own children later in life. Members of a family unit learn patterns of behavior, and those patterns may include the abuse or maltreatment of children (Gosselin 2010).

Some family violence researchers feel that this assessment is accurate (McCabe 2003); however, not all victimologists (individuals who study victims) share this opinion, since scholars maintain that there exists no sound empirical proof for the notion of the intergenerational transmission of violence (Doerner 2015). This rationale includes the fact that the majority of caretakers who have been abused as a child become extremely loving, supportive, and nurturing parents.

Control theories are based on the concept of why some people do not engage in criminal activity. From this perspective, theorists discuss two kinds of controls: (1) personal and (2) social (Reiss 1951). Personal controls involve individual conscience, a commitment to law, and a positive self-concept, whereas social controls are concerned with social institutions such as family, schools, and religion (Barkan 2015). The purpose of this section is to discuss control theories as related to the abuse of a child.

The containment theory stresses that inner and outer containment helped prevent juvenile offending (Reckless et al. 1956). Inner containment includes a positive self-concept, tolerance for frustration, and the ability to set realistic goals. Outer containment includes institutions such as the family (Barkan 2015). Although the concept of this theory was originally proposed to address juvenile delinquency, these same principles can be applied in discussing violent or abusive behavior directed toward children. Negative self-concepts and low self-esteem have been frequently noted as characteristics of those who abuse or neglect children (Marshall et al. 1999). A caretaker with a high level of inner containment, who has a child that is *acting out*, may not lash out at the child but rather set realistic goals as related to the child's behavior. Caretakers who have a support system within their family can use them as a resource to assist them in dealing with their frustrations, as these support members may provide them a much-needed break from parenting.

Finally, research suggests that individuals with low self-esteem are more likely to commit various types of offenses and have other types of problems (Rocque et al. 2013). This lack of self-control often results from ineffective child rearing on their parents' part and continues throughout their lifetime. Those who have low self-control act impulsively and place their needs above the needs of the group—to include their need for pleasure. Thus, individuals who place their needs and desires above those of others are more likely to abuse a child if it is their desire.

The ecological theory focuses on the abnormalities in the parent–child relationship (Bavolek 2000). From this perspective, there are four abnormities in the parent–child relationship that can lead to abuse or neglect: (1) inappropriate parental expectations of the child, (2) lack of empathy toward the child's needs, (3) parent's belief in physical punishment, and (4) parental role reversal. Included as examples of the abnormalities are a parent who expects their child to always be the star athlete, a parent who expects their child to always receive the best of grades, and a parent who expects the child care for the younger children to always be provided by the older child.

> Jackie (age 55), a mother of three children from three different men, is a recovering alcoholic and has been homeless at least six times since leaving her father's home over 30 years ago. When Jackie was young (age 10), her mother left the family, leaving Jackie to care for her father and two brothers. For the next nine years, Jackie was the housekeeper, the cook, the mother, and the wife. Only now does Jackie discuss the abuse (physical, sexual, and emotional) at the hands of her father.

Parents' feelings about and behaviors toward their child are influenced by the characteristics of the child. The ecological theory includes environmental circumstances that can elicit stressful behaviors, including family structure, and extreme levels of economic deprivation. (Burgess et al. 2013). A parent's ability to care for their children is influenced by their surroundings, which could well create parents who neglect. In today's research, the ecological perspective is an encompassing theory that covers many aspects of neglect (Crosson-Tower 2010).

Social disorganization is another theory that describes the breakdown of social bonds and social control, thus creating a confusion of behaviors to include child abuse (Akers and Sellers 2013). Many of these neighborhoods, which are continually in transition, may have residents living in dilapidated housing where the families experience high divorce rates. A single parent who may be unable to afford child care is forced to leave his or her children alone while they work or seek employment.

With the goal of survival or the objective of moving to an improved neighborhood, residents will not have concern for community; thus, they may not spend time getting to know their neighbors. This type of environment can make it more challenging to know who *belongs* in the neighborhood and who is an outsider, thus creating a situation where it is difficult to be cognizant of a person who may potentially be a threat to a child.

In these environments, parents may also not seek out or benefit from community resources, such as those associated with schools and social services. Children living in a society of social disorganization are often lacking guardianship, which can make them a more attractive target for predators. Hence, poverty in transitional neighborhoods is believed to contribute to lawlessness (Gosselin 2010). Multiple moves and unsupported neighborhoods place parents under a great deal of pressure as they try to raise their child within a disorganized environment. In a nutshell, unemployment, poverty, and a stressful relationship within a family can facilitate abusive behavior by a parent toward their child (Crosson-Tower 2010).

Finally, the routine activities theory, developed by Lawrence Cohen and Marcus Felson in 1979, argues that a person's activities or daily routines influence their likely victimization (Daigle 2012). This theory, based on three conditions, suggest that when conditions exist, victimization will occur. This victimization includes child abuse and neglect. The three conditions are (1) a target, (2) a motivated offender, and (3) a lack of guardian(s). A target is someone or something that another person might desire. In the case of individuals, the target may be someone easier to victimize, such as an elderly person or a child. Both of these individual types may be classified as vulnerable prey. What is it about these categories of victims that would make them vulnerable? Both may be considered physically weaker than their offender and may not have the ability to fend off an attack. Their lifestyle could also be a contributing factor to make them an attractive target, despite the elderly being considered the least likely segment of the population to be victimized. However, some children may be easier marks as their lifestyle may make them more accessible to a motivated offender.

A motivated offender is anyone who is willing to victimize a potential target if they feel that there is an attractive victim, and the opportunity to commit this crime exists due to a lack of guardianship. Under this condition, one must assume that, given the correct conditions (internal or external), an individual who is willing to hurt another person or damage someone's property exists. In terms of child abuse, one assumes that there exist individuals motivated and willing to cause harm to a child for either personal pleasure and/or personal profit.

Finally, a lack of guardianship develops when individuals or conditions do not exist to intervene. For example, an alarm system may be an appropriate guardian to reduce or eliminate the chance that a home may be burglarized. For potential child victims, the presence of other individuals, such as a police officer or a parent, may be the guardian who prohibits their victimization. Unfortunately, when a child does not have anyone to serve as a guardian, victimization is possible. As previously discussed in this section, with social disorganization, a child may be left alone as a single parent works, and, as there is a lack of community in some neighborhoods, there is not a guardian or no appropriate adult supervision. Hence, no one is present to prevent the victimization of the child.

Jeannine is a single mother who rented a two-bedroom apartment in the projects of New York City since her divorce. She works a full-time manual job trying to keep her head above water, as her ex-husband has not been paying child support for their 11-year-old son. Robbie, her son, is currently a middle-school student in the seventh grade and has not made any friends since he was new to the neighborhood. Jeannine currently does not make enough money to pay for a sitter and has not found time or a desire to acquaint herself with any neighbors, as her focus has been to work and save enough money to move to a more desirable area. Robbie walks the same route home each day from school, where he usually arrives home at approximately three o'clock. One day, coming home, Robbie is approached by a man who offers to give him a ride. Jeannine arrives home at six o'clock after a long day's work and finds that Robbie is nowhere to be found. She promptly calls the police as she realizes that Robbie may have been missing for over two hours. Robbie is never seen again.

☐ Feminism

Finally, a commonly utilized contemporary theory to explain child abuse is the feminist pathways perspective, which suggests that girls who are victimized by child abuse or who witness intimate partner abuse may also become active in criminal behavior later in life as a result of these childhood experiences. Adult survivors of childhood sexual assault are more probable to engage in high-risk sexual behavior (Reid 2010). Criminal offenses can include prostitution, robbery, or sexual assault. Research has shown that incarcerated girls are nearly four times more likely to have been abused when compared to their male counterparts (Mallicoat and Ireland 2014).

The effects of sexual abuse can lead to drug dependency and alcohol addiction, as well as mental health issues such as post-traumatic stress disorder. These can be the catalysts of runaway behavior. Many girls will often attempt to flee their homes in an effort to avoid further abuse but can find themselves revictimized when it becomes apparent that they are desperate and vulnerable by those who desire to take advantage of their plight. A women's decision to engage in sex work or to become homeless is directly correlated with their decision to leave home at an early age to avoid physical or sexual abuse by their parents or another family member.

Ashley (age 14) has been sexually abused by her father for over two years. She has turned to alcohol and drugs in an attempt to *block out* what is happening to her. Out of pure desperation, she runs away from home to escape this endless abuse. After just one night, Ashley finds herself desperate for shelter and food. A man approaches her with what appears to be compassion and offers her a place to stay. This stranger takes her to his home and immediately starts to sexually assault Ashley. Ashley is scared as she does not know where she is and finds herself locked inside this stranger's basement. After two weeks of relentless sexual assaults, Ashley is transported to another man, who takes her across state lines where she is forced to engage in prostitution. Ashley never sees her family again as she is continuously transferred from one area to another as a victim of child sex trafficking.

Finally, children are usually cared for by their mother or another female caretaker, who in many cases is taking on that responsibility as a single parent. The stressors associated with caring for a child may explain why some women abuse their child, but there does not seem to be any concise reasoning as to why this abuse occurs. Throughout history, most research of criminal behavior has been based on men. Mothers typically spend a greater amount of time with their children leaving them with more of an opportunity to abuse them. Women are the primary offenders against children, which might explain the lack of research (Gosselin 2010).

☐ Summary

Research in the area of child abuse often focuses on the incidents of crime without considering the theoretical foundations for explaining these behaviors. This chapter attempts to address that gap in much of the child abuse research by providing various theoretical foundations in an attempt to explain the victimization of children. Specifically, this chapter, although not providing concrete explanations for the victimization of children, provides explanations for child maltreatment through a variety of classical and contemporary perspectives to include demonology, intraindividual perspective theories, sociological explanations, and a discussion on the feminist perspective.

In these perspectives, contemporary explanations, such as mental illness on the part of the parent, the opportunity for child abuse because of a lack of guardian(s), and child abuse as a result of substance abuse, are explained from theoretical perspectives. In summary, a theory provides a systematic way of studying and explaining events. In this chapter, theories were provided as foundations for beginning the systematic study of child maltreatment. Hence, this chapter provides theoretical explanations to better understand child abuse and neglect.

CHAPTER QUESTIONS

1. What are some of the theories offered as explanations for child abuse?

2. How have many of the contemporary theories of child abuse mirrored the classic theories?

3. What are some external factors used to help explain child abuse?

QUESTIONS FOR FURTHER THOUGHT

1. Should sex offenders be hospitalized instead of incarcerated if they are unable to control their actions?

2. If child abuse is a result of mental illness, how can we end the victimization of children?

3. Can child abuse truly be explained?

☐ References

Akers, R. and Sellers, C. 2013. *Criminology Theories: Introduction, Evaluation, and Application.* New York: Oxford University Press.

Bandura, A. 1973. *Aggression: A Social Learning Analysis.* Englewood Cliffs, NJ: Prentice Hall.

Barkan, S. 2015. *Criminology: A Sociological Understanding* (6th ed.). Englewood Cliffs, NJ: Prentice Hall.

Bavolek, S. 2000. *The Nurturing Parenting Programs.* Washington, D.C.: Office of Juvenile Delinquency and Prevention, US Department of Justice.

Bialystok, E. and Craik, F. 2006. *Lifespan Cognition: Mechanisms of Change.* Oxford, United Kingdom: Oxford University.

Bienstock, S. 2003. *Mothers Who Kill Their Children and Postpartum Psychosis,* 32 Sw. U.L. Rev. 451 (Southwestern University Law Review).

Bund, J. 1997. Did you say chemical castration? *University of Pittsburgh Law Review,* 59(1), 157–192.

Burgess, A., Regehr, C., and Roberts, A. 2013. *Victimology: Theories and Applications* (2nd ed.). Burlington, MA: Jones and Bartlett Learning.

Burke, R. 2005. *An Introduction to Criminological Theory.* Portland, OR: William Publishing.

Cox, S. Allen, J., Hanser, R., and Conrad, J. 2014. *Juvenile Justice: A Guide to Theory, Policy, and Practice.* Thousand Oaks, CA: SAGE.

Crosson-Tower, C. 2010. *Understanding Child Abuse and Neglect* (8th ed.). Boston: Allyn & Bacon.

Daigle, L. 2012. *Victimology*. Thousand Oaks, CA: SAGE.

Doerner, W. and Lab, S. 2012. *Victimology* (6th ed.). Burlington, MA: Anderson Publishing.

Durkheim, E. 1895. *The Rules of the Sociological Method*. New York: Free Press.

Freud, S. 1920. *A General Introduction to Psycho-Analysis*. New York: Liveright.

Gosselin, D. 2010. *Heavy Hands: An Introduction to the Crimes of Family Violence* (4th ed.). New Jersey: Prentice Hall.

Hiday, V., Swartz, M., Swanson, J., Borum, R., and Wagner, H. 1999. Criminal victimization of persons with severe mental illness. *Psychiatric Services*, 50(1), 62–68.

Lanier, M. and Henry S. 1998. *Essential Criminology*. Boulder, CO: Westview.

Mallicoat, S. and Ireland, C. 2014. *Women and Crime: The Essentials*. Thousand Oaks, CA: SAGE.

Marshall, W., Cripps, E., Anderson, D., and Cortoni, F. 1999. Self-esteem and coping strategies in child molesters. *Journal of Interpersonal Violence*, 14(9), 955–963.

McCabe, K. 2003. *Child Abuse and the Criminal Justice System*. New York: Peter Lang Publishing.

Moyer, I. 2001. *Criminological Theories: Traditional and Nontraditional Voices and Themes*. Thousand Oaks, CA: SAGE.

Raine, A., Rocque, M., and Welsh, B. 2013. *Criminology: Prospects for Advancing Science and Public Policy*. New York: Cambridge University Press.

Reckless, W., Dinitz, S., and Murray, E. 1956. Self-concept as an insulator against delinquency. *American Sociological Review*, 21, 744–756.

Reid, J. 2010. Doors wide shut: Barriers to the successful delivery of victim services for domestically trafficked minors in Southern US metropolitan area. *Women and Criminal Justice*, 20, 1–2.

Reiss, A. 1951. Delinquency as the failure of personal and social controls. *American Sociological Review*, 16(1), 196–207.

Rocque, M., Posick, C., and Zimmerman, T. 2013. Measuring up: Assessing the measurement properties of two self-control scales. *Deviant Behavior*, 34(3), 534–556.

Siegel, J. and Williams M. 2003. The relationship between child sexual abuse and female delinquency and crime: A prospective study. *Journal of Research in Crime and Delinquency*, 40, 71–95.

Sutherland, E. 1939. *Principles of Criminology* (3rd ed.). Philadelphia: J.B. Lippincott.

Child Trafficking

Mary was born in the United States but sold into slavery by her mother when she was four. She spent the next 12 years of her life as a sex slave for a group of American businessmen. She traveled to multiple states, which included California, Oregon, and New Jersey, before being rescued. (Salvation Army 2003)

Child abuse, for many, is considered intimate, and personal child abuse through trafficking is considered global and revenue generating. Human trafficking and, in particular, the trafficking of children have recently become recognized as one of the most profitable criminal enterprises involving the maltreatment of children. Human trafficking is defined by the United Nations as

> the recruitment, transfer, harboring or receipt of persons by threat or use of force. (UNODC 2006)

This criminal enterprise involves men, women, and children, who are viewed as a product worthy of victimization for profit. In general, the majority of the individuals who are victims of human trafficking are trafficked for one of two reasons: (1) sex or (2) labor. In discussions of human trafficking, much of today's focus is on the trafficking of women, their stories, and the conditions in which the trafficking occurred as most research suggests that the majority of the victims are female and under the age of 24.

The International Labour Organization and the Federal Bureau of Investigation estimate that human trafficking generates over $32 billion annually and is quickly increasing in revenue (Wilson 2013). Unfortunately, human trafficking is not limited to adult victims: children, some of whom are very young, constitute the over 5 million victims of human trafficking. It is these child victims of human trafficking that are the focus of this chapter.

Based upon estimates by the US Department of State, for every 6000 victims of human trafficking, approximately one trafficker is convicted.

Essentially, there are four categories of victim of human trafficking. The first category includes adults and children, who, through force, fraud, or coercion, are forced into labor. The second category includes adults who, through force, fraud, or coercion, are forced into the sex industry. The third category includes children who are forced into the sex industry. The fourth category includes children who are trafficked for reasons other than labor or sex.

Incidents of human trafficking have existed for generations; however, Vinkovic (2010) suggests that child trafficking became more prevalent in developed countries with the fall of the communism in the 1980s. The overwhelming presence of poverty, job insecurity, and an inadequate education system created a favorable environment throughout Europe for the shift to smuggling and human trafficking (McCabe 2008). In fact, Hubbard et al. (2008) suggest that child trafficking facilitated the worst form of child labor in Europe. The current annual report produced by the US Department of State suggests that child trafficking cases continue to increase.

For clarity of this chapter, it is acknowledged that the trafficking of persons, although different from smuggling, is often identified as people smuggling. People smuggling is also a problem in the United States and other developed countries as criminal networks exist to move individuals across the borders as the individual desires.

Human trafficking involves exploitation and/or coercion. With smuggling, the movement is always transnational (across borders) and without coercion. Human trafficking may occur transnationally or within geographic borders and involves an element of force, coercion, and fraud. Hence, human trafficking is not smuggling; however, some smuggling cases may become cases of human trafficking if the choice to leave or not participate becomes not available to the smuggled individual (McCabe 2008).

The distinction between smuggling and trafficking is significant in that not only are the dynamics behind the two different, but also individuals who have been smuggled are not eligible for services provided to trafficking victims; this includes the services designed for child victims of trafficking. It is also important to note that a person under the age of 18, regardless of country of origin, cannot give his or her consent to move from one country to another. In addition, parents cannot provide consent for children to be moved for the purpose of forced labor or sexual exploitation; hence, child trafficking is identified (UNODC 2006).

Cases of child trafficking are often identified in reports of human trafficking; however, specific information on the young victims is limited. In fact, historically, information on adult trafficking has been assumed to apply to child trafficking in regard to the number of children trafficked, the conditions of child trafficking, and the perpetrators behind child trafficking. Recent research suggests that these assumptions may not be true (McCabe and Manian 2010, 2008; McCabe 2008). Today, the United Nations and the United States have identified the trafficking of minors for sex and labor as a serious global issue and one worthy of not only public attention but also legislative attention. In 2003, the Prosecutorial Remedies and Other Tools to end the Exploitation of Children Today (PROTECT) Act was adopted to seek and punish aggressively those Americans involved in traveling to participate in child sex rings (Miller 2006). However, day after day in the United States and abroad, one case after another is discovered involving a trafficked child.

In the late 1980s, there were approximately 150,000 victims of child prostitution in the United States (Champagne and Poffenberger 1988). These estimates did not distinguish between national and international minors or child prostitutes who chose to sell their bodies and children who were trafficked into a life of sexual exploitation. Researchers estimate that today, approximately 2 million people are slaves in the international sex market and that many of these individuals are children (Zoba 2003). In addition, the United Nations Children's Emergency Fund (UNICEF) estimates that today, more than 200 million children between the ages of 5 and 17 are forced to work in situations of child bondage.

In the global arena, the United States has been a leader in attempting to support the rights of children and to end child abuse (McCabe 2003). With AMBER alerts and Megan's Law for missing children, it is difficult to believe that child trafficking might occur in the United States; however, it does occur every day.

United States v. Satia and Nanji (2001)

Two Maryland residents were sentenced to 108 months in prison after being convicted of holding a 14-year-old girl prisoner and forcing her to work as a domestic servant in their home.

Historical research on immigrants has traditionally been conceptualized around adult men's movements, with women and children typically accompanying these men as a family (King 2002); however, with child trafficking, a new aspect of immigration and abuse emerges. This aspect involves the focus of child trafficking.

Over the last two decades, Estes and Weiner (2001) suggested that over 10,000 children between the ages of 10 and 17 are brought into the United States from other countries annually for sex and that most of these children are forced to work in the sex industry. Today, the US State Department (2015) suggests that the number of child victims of trafficking into the country has doubled only in the past few years. Reports from the National Center for Missing and Exploited Children suggest that in the 1980s, American motorcycle gangs were heavily involved in the trafficking of vulnerable youths; however, today, these gangs appear to have little involvement in the trafficking of children.

The trafficking of children or those victims under the age of 18 refers to the category of trafficking identified in the 2003 Trafficking Victims Protection Reauthorization Act (TVPRA) as a severe form of trafficking. As inferred in the term *severe*, harsher penalties accompany the trafficking of children. Unfortunately, as trafficked children are usually subsumed under the classification of women and children, and, as it is often difficult to determine a child's age through physical characteristics alone, distinguishing between a child and a young man or woman is often difficult.

Researchers who attempt to generate a profile of child victims of human trafficking often use cases from source institutions and nongovernmental organizations for which age and gender are known (Kangaspunta 2006). It is from these cases that it is determined that child victims comprise the largest percentage of the persons reported as victims of human trafficking outside the United States. It is also from these cases that it is concluded that most child victims come from families with many (four or more) children and with only one or two of the family members contributing to the family income. In these cases, child trafficking is profitable not only for the trafficker but also, in many ways, for the child's family. Even if a family member is not paid for the child, they save the cost of caring for the trafficked child. Although it is difficult to imagine a parent allowing for the trafficking of their child to avoid the cost of care for that child, it is a reality for many adults in need of money to either support an addiction or their remaining children.

☐ Why Children Are Trafficked

To understand the trafficking of children, one must first eliminate from their mind the concept of a child as a person and view the child as a product, one that is worthy of much effort in its care and very profitable to its owner. In this scenario, the customer is the consumer of the product, and the trafficker is the means of production and distribution for the product. The victimization of a child is simply the outcome of the consumer's desire. Hence, child trafficking is a business.

Children are trafficked for a variety of reasons in addition to sex and labor. Specifically, children are trafficked for labor, adoption, drug smuggling, sex, their healthy internal organs, and (in some countries) soldiering and camel jockeying. Each use of a trafficked child equates to profit to his or her trafficker. As the child is moved when necessary for consumption by the consumer, there rarely exists an opportunity for the detection of the victimization by an individual outside of the organized criminal unit.

Currently, there is no national system for tracking unaccompanied minors; therefore, the movement of these children from place to place and from country to country is often accomplished without restriction (McCabe 2008). Many international children enter the United States on a family immigration visa. With the family member visa, the child is sponsored by an individual within the United States (such as an uncle, aunt, cousin, or an individual claiming to be a relative) and allowed entry into the country. Children who appear to be at least 18 years old may also enter the United States under false temporary (nonimmigrant) visas. Unless the child's documentation is determined to be false, and the child is identified and taken into the custody of immigration officials, he or she is virtually undetectable and therefore at the mercy of the trafficker once they reach their destination (McCabe 2008).

In the late 1990s, the US Department of Labor began to take notice of human trafficking when it was revealed that American companies such as Gap and Nike were selling items made in sweatshops with trafficked child labor (Bales 2004). In cases such as these, the criminals were the *respectable* businesspeople with the goal of maximum profit, and the product was some material item that everyone in the country desired. The realization that child trafficking was the means to obtain those desired products was a wake-up call for many people in the United States.

Historically, research in the area of forced labor indicates that many of the persons, including children, identified as working in exploitative conditions (including domestic servitude), gave their consent and, therefore, are of little interest to the criminal justice system (Clawson 2009; Munro 2006). Nearly 20 years ago, the concept of *consent* began to be questioned. Again, as the lines between trafficking and smuggling are often blurred, the notion of consent (even for a child who cannot legally provide consent) leaves law enforcement officials conducting very few investigations in terms of labor exploitation.

As children are placed in these positions of servitude by their parents or caregivers (Melrose 2002; Aronowitz 2001), the majority of these children continue to work under deplorable conditions without complaint and without ever attempting to leave their work environment. In addition, many of these child victims do not report their abuse as they are often terrified to return home given that their parents or another family member arranged their *employment*.

Attempts to determine whether any financial yield is received by the trafficked children suggest that, for the most part, the child victim receives little or no compensation. For a child from a country mired in poverty and neglect, labor trafficking provides them the opportunity to escape the country and to receive food and shelter. The food and shelter, which, for many, far exceeds the conditions they left in their homeland, are an attractive incentive for the children and their parents, and hence the exploitation begins. As suggested by many researchers, poverty supports the environment of human trafficking (McCabe and Manian 2011).

Labor trafficking continues, and children work in below-standard conditions in agriculture, mining, or manufacturing. This arrangement works well for the traffickers; they receive money from the labor of the children, and, in most cases, the children are easier to control than adults, have a longer working-time potential, and, in many countries, are more in number and easier to obtain than adults. Therefore, children are desirable for those individuals interested in the trafficking of individuals for labor.

Children are also trafficked for adoption. In many cases of child adoptions, government officials are recognizing the involvement of organized crime. Specifically, in international cases revealed over the past few years, there have been a number of organized child trafficking rings involved in the criminal activity (Binh 2006). These crime organizations provide infants to desperate couples seeking to adopt a child. The traffickers involved in this type of child trafficking typically purchase desired international babies from the poorest of families, orphanages, or single mothers. Those most desired babies in the United States and across

Europe are white newborn babies (McCabe 2008). With couples in the United States willing to pay $30,000 or more for a baby, the demand is always present. In the children's country of origin (including many of those countries previously governed by the Soviet Union), traffickers will identify possible children or babies on the basis of their physical characteristics and/or the physical characteristics of their parents and then either attempt to purchase the children from their parents or kidnap the children. Again, one must consider the child as a product and the trafficker as the distributor.

Children trafficked for adoption are not unique to areas outside of the United States or within the United States. Specifically, children born to unwed mothers, and especially children born to single white mothers, are targeted by traffickers in the United States. Nationally, traffickers involved in the trafficking of babies for adoption understand the demand in the United States and other developed countries. Therefore, child victims with the desired physical characteristic of *whiteness* are often the targets of traffickers for adoptions.

The Coalition Against Trafficking in Women and the Bilateral Border Safety Coalition focus on reducing human trafficking between Mexico and the United States.

Children are also trafficked for use in the smuggling of drugs. According to Estes and Weiner (2001), children serve as *drug mules* in transporting illegal narcotics from other countries into the United States. Historically, adult men and even women who appeared to be pregnant were used to transport drugs, particularly from Mexico and South America, into the United States; however, as security measures have increased, and the searching of baggage and persons has become more prevalent in airports and land-border crossings, individuals, including children, are transporting drugs by means of ingestion. Children, from a trafficker's perspective, are excellent hosts for the movement of drugs across borders. Children often do not receive the scrutiny of customs or immigration officials as they enter the country accompanied by an adult (usually a female). If the small bag of drugs that is swallowed by the child dissolves or leaks into the stomach, then death is common. However, as the child is viewed as cheap, disposable, and easy to replace, the trafficker involved in drug smuggling suffers less of a financial loss with a child than with an adult, and another child is quickly obtained and is then trafficked as a replacement.

The most commonly offered explanation for the human trafficking of women is sex trafficking. Sex trafficking is also the most common reason for the trafficking of children—for sex and the support of the commercial sex industry (Lulo 2013).

Dalton (2013) discussed child sex trafficking as it was found in men's clubs and bars. McCabe (2007) focused on the children involved in trafficking for reasons of pornography. Davidson (2005) identifies the children in the sex trade across the globe. Somerset (2004) discussed the children trafficked for prostitution. Hence, included within the reasons for the sex trafficking of children are child pornography, child prostitution, sex rings, molestation, the supporting sex tourism industry, and nude dancing. As sex involving children is supported by the human desires for gratification, profit, and fulfillment, it is neither a phenomenon easily remedied nor an activity easily identified and/or investigated.

Many individuals, including recruiters, trainers, purveyors, creators of false documentation, transporters, money collectors, enforcers, and parents, are involved in the sex trafficking of children (Estes and Weiner 2001). Sex involving a child sells, and traffickers are aware of the profits (McCabe 2008). Whether these children are born in the United States or another country and brought into the United States under the legalized family immigrant visa, through the unregulated industry of mail-order brides, or under false pretenses, all of these children are potential victims of child trafficking in the United States, and all are trafficked into the country for a profit.

The sex trafficking of children provides income for many individuals involved in the enterprise, including, in some instances, individuals involved in organized criminal networks. Recent work by the United Nations Office of Drugs and Crime (UNODC) suggests the existence of a strong link between child sex trafficking and organized crime, and it continues to be one of the most profitable industries in the world (Wilson 2013). This includes the payment of debts to criminal organizations through the exchange of girls in marriage and the recruitment and/or abduction of children for sexual exploitation (Sheldon 2011). In these cases, the UNODC suggests the existence of small core criminal organizations whose members maintain very high levels of secrecy, more because of fear of community outrage than a fear of detection by law enforcement officials.

According to UNICEF, girls as young as 13 are trafficked as mail-order brides.

Another reason for the trafficking of individuals and, specifically, the trafficking of children is the desire for healthy internal organs. In 2003, it was reported that over the past decade, hundreds of women and children have been reported missing or murdered in the northern

Mexican border town of Ciudad Juarez (Miles 2003). It was speculated that one of the reasons for the murders was organ smuggling. In London, during the same period, a young Nigerian boy's body was found in the River Thames with some of his organs missing. With the ever-pressing need for organs for transplantation in the United States and other developed countries, and fueled by the fear of AIDS in adults, a child is the perfect victim of human trafficking for internal organs. The child's organs are more likely to be healthy and HIV negative; thus, it is very profitable for those involved in trafficking and for those not deterred from murdering a child for profit (McCabe 2008).

Finally, child soldiering and camel jockeying, although not documented to exist in the United States, are also reasons for the trafficking of children. It is not uncommon in developing countries for children to be kidnapped, their families bribed, or the families and/or children enticed through false promises of financial compensation into being trained as soldiers or to serve as camel jockeys.

Cases of child soldiering and jockeying most often involves male children exploited for labor; however, some female children may also be trafficked for these reasons. International standards exist prohibiting the use of children as soldiers, although the United Nations has information indicating that child soldiers are being used in more than 30 countries (Wallace and Roberson 2015). Hence, child trafficking occurs for not only sex and labor but also reasons that exclusively involve the need for children.

☐ How Is Trafficking Facilitated?

The trafficking of children, with perhaps the exception of trafficking for adoption, is essentially a financial investment (McCabe 2008). A single trafficked child can earn the trafficker thousands of dollars, and, if more children are trafficked, the profits only increase. In identifying children to be trafficked, the country and family background of the child must be considered, as well as the physical characteristics of the child. Just as McCabe (2003) suggested in the abuse of children by family and strangers and the importance in the existence of an opportunity, the opportunity must exist for child trafficking. Specifically, in child trafficking, the conditions that exist within the child's country and family often provide the opportunity for victimization (Bush 2011).

Countries with deepening poverty, long-term unemployment, and population explosions are often identified as source countries for child trafficking. These countries, often with political instability, public corruption, and insufficient or uncaring law enforcement, provide many of the children who will one day become victims of child trafficking (Kendall and Funk 2011; Kapustin 2006). For parents and the children in these countries, the desperation for a better life facilitates the trafficking.

Parents within source countries for child trafficking often lack educational opportunities and are ignorant of the tactics of experienced traffickers; hence, the parents may allow another adult the opportunity to care for their child (Mirza 2010). In particular, parents in rural areas of source countries may have had no exposure to child traffickers (Ali et al. 2013). In addition, with gender inequality and the customary practice of purchased marriage in the family's culture, child trafficking is not an unrealistic outcome (Chung 2006).

Trafficked children are not a homogeneous group (McCabe 2008). In fact, variations in terms of gender, class, race, age, nationality, and immigration status are related to demand, their cost, and the amount of risk their traffickers are willing to take (Davidson 2005). The tracking or identification of a child victim, once he or she begins the shuffle associated with trafficking in the United States or any country, is nearly impossible. The children, often in the same situation as trafficked adults, are often unable to speak English or the country's native language, are unable to seek help from law enforcement, and are subjected to repeated victimization.

☐ Why Don't Children Leave Their Captors?

Although many victims are under close scrutiny and are unable to escape their captors due to physical constraints, others may have the opportunity to leave but are unable as they still find themselves under the control of their traffickers. For these children, the dependence is not only physical but also emotional.

Traffickers use number-coercive methods and psychological manipulations to control their victims (Rafferty 2007). Some child victims are manipulated by threats the trafficker makes against their family if the child attempts to leave. Girls who are imprisoned in a brothel are beaten into compliance (Mallicoat 2015), thus continuing control of the child. Most girls in these brothels are unable to see or communicate with their family members, which they have left behind (Mallicoat 2015). Many children taken to a region they are no longer familiar with find themselves dependent on their traffickers. These children find themselves in a situation where they must rely on their traffickers for basic needs such as food, shelter, clothing, and even their safety (Mallicoat and Ireland 2014). In addition, when some girls are able to escape their captors, they may return home and be viewed as *damaged goods* and, as a result, are shunned by society and their family members (Simkhada 2008).

Finally, just as the concept of a *bad parent* is better than *no parent* exists for many child victims of abuse and neglect, victims of child trafficking often view their traffickers as their protectors and their security. For these children who have no other adults in their lives to care for them, by continuing their contact with their trafficker, even if it means continuing their victimization, the traffickers are their safety and support.

☐ Why Child Trafficking Continues

Explanations as to why child trafficking continues go beyond the conditions of the countries of origin. It is suggested that recent economic crises in Asia and other countries have made children particularly vulnerable to traffickers as more and more children are not attending school and seeking employment (McCabe 2008).

Individuals who traffic children are experienced in subtle psychological manipulation and have found it to be more effective with children than overt control through force and violence. The trafficker is most often perceived as a young, rich, and good-looking man; however, this is not always the case. Just as with the trafficking of adults, traffickers of children may be male or female, and, the younger the children, the more often a woman (because of a gender-biased perception of love and mothering) is involved. These women, in cases of child trafficking, occupy the position of a mother or a caregiver in travel with the children to gain entry into the country (McCabe 2008).

Once the children are in the county, the women often continue their day-to-day care until the children are moved to other caregivers or are killed because of their abusive situations. There have also been cases identified in which babies are taken or purchased from their families, raised to the age of five or six, and then trafficked for either sex or labor.

Those involved as clients of trafficked children are not always men, as many child domestics will report to and be controlled by women (Barnitz 2000). Traffickers, especially those involved in the trafficking of children, have become increasingly flexible in adapting to situations and may change faces or appearances to allow the use of different travel routes to avoid detection (Lazaroiu and Alexandru 2003). Customers seeking a child will search through word of mouth, existing brothels, phone booth advertisements, bartenders, taxi drivers, and Internet chat rooms (Dalton 2013).

> Mary, 15, was a victim of child sexual abuse at the hands of her step-father and then her mother's new boyfriend. She repeatedly ran away from home and missed school. Eventually, her mother stopped looking for her. In the meantime, Mary met a handsome young man, who promised her a career as a dancer. With a fake ID, Mary began dancing in strip clubs, and, by 16, she was addicted to heroin. Mary was forced to continue dancing throughout the southern part of the United States and then forced into prostitution by one of her club *bosses*. Mary was a victim of child trafficking.

Police often patrol well-known street prostitute areas; however, it is rare that a trafficked child will be identified in these areas. In fact, most law enforcement officers will never be exposed to an individual who admits to being a victim of human trafficking (Peet 2006).

This ability of the traffickers to adjust their plans, along with their often-decentralized modes of transporting individuals, creates a very difficult environment for detection. Without the centrality of leadership and control often found in adult trafficking operations and historically in organized crime, the individual traffickers involved in child trafficking are among the most important elements in the activity (Sheldon 2000).

Traffickers may pose as a family member, a friend to the child, an adopting adult, or the head of a modeling agency, and all within the role of trafficking the child (Lazaroiu and Alexandru 2003). The home country does not miss the child, the traffickers are organized, and work in the United States is ideal. Traffickers to the United States are encouraged by large tax-free profits, the continued income from the same victim, and the relatively minor penalties (Miko 2004). Hence, the trafficker facilitates the victimization by communicating with the buyer and procuring the victim (Siddharth 2010). Finally, recent research on human trafficking, similar to research on chronic child abuse, suggests that many survivors of child sex trafficking do not realize that they were victims until years later.

The growth of child pornography is another explanation for the increase in child trafficking (McCabe and Johnston 2014). Online child pornography fuels the demand for child victims, and child pornography and trafficking are a gateway to the victims of these types of sexual exploitation (McCabe 2007). As it becomes easier to identify and contact children via the Internet, it becomes easier for traffickers and those interested in the exploitation of children to identify a potential victim.

Recent US legislation has expanded the penalties for those who profit by human trafficking and specifically child trafficking; however, further legislation is needed to provide support for these child victims of trafficking, including the decriminalization of the minor and additional services uniquely required by children such as education and the supervision of an adult. The child victim of trafficking, depending on his or her age, may need the services typically provided in toddler care, medical and growth checkups, or remedial education. In addition to their physical and educational needs, child victims of human trafficking will require socialization, counseling, social services interventions, patience, and perhaps even mental health treatment to begin their acclimation into mainstream society.

When exploiters are hard pressed, and law enforcement begins targeting the perpetrators of child trafficking, the demand for trafficked children increases. Unfortunately, in these cases, the traffickers will then refine the process of trafficking and become more difficult for law enforcement to identify (McCabe 2008). In the United States, the majority of the trafficked children are not US citizens, and they are perceived by many of the country's citizens as having been given an opportunity for a better quality of life. Hence, the fact that these children are victims of human trafficking is not even considered.

Law enforcement agencies, because of limited reporting by the public, the child's fear of the police and of deportation, and the child's lack of English skills, are often unaware of child trafficking cases (Kendall and Funk 2011). Without awareness, law enforcement cannot act. Finally, child victims are more difficult cases than adult cases for law enforcement as the demographic characteristics of age are related to sanctions, and those sanctions vary by time and place.

☐ Legislative Measures

During the 20th century, there was no single agency responsible for the collection of data on human trafficking and little interest in the activity even though, in 2000, President William Clinton signed the Trafficking Victims Protection Act (TVPA). However, after Secretary of State Colin Powell announced that monies acquired through human trafficking helped to support the 9/11 hijackers while they lived in Florida, the public and the government began to recognize the criminal activity and initiate combative efforts (McCabe 2008).

In 2002, President George W. Bush signed an executive order to establish an Interagency Task Force charged with strengthening efforts among agencies and identifying the needs of trafficking victims while punishing traffickers and preventing future trafficking (Miko 2004). The TVPA was amended and signed in 2003 as the TVPRA, which mandated responsibilities and duties for federal agencies regarding human trafficking. It was also established with the 2000 TVPA and the 2003 TVPRA that the Office to Monitor and Combat Trafficking Persons would be established as an Interagency Task Force to strengthen and coordinate efforts among agencies and identify the needs of trafficking victims.

Included in the responsibilities of this office is an annual Trafficking in Persons (TIP) Report, which classifies countries with a tier rating system based upon their number of human trafficking cases and their legislative responses to human trafficking. In the TIP report, countries are rated as Tier 1, Tier 2, Tier 2 Watch, and Tier 3. Tier 1 countries are those countries that fully comply with the act's minimum standards. Tier 2 countries are those countries that do not fully comply with minimum standards but are making significant efforts. Tier 2 Watch was established for Tier 2 countries that have shown a significant increase in the number of trafficking victims and are failing at their efforts to reduce human trafficking, and Tier 3 countries do not comply with the minimum standards. As displayed by an empirical assessment utilizing 2014 TIP countries (see report in Appendix A), a variety of demographic characteristics are related to tier classification.

In 2003, the United States strengthened its role in fighting human trafficking by passing legislation specifically to fight child sex tourism. This legislation, the PROTECT Act, increases penalties for those involved in child sex tourism to a maximum of 30 years in prison. This measure, along with the various states passing laws against forced child labor and child sexual exploitation, demonstrates the commitment by the United States to end child trafficking because now, in most states, convicted traffickers face a minimum of 25 years in prison.

In addition, the Department of Homeland Security has developed Operation Predator to combat child exploitation, child pornography, and child sex tourism. Finally, in Cancun, Mexico, the hottest destination for American tourists in Mexico, training and awareness efforts on the subject of child trafficking have been introduced to hotel staff and US tourists (ECPAT 2007).

To reduce the number of incidents of child trafficking, the US government has supported several research initiatives focusing on sexual exploitation. Specifically, beginning in 2006, the Office of Juvenile Justice and Delinquency Prevention began supporting million-dollar research studies on the sexual exploitation of children through trafficking and prostitution. In addition, juvenile justice officials have developed a number of prevention and intervention programs focused on assisting these exploited children (*Corrections Digest* 2006).

It is now realized by US law enforcement and government officials that child trafficking may be addressed only through national and international efforts. The United Nations Protocol to Prevent, Suppress, and Punish Trafficking in Persons, especially Women and Children, is an international agreement to address human trafficking, especially the trafficking of children on an international level (Ejalu 2006). It creates the global language necessary to define trafficking in persons, assist victims, and prevent trafficking. Also within the protocol, parameters for judicial cooperation and exchanges of information among countries are intended to facilitate the establishment of laws and synchronized legislation across borders.

☐ Summary

Child trafficking has gained global attention in the past few years. Child trafficking occurs for many reasons to include labor, adoption, drug smuggling, sex, and the trade in healthy internal organs. Unfortunately, the extent of child trafficking in the worldwide is unknown as there exists no national system for tracking unaccompanied minors within or outside of the United States.

The trafficking of children is essentially a financial investment. A single trafficked child can earn the trafficker thousands of dollars, and, many times, the family of the trafficked child has no knowledge of the child's abuse. The most common reason for child trafficking is sexual exploitation.

Trafficked children vary by gender, race, and age, with these characteristics influencing the demand for them and their traffickers' profits. To address child trafficking for sexual exploitation, the United States and other governments have passed legislation to reduce the criminal activity. In addition, funding has been made available to support proactive programs to address child trafficking. However, the trafficking of children is currently one of the most profitable avenues for organized crime. Thus, child abuse and neglect, crimes that are most often intimate and personal, are now broadly publicized and supported as a revenue-bearing enterprise of child victimization.

CHAPTER QUESTIONS

1. What are the reasons children are trafficked, and how do these traffickers procure their victims?

2. Why and how are children used to transport drugs?

3. Why is child trafficking such a profitable business?

QUESTIONS FOR FURTHER THOUGHT

1. What additional legislation can be implemented to help fight child trafficking?

2. If children are poor and want to be trafficked, is it okay?

3. As child trafficking is a crime of relative low risk for traffickers, why don't more people traffic children?

☐ References

Ali, S., Muhammad, N., Shah, M., and Abdullah, I. 2013. Application of demographic variables in measuring the perception of child trafficking in Khyber Pakhtunkhwa, Pakistan. *Pakistan Journal of Criminology*, 5(2), 181–189.

Aronowitz, A. 2001. Smuggling and trafficking in human beings: The phenomenon, the markets that drive it and the organizations that promote it. *European Journal on Criminal Policy and Research*, 9(1), 163–195.

Bales, K. 2004. *New Slavery: A Reference Handbook* (2nd ed.). Santa Barbara, CA: ABC–CLIO.

Barnitz, L. 2000. *Commercial Sexual Exploitation of Children*. Washington, D.C.: Youth Advocate Program.

Binh, V. 2006. Trafficking of women and children in Vietnam: Current issues and problems. In K. Beaks and D. Amir (eds.) *Trafficking and the Global Sex Industry*, pp. 33–46. Lanham, MD: Lexington Books.

Bush, M. 2011. Afghanistan and the sex trade. In McCabe and Manian (eds.) *Sex Trafficking: A Global Perspective*, pp. 111–118. Lanham, MD: Lexington Books.

Champagne, D. and Poffenberger, D. 1988. *The Sexual Trafficking in Children*. Westport, CT: Auburn House.

Chung, R. 2006. Cultural perspectives on child trafficking, human rights, and social justice: A model for psychologists. *Counseling Psychology Quarterly*, 22(1), 85–96.

Clawson, H. 2009. *Human Trafficking Into and Within the United States: A Review of the Literature*. Washington, D.C.: US Department of Human and Health Services.

Corrections Digest. 2006. Research on sexual exploitation of minors. *Corrections Digest*, 37(2), 9–10.

Dalton, R. 2013. Abolishing child sex trafficking on the Internet: Imposing criminal culpability on digital facilitators. *The University of Memphis Law Review*, 43(4), 1097–1144.

Davidson, J. 2005. *Children in the Global Sex Trade*. Cambridge: Polity Press.

ECPAT. 2007. Info ECPAT. *ECPAT Groups' Monthly Newsletter*. Washington, D.C.: ECPAT, March 20, p. 4.

Ejalu, W. 2006. From home to hell: The telling story of an African woman's journey and stay in Europe. In K. Beeks and D. Amir (eds.) *Trafficking and the Global Sex Industry*, pp. 165–186. Lanham, MD: Lexington Books.

Estes, R. and Weiner, N. 2001. *The Commercial Sexual Exploitation of Children in the US, Canada, and Mexico*. Philadelphia, PA: University of Pennsylvania.

Hubbard, P., Matthews, R., and Scoular, J. 2008. Regulating sex work in the EU: Prostitute women and the new space of exclusion. *Gender, Place, and Culture*, 15(2), 137–152.

Kangaspunta, K. 2006. *Trafficking in Persons: Global Patterns*. Vienna, Austria: United Nations Office on Drugs and Crime, April.

Kapustin, E. 2006. The new global slave trade. *Foreign Affairs*, 85(6), 103–115.

Kendall, V. and Funk, T. 2011. *Child Exploitation and Trafficking: Examining the Global Challenges and US Responses*. Maryland: Rowman and Littlefield.

King, R. 2002. Towards a new map of European migration. *International Journal of Population Geography*, 8, 89–106.

Lazaroiu, S. and Alexandru, M. 2003. *Who Is the Next Victim?* Oslo, Norway: International Organization for Migration.

Lulo, S. 2013. Child exploitation and trafficking. *Criminal Justice*, 28(1), 63–65.

Mallicoat, S. 2015. *Women and Crime* (2nd ed.). Thousand Oaks, CA: SAGE.

Mallicoat, S. and Ireland, C. 2014. *Women and Crime: The Essentials*. Thousand Oaks, CA: SAGE.

McCabe, K. 2003. *Child Abuse and the Criminal Justice System*. New York: Peter Lang.

McCabe, K. 2007. The role of Internet service providers in cases of child pornography and child prostitution. *Social Science Computer Review*, 25(2), 1–5.

McCabe, K. 2008. *Human Trafficking: National and International Responses*. New York: Peter Lang.

McCabe, K. and Johnston, O. 2014. Perceptions on the legality of sexting. *Social Science Computer Review*, 32(6), 765–768.

McCabe, K. and Manian, S. 2010. *Sex Trafficking: A Global Perspective*. Lanham, MD: Rowman and Littlefield/Lexington Books.

Melrose, M. 2002. Labour pains: Some considerations of the difficulties of researching juvenile prostitution. *International Journal of Social Research Methodology, Theory, and Practice*, 5(4), 333–351.

Miko, F. 2004. *Trafficking in Women and Children: The US and International Response*. Washington, D.C.: Library of Congress.

Miles, N. 2003. Organ traffick link in Mexico murders. *BBC News*, May 1. Available at http://newsvote.bbc.co.uk. Accessed on August 6, 2015.

Miller, J. 2006. Modern day slavery. *Sheriff*, 58(2), 34–36.

Mirza, M. 2010. The menace of human trafficking. *Pakistan Journal of Criminology*, 2(4), 151–164.

Munro, V. 2006. Stopping traffic? A comparative study of responses to the trafficking of women for prostitution. *British Journal of Criminology*, 46(2), 318–333.

Peet, D. 2006. Human trafficking: Using analytics to address a faceless crime. *Deputy and Court Officer*, 3, 40–43.

Rafferty, Y. 2007. Children for sale: Child trafficking in Southeast Asia. *Child Abuse Review*, 16(6), 401–422.

Salvation Army. 2003. *Human Trafficking: Modern Day Slavery in America*. Washington, D.C.: Salvation Army.

Sheldon, K. 2011. What we know about men who download child abuse image. *British Journal of Forensic Practice*, 13(4), 221–234.

Sheldon, R. 2000. Perspectives on trafficking migrants. *International Migration*, 38(3), 99–115.

Siddharth, K. 2010. *Sex trafficking: Inside the business of modern slavery*. New York: Columbia University Press.

Simkhada, P. 2008. Life histories and survival strategies amongst trafficked girls in Nepal. *Children and Society*, 22, 235–248.

Somerset, C. 2004. *Cause for Concern?* London, United Kingdom: ECPAT.

United Nations Office on Drugs and Crime (UNODC). 2006. *Trafficking in Persons: Global Patterns*. UN: Human Trafficking Unit.

US Department of State. 2015. *Trafficking in Person Report, June 2014*. Washington, D.C.: Office to Monitor and Combat Trafficking in Persons.

Vinkovic, M. 2010. The unbroken marriage—Trafficking and child labour in Europe. *Journal of Money Laundering Control*, 13(2), 87–102.

Wallace, H. and Roberson, J. 2015. *Victimology: Legal, Psychological, and Social Perspectives* (4th ed.). Upper Saddle River, NJ: Pearson.

Wilson, A. 2013. Using commercial driver licensing authority to combat human trafficking related crimes on America's highways. *The University of Memphis Law Review*, 43(4), 969–1012.

Zoba, W. 2003. The hidden slavery. *Christianity Today*, November, pp. 68–74.

CHAPTER

Child Abuse and Technology

Emma was a 13-year-old girl from Virginia. In the afternoons and evenings, she would communicate with an 18-year-old college student through a young adults' chat room. Three days after she left her home to meet her boyfriend, her body is found. She has been stabbed and died as a result of her injury.

Technology has improved so many aspects of modern living. Medical advances have increased life spans. Travel between locations occurs within hours, not weeks. Information is available at the touch of a button. Unfortunately, technology has also promoted vulnerabilities for victims in a variety of modalities. This includes an increase in the vulnerability of children for victimization via technology. In 2015, a 31-year-old former Top Gun navy instructor and veteran of Iraq, living in Virginia, was convicted of posing as a teenager on the Internet and extorted young girls into sending him sexually graphic photos of themselves and each other. Also, in 2015, three Michigan high school teens were found guilty of sexting multiple images of child pornography. Finally, in 2006, a 13-year-old Missouri teen, who was a victim of cyberbullying, hanged herself in a bedroom closet. Each of these cases involved crimes against children, and each of these cases involved either the Internet or a cell phone or both.

Today, it is not unusual to read reports or view television shows that focus on Internet crimes against children (ICAC). The Internet, originally designed to benefit an individual, now provides individual access to other individuals, which includes predators focused on the abuse of children. This chapter is provided not to suggest that predators seeking children are more prevalent on the Internet, or that ICAC are more detrimental to children, but simply to document the increasing numbers and the ever-pressing need for assistance in combating ICAC in society as a whole.

Adam Walsh, Jacob Wetterling, Polly Klaas, and Megan Kanka were historical cases of child sexual abuse that have led to legislative efforts and increase in public awareness of child victimization (Crosson-Tower 2010; Morrissey 2006; McCabe 2003). However, none of these historical cases involved the Internet, a new avenue for predators seeking to identify, obtain, and abuse children. Today, the Internet, which allows predators the tool to target children who they have not met in person, plays a significant role in the victimization of children (McCabe 2008). In addition, bullying, which has existed throughout the history of schools, now includes bullying via the Internet (or cyberbullying), stalking, which gained national attention under the umbrella of violence against women, now includes cyberstalking, and sexting, with the use of a cell phone, has become almost a norm for couples involved in sexually explicit conversations (McCabe and Johnston 2014).

This chapter focuses on the extrafamilial sexual abuse of children and, in particular, the ICAC involving child pornography, child solicitation, cyberbullying, and sexting, as well as the perpetrators of those crimes and the victims of those crimes. For clarity, child pornography is defined as a photo, film, or other visual representations of a person under the age of 18 engaged in sexual activity or a photo, film, or other visual representations of the genitalia of a person under the age of 18. Cyberbullying is defined as the repeated harassment of threatening or embarrassing pictures through the use of a computer, a cell phone, or other electronic devices (Hinduja and Patchin 2009). Sexting is defined as the sending and/or receiving of sexually suggestive images or messages to peers through a cell phone (Mitchell et al. 2012). Each of these activities is common in today's virtual world. Each of these activities may involve children, and each of these child-involved activities is illegal.

According to the Office of Juvenile Justice and Delinquency Program, during 2014, there were over 8000 individuals arrested through law enforcement task forces focused on ICAC.

According to Crosson-Tower (2010), the majority of the perpetrators of child abuse are family members or familial. This is not the case for ICAC, as the majority of perpetrators of ICAC are extrafamilial or someone outside of the family (McCabe 2003). In addition, persons involved in ICAC are significantly more likely to have also committed the contact crime of child sexual abuse (Bourke and Hernandez 2009). With cases of child maltreatment, acute extrafamilial abuse is the category of child abuse most likely to be reported to police; however, the use of the Internet creates a difficult environment for the detection of such crimes and often results in nonreporting. Therefore, the information and data discussed in this chapter are based upon reported cases of ICAC.

In today's world of technology and virtual reality, the label of *friend* is often applied to a chat-room partner whom the child has met online. In reality, this friend is often a perpetrator of child abuse in search of his or her next victim for child sexual exploitation. Unfortunately, this notion of familiarity, for many cases of ICAC, creates a confusing environment for child victims as they may perceive a stranger as a friend, and a friend would certainly not cause them harm. Thus, in the child's mind, his or her Internet friend is harmless. Therefore, ICAC are often not reported by the child or their parent and continue to occur without interventions from the criminal justice community.

☐ Child Pornography

Current research suggests that child pornography, cyberbullying, and sexting are often the result of peer-to-peer networks (Fagundes 2009; McCabe and Martin 2005). In addition, homemade images, which are not commercially produced, comprise a substantial proportion of child pornography (Huang et al. 2009).

Offenders involved in these activities are oftentimes younger than most offenders of traditional incidents of child sexual abuse (Reijnen et al. 2009). Research also suggests that pedophiles aggressively target specific victims and that most of those victims utilize the Internet (Middleton et al. 2006). In addition, the majority of those offenders who commit any type of ICAC are also in possession of child pornography (Wolak et al. 2003).

During February of 1996, President William Clinton signed the Telecommunications Reform Act, which included regulatory reform and obscenity prohibitions. Within the Telecommunications Reform Act is the Communications Decency Act (CDA)—an attempt to censor the Internet of obscene, indecent, or annoying communications, written or otherwise, and impose penalties on those convicted of CDA violations (McCabe and Lee 1997). Unfortunately, the enforceability of the Telecommunications Reform Act is difficult as the Internet is a global community without boundaries, technology that changes daily, and with over 1 billion online users every day.

Specifically, a report released by the Office of Victims of Crime suggested that the sheer number of young people using computers on a daily basis causes the concern for their safety to be well founded. By the end of the 1990s, approximately 40% of all American homes had a computer, and 25% of those homes had Internet access. By 2005, approximately 75 million youths were online.

Today, there are more than 100 million young people using the Internet every day. With the use of the Internet as a tool for criminal activity, and this increased use of the Internet, sexual crimes against children have changed. Thus, there are certainly more victims of child sexual abuse via the Internet than ever reported to police. In response, law enforcement agencies have begun to recognize the utility of the Internet and sexting in the sexual abuse of children; however, few of these agencies are providing specialized investigations in this area. Some law enforcement agencies will avoid computer crime investigations and, in particular, the case of ICAC as they are complex, demanding, and not always considered a high priority when compared to other traditional crimes such as robbery or assault.

In addition, the investigations of ICAC often require a great deal of time, and most law enforcement agencies operate under the *report, respond, and move on* mode (Schmalleger 2016). This lack of support by law enforcement agencies fuels the problem of ICAC. Not only are many of these crimes not investigated, but also many are never reported as the public also views these crimes as a low priority. In considering ICAC, one must not only consider child sexual abuse and those victims but also those offenders and their actions upon which the victimization of children is the ultimate outcome. In a review of ICAC cases investigated by the Southern Virginia Internet Crimes Against Children Task Force in Virginia during 2008 and 2014, an increase was determined to exist in cases of child enticement, the proportion of male victims, and the use of sexting to facilitate the crime (see Appendix B for the abridged report).

Sextortion is defined as a form of sexual abuse where an abuser threatens to reveal sexually explicit images of a victim unless that victim meets the specific demands of the abuser.

Annual reports of child abuse suggest that approximately 10% of all incidents are sexual abuse (Children's Bureau 2014). Since the 1980s, a number of multifactorial theories have been developed in an attempt to explain child sexual abuse. One of the most influential of those theories is Finkelhor's (1984) model of child sexual abuse, which suggests that before a sexual assault of a child occurs, there is a progression of stages (or preconditions) that must be completed. As discussed under sexual abuse, once all of these preconditions have been satisfied, the child's sexual assault will likely occur with the Internet, and a new element exists in child abuse. Later, with the introduction of the Internet and social media, Lanning (2001) expanded Finkelhor's preconditions to include a typology of individuals utilizing the Internet to access and distribute child pornography. However, it should be noted that predators, utilizing sexual solicitations, were nearly twice as likely to target females (Mitchell et al. 2003).

Specifically, Lanning's (2001) four typologies of individuals utilizing the Internet and child pornography include (1) periodically prudent offenders, (2) fantasy-only offenders, (3) direct victimization offenders, and (4) commercial exploitation offenders. Essentially, periodically prudent offenders access images out of impulsivity or curiosity with the images not necessarily of children. This typology of offender is generally not the perpetrator of ICAC. Fantasy-only offenders trade images to fuel their sexual interest in children; however, they do not have a history of actively offending children.

This typology utilizes the child pornography for their own sexual excitement; however, it rarely attempts to sexually abuse a child through molestation. Direct victimization offenders use the online community to offend both directly by downloading pornography and indirectly as a means of grooming future victims. This typology will often be identified as the perpetrators of ICAC, as well as the sexual abuse of children. Finally, commercial exploitation offenders utilize the online community to assist in the production and distribution of child pornography for economic gain. For this typology, the child is simply the product of consumption, and they may not be attracted to the physical characteristics of a child.

Ward and Siegert (2002) expanded the discussion on Internet users and their propensity toward child pornography as related to a variety of psychological pathways, which, when satisfied, result in abuse. Those pathways include intimacy deficits, distorted sexual scripts, emotional deregulation, and antisocial cognitions. In other words, individuals who utilize the Internet to abuse children are socially isolated or rejected, possess cognitive disorder, which then misguide their sexual behaviors, have difficulties regulating their moods and emotions, and have general procriminal beliefs and actions.

Taylor and Quayle (2003) suggested that viewing child pornography helps the pedophiles to normalize the viewing of children as sexual objects. Calder (2004) suggested that Internet child pornography fuels the desire for offenders to sexually abuse a child. In contrast, Seto and

Eke (2005) suggested that only a minority of the viewers of child pornography actually sexually abuse children; however, some viewers do victimize children.

By 2014, the National Center for Missing and Exploited Children had initiated reviews of over 22 million images for potential cases of child sexual abuse provided by the law enforcement community.

Regardless of the associations between child pornography and child sexual abuse, child pornography via the Internet is accessible, inexpensive, and anonymous; hence, it facilitates the abuse of children without the face-to-face interactions historically required to exist between an adult perpetrator and a child victim prior to our technology age.

To address the issue of child pornography and computer technology, the 1977 Sexual Exploitation of Children Act prohibited the transportation of child pornography by mail or the computer. In 1984, the Child Protection Act defined anyone younger than 18 as a child. In 1988, the Child Protection Enforcement Act made it unlawful to use a computer to transport child pornography and provided a specific age definition of a child based upon the physical characteristics of the child, and, in 1996, the Child Pornography Act amended the definition of a child to include computer-generated children (McCabe 2000). (Unfortunately, in 2002, the Supreme Court ruled that computer-generated children were not actually children.) In 2010, the Child Abuse, Prevention, and Treatment Act was reauthorized and continues to be recognized as the largest body of legislation intended to protect children. In 2014, the Child Victims' and Child Witnesses' Rights allows victims of child abuse to provide their testimonies via videos.

This research acknowledges that the effects of social networking, sexting, and instant messaging are new and unclear in this progression of child abuse via the Internet (Amerson 2009). This research also acknowledges that not all perpetrators of ICAC are the same, and, whereas most are motivated by a sexual attraction to children, some are motivated by profit. In fact, cases of child sexual abuse and ICAC involve a variety of offenders such as sexual addicts, pedophiles, consumers of child pornography, child traffickers, and those involved in child sex rings.

In regard to offenders of ICAC, the research is extremely scarce with only a few historic details available on the demographic characteristics and limited information on psychological characteristics. Howitt and Sheldon (2007) suggest that the perpetrators of ICAC have many cognitive distortions regarding children as sexual beings. Webb et al. (2007) suggest that perpetrators of ICAC are more antisocial and prone to breaking rules. Finally, Elliott and Beech (2009) suggest that perpetrators of ICAC share symptoms relating to intimacy and social skill deficits. Regardless of the explanation for the abusers, children are victims.

Research suggests that children who are victims of sexual abuse are, in most cases, female. However, in the cases of child pornography and child sex rings, some research suggests that the victims are more likely to be male (McCabe 2003). In regard to victims of ICAC, research suggests that a distinction can be made between victims of sexual abuse and victims of child pornography (Cuijpers and van der Knaap 2010). The first group includes victims exposed to online solicitations. Most victims of child pornography, although rarely identified, have not yet reached puberty (O'Donnell and Milner 2007). Victims of child pornography tend to be female, use chat rooms, talk about sex online, and have experienced physical and/or sexual abuse off-line, generally at the hands of a family member (Mitchell et al. 2007).

Later, Ward and Beech (2006) suggested that Internet offenders are uncomfortable in face-to-face interactions; therefore, they utilize the Internet as a means to escape stressful situations. In addition, offenders who utilize the Internet often lack a general regard for future consequences and view children as simply sexual objects. Since these individuals are only viewing child pornography, in their mind, there exists no real harm to the child. However, by all accounts, pedophiles are these individuals most identified by the media in stories on child sexual abuse and often involved in ICAC (McCabe 2003).

Again, aside from blurring the boundaries of social convention, one of the most popular discussions of ICAC concerns the relationship between pornography through the Internet and child abuse (Wethal 2009; Sheldon and Howitt 2007). Sullivan's (2002) spiral of abuse suggests that the habituation of viewing child pornography can trigger passive pedophiles into active sex offenders.

Researchers suggest that peers often request more child pornography than strangers (Strassberg et al. 2012). However, child pornography posted on the Internet is used by offenders to justify beliefs and the acceptability of adult–child sexual relationships (Burges et al. 2013). The spiral describes how pedophiles are initially satisfied by images, but, as their fantasies grow, they eventually sexually abuse a child. Individuals who view these images become desensitized and will seek more stimulating materials to meet their addiction (Schell et al. 2007). Of course, the computer and the Internet are today's tools to provide the images and help to initially satisfy those desires. For those interested in abusing a child, those images are child pornography, and research suggests an availability of images too numerous to count. In additional to the countless images of real child pornography available through the Internet, there is, through advanced technology, digital imaging (virtual child pornography) of children engaging in sexual acts. Since these images do not involve real children, the US Supreme Court ruled in 2002 that these images were not illegal to possess or distribute, thus leaving a pedophile the legal right to view pornographic images of virtual children to satisfy their desires.

Nationally and internationally, child pornography is prevalent. Specifically, in 2008, the International Criminal Police Organization (Interpol) had identified over 500,000 images and approximately 700 victims. During 2014, Interpol has identified over 1 million images of child pornography. Victims of child pornography are similar in gender and age to child victims of sexual abuse; hence, victims include both males and females of all ages.

Historically, child pornography was produced and distributed through the work of pornographic groups or sex rings and adults who work together to exploit children for sex (Abel 1987). In these cases, the adults who controlled the sex ring used a position of trust to recruit the children and then exploited them through a combination of material and psychological rewards. The Internet and the online community have changed the technical mode for child pornography and sexual solicitations. Sheldon (2011) suggests that offenders utilizing the Internet and child pornography are similar in many ways to pedophiles; they seek children for their sexual gratification. Although illegal in most states, the production and distribution of child pornography are another type of ICAC (McCabe 2000), and child victims of pornography often display behaviors associated with victimization.

A law enforcement officer in California contacted police in New England, reporting that, while working undercover, the officer had been receiving child pornography online originating from a resident in the their jurisdiction. The suspect was identified as Martin, who was known to law enforcement due to his extensive criminal record. The police in that community issued a search warrant to seize the computer within the residence. Examination of the computer revealed several hundred pornographic pictures involving children of various ages engaged in explicit sexual acts. None of the children in the pictures could be identified, but Martin was charged with felony possession of child pornography. Due to the magnitude of this offense, this investigation was turned over to the Federal Bureau of Investigation, as it appeared that Martin was networking with other offenders throughout the country; there was a hope that some of the victims could be identified.

Behavioral Indicators

Children involved in either the viewing or creation of child pornography often display behavioral indicators similar to victims of other forms of child abuse. Specifically, a child involved in child pornography may appear withdrawn or depressed and often lies about their computer usage (McCabe and Gregory 1998). In addition, the child involved in viewing child pornography may begin to notice the bodies of others and show a tolerance for previously ignored sexually graphic movies. Finally, children involved in the viewing of child pornography will begin spending time out of the home and in restaurants or cafes with Internet access. They will begin locking their door when using the computer in their room, turn the computer off or switch sites when someone enters the room while they are on the computer, and often delete their search histories.

Children involved in not only the viewing of child pornography but also the production of child pornography will often display actions similar to those child victims of sexual abuse (McCabe and Ore 2007). In addition, many victims of child pornography receive calls and gifts from adults unknown to parents and or known to parents; however, these adults are the ones who have achieved a significant role in the child's life. Also, it is not unusual for victims of child pornography to use other's accounts (usually their abuser's) for online calls and merchandise.

With improved technology, increases in voyeurism, and more exhibitionism sites, the use of the Internet has increased, and the cases of child pornography have multiplied. Sex offenders are now using the privacy of the Internet to identify those vulnerable children who use the Internet unsupervised (Medaris and Girouard 2002). Despite federal and state laws that prohibit the transmission of child pornography over the Internet, child pornography is often easily accessed (McCabe 2003).

In the cases of child pornography that involve a real child and sexual abuse, the children are victimized during the production of the pornography and then are repeatedly victimized as the pornography is distributed to the thousands of viewers in the market for child pornography. The statement *once it's on the Internet, it's there forever* is true.

☐ Child Solicitation

The computer and the Internet provide individuals the opportunity to interact. Unfortunately, the Internet also provides an individual wishing to contact a child the opportunity to interact. Pedophiles engage children for many purposes including for a sexual chat or to obtain child pornography (Crosson-Tower 2010). These abusers, skilled at initiating conversations with children, can use an array of strategies to engage in sexual conduct with a minor to include talking about animals, the environment, or unfair parents. Thus, the Internet is an invaluable tool for individuals who wish to prey on young victims. Sexual predators are able to access chat lines to contact children or communicate with other adults who share the same fantasies.

In early 2000, there were approximately 40,000 Websites for chatting (or chat rooms) that advocate for adult–child sexual relations; today, many more exist (Sinclair and Sugar 2005). Through their anonymity, these predators can pretend to be the same age as the child and bond with the child as they provide false information about themselves or the interests they may share. Using this tactic, they are able to, at times, convince the child to meet with them resulting in potential victimization. Other adult offenders may admit to their age and befriend the child through flattery and expressing mutual interest in whatever will enhance their bond. Some offenders may openly solicit a child to engage in sexual conduct and make arrangements to meet with them. This occurs even in cases where the child, through their Internet chat, has revealed that he or she is under the legal age to consent to having sex. Law enforcement officers, working in an undercover capacity, have posed as child sex offenders to lure unsuspecting predators into custody. In fact, research suggests that approximately one-third of these cases were identified through the proactive efforts of law enforcement (McCabe 2003).

☐ Cyberbullying

Cyberbullying is essentially the bullying of an individual through the use of computers and other electronic devices. Cyberbullying relies on technological programs, such as emails, Websites and chat rooms, to intimidate, embarrass, or humiliate their victim (Beale and Hall 2007). For some children, cyberbullying may begin as early as second grade (Sabina et al. 2008). Other types of cyberbullying can include posting embarrassing or compromising pictures where a child's face may be attached to a pornographic picture (Burgess et al. 2013). Once these pictures are posted, they can no longer be retrieved leaving the victim with a constant reminder of their victimization. In fact, nearly 20% of school-age children report sending child pornography to their peers, and 40% report receiving child pornography from a peer (Strassberg et al. 2012).

Although bullying tends to peak during the middle-school years, there are reports of incidents occurring in earlier or later years (McCabe and Martin 2005). Coloroso (2003) has identified four elements of bullying: (1) an imbalance of power, (2) an intent to harm, (3) a threat of further aggression, and (4) terror. These elements always exist in cases of bullying. In bullying, the bully is usually older, physically larger, or from a higher social class (McCabe and Martin 2005). This is not always the case with cyberbullying.

Incidents of cyberbullying, just as with incidents of bullying, are more likely to occur in middle school (Williams and Guerra 2007). Although both males and females are perpetrators of cyberbullying (Elledge et al. 2013), males are oftentimes the perpetrators of cyberbullying and females the victims (Sourander et al. 2010). However, other studies have shown that girls are twice as likely than boys to be both the perpetrator and the recipient of cyberbullying (Kowalski et al. 2005; Mitchell et al. 2003). In addition, the majority of the children who are involved in cyberbullying are involved in more traditional types of bullying (Raskauskas and Stoltz 2007).

Victims of cyberbullying are similar to the victims of bullying in that they are often socially isolated, disliked by their peers, children with disabilities, or members of the lesbian, gay, bisexual, or transsexual community (Smith et al. 2008). Whereas the victims of bullies are often siblings, the victims of cyberbullying are often acquaintances. Just as with bullying, if a child's friends are being cyberbullied, then the child will often be cyberbullied as well. Finally, if a child is a victim of bullying, they are also likely to be a victim of cyberbullying (Erdur-Baker 2010).

In 2000, less than 10% of youths reported being victims of cyberbullying (Finkelhor et al. 2000). In 2007, over 70% of youths reported being victims of cyberbullying (Juvonen and Gross 2008). Unlike bullying, which often occurs either during school hours or home hours, cyberbullying may occur 24 hours a day, seven days a week, and is not location specific. The most common form of cyberbullying is the posting of hurtful comments (Hinduja and Patchin 2013). Unfortunately, once these comments are posted via the Internet, the cyberbullying may occur over and over. In addition, the anonymity of the perpetrators of cyberbullying not only protects the abusers but also leaves the victim even more fearful as the unknown offender is often perceived worse than the known offender.

Behavioral Indicators

In cases of bullying, physical signs, such as unexplained injuries or the destruction of property, are often revealed (McCabe and Martin 2005).

However, with cyberbullying, the indicators are often entirely behavioral as there is no physical confrontation. This does not indicate that the effects are any less damaging to the child victims.

Specifically, many child victims of cyberbullying suddenly lose their friends and appear sad, embarrassed, or fearful during their social interactions (Patchin and Hinduja 2011). Over 25% of teens report forwarding child pornography to other teens (Strassberg et al. 2012). As this type of bullying can occur without the child's knowledge, a child may find themselves ostracized by their peers without ever understanding the dynamics of why this is occurring. In addition, these child victims report a variety of pains or stress-related illnesses, display changes in their eating habits, and have difficulties sleeping. Also, child victims of cyberbullying may begin to use alcohol or drugs, miss or fight in school, and drop out of school (Hinduja and Patchin 2010). Finally, it is not unusual for victims of cyberbullying to report suicidal thoughts or attempt suicide.

☐ Sexting

Statistics indicate that approximately 80% of all US teens have their own cell phones and that at least 50% of those with cell phones send text messages (Madden et al. 2013). For many teens, those text messages are considered sext messages. Sexting is vaguely defined to include the sending or receiving of sexual images (Agustina and Gomez-Duran 2012); however, state laws generally focus only on the nude or seminude pictures of minors and only if the images are reported to law enforcement by parents. Unlike adults, teens without the capacity to make rational choice decisions are some of the main perpetrators of sexting (Martinez-Prather and Vandiver 2014). Those teens who generally send the original sext messages are females. Those teens who generally distribute the sext message are males. Unfortunately, there are multiple risks to the victim from sexting after the original message is sent.

Teens who have participated in sexting place themselves at risk for other forms of victimization. Specifically, many teens who have sexted a message to one certain individual may later discover that their *private* picture message has now been viewed by hundreds of individuals within the virtual community; thus, they are now victims of child pornography (Strassberg et al. 2012). Teens who have sexted messages may also find themselves victims of harassment and/or cyberstalking by an individual or individuals who have viewed their message. In addition, teens who have sexted may find themselves *outed* in a community that may not respect or support their lifestyle or choices; thus, this individual may become an isolated victim among his or her peers. Finally, teens who have sexted may find themselves victims of identity theft or impersonation on sites such as Facebook with the blame or responsibilities of another's action(s) placed on them.

Behavioral Indicators

In most cases, sexting does not produce negative consequences for the perpetrator; however, on some cases, sexting, combined with teen experimentation, presents a new type of problem and risky behavior (Willard 2010). Indicators of those problems include a sudden reluctance by the teen/victim to socialize with their peers. Another indicator, similar to cyberstalking, is the victim's desire to miss school or stop participating in sports or other extracurricular activities as a means to avoid contact and interactions with their peers. Hence, sexting, which may occur between teens in a dating relationship, has now lead to the victimization of those involved in the relationship.

☐ Summary

With ICAC, physical contact between the child and the perpetrator does not need to occur for a child to become a victim or for a crime to be committed as innocent pictures of children can be digitally transformed into pornographic material and distributed across the Internet without the victims' knowledge. In addition, the Internet provides a source for repeated victimization that can last for years without the victim's knowledge. ICAC transcend jurisdictional boundaries, as the geographic location of a child is not a primary concern for most perpetrators who may travel hundreds of miles to different states and countries to engage in sexual acts with children they have met over the Internet. The anonymity of the Internet provides a sense of security and secrecy for both the perpetrators and the victims.

Research on the online victimization of youth suggests that unwanted exposure to sexual materials have increased over the years. Others suggest that online child pornography, sexting, and interactive stripping have helped to increase the number of child victims of sexual exploitation (McCabe and Johnston 2014). Finally, as if the sexual exploitation of children is not bad enough, the growth of child exploitation through sexting via the Internet is another explanation for the increase in child abuse. Again, as technology changes, criminal justice efforts must also change.

Much of the research on ICAC focuses on general profiles of perpetrators (white, male, with difficulty in maintaining interpersonal relationships) and a general profile of child victims (female, socially isolated, history of family abuse). However, few projects attempt to examine the dynamics (e.g., mode of contact, number of contacts) of the victimization or the dynamics associated with specific offenders. According to McCabe (2000), sexual offenders who utilize the Internet target children with particular characteristics. Often, these child victims have experienced prior abuse or neglect, are emotionally immature with learning and social difficulties, and often have problems with peer friendships. In addition, these targeted children are deprived of attention but still have a strong respect for adult status.

The offenders, as reported by their child victims, were most often male (approximately 67%) and most often perceived to be under the age of 25 (Wolak et al. 2009). For those offenders interested in a sexual relationship with a child, child pornography was often relayed through the Internet as a means of desensitizing the victims. However, little research exists on those perpetrators who do not use child pornography as a gateway to further ICAC (Howitt 1995).

Longitudinal studies of the perpetrators of ICAC are essentially nonexistent (McCabe 2008). According to researchers at the University of New Hampshire's Crimes Against Children Research Center, arrests increased over 20% in the years of 2000–2006 for online solicitations of youths with nearly a 400% increase in offenders posing as a youth themselves (Wolak et al. 2009). Reijnen et al. (2009) assert that there is no specific psychological profile established for offenders of Internet child pornography.

Those responsible for the legal protection of children know firsthand the limitations in research and practice in reducing ICAC and know that the problem is becoming more significant with the passing of time. Today's efforts have been largely reactive—what is needed is proactive approaches to end ICAC.

CHAPTER QUESTIONS

1. How does technology facilitate child pornography?

2. Is sexting a new avenue for child pornography?

3. How is cyberbullying different from bullying?

QUESTIONS FOR FURTHER THOUGHT

1. Why is child pornography such a problem with child abuse and now the computer?

2. If sexting involves only young people (under the age of 18), is it illegal?

3. Why is there a new interest in cyberbullying as bullying has always existed?

☐ References

Abel, G. 1987. Self-reported sex crimes of non-incarcerated paraphiliacs. *Journal of Interpersonal Violence*, 2(1), 3–25.

Amerson, L. 2009. Internet safety. *Sheriff*, 61(6), 26–27.

Agustina, J. and Gomez-Duran, J. 2012. Sexting: Research criteria of a globalized social phenomenon. *Archives of Sexual Behavior*, 41(6), 1325–1328.

Beale, A. and Hall, K. 2007. Cyberbullying: What school administrators (and parents) can do. *The Clearing House*, 18, 8–12.

Bourke, M. and Hernandez, A. 2009. The Butner Study redux: A report of the incidence of hands-on child victimization by child pornography offenders. *Journal of Family Violence*, 24(3), 183–193.

Burgess, A., Regehr, C., and Roberts, A. 2013. *Victimology: Theories and Applications* (2nd ed.). Burlington, MA: Jones & Bartlett Learning.

Calder, M. 2004. *Child Sexual Abuse and the Internet: Tracking the New Frontier*. Lyme Regis, United Kingdom: Russell House.

Children's Bureau. 2014. *Child Maltreatment 2013*. Washington, D.C.: US Department of Health and Human Services. Administration for Children and Families.

Coloroso, B. 2003. *The Bully, the Bullied, and the Bystander*. New York: Harper Collins.

Crosson-Tower, C. 2010. *Understanding Child Abuse and Neglect* (8th ed.). Boston: Allyn and Bacon.

Cuijpers, C. and van der Knaap, L. 2010. Cyberpaedophilia. In M. Herzog-Evan (ed.) *Transnational Criminology Manual*, vol. 2, pp. 129–147. Nijmegen, Netherlands: Wolf Legal Publishers.

Elledge, L., Williford, A., Boulton, A., DePaolis, Little, T., and Salmivalli, C. 2013. Individual and contextual predictors of cyberbullying: The influence of children's provictim attitudes and teachers' ability to intervene. *Journal of Youth Adolescence*, 42(3), 698–710.

Elliott, I. and Beech, R. 2009. Understanding online child pornography use. *Aggression and Violent Behavior*, 14, 180–193.

Erdur-Baker, O. 2010. Cyberbullying and its correlation to original bullying, gender, and frequent risky usage of Internet-mediated communication tools. *New Media and Society*, 10(11), 146–151.

Fagundes, P. 2009. Fighting Internet child pornography—The Brazilian experience. *The Police Chief*, 76(9), 48–49.

Finkelhor, D. 1984. *Child Sexual Abuse: New Theory and Research*. New York: Free Press.

Finkelhor, D., Mitchell, K., and Wolak, J. 2000. *Online Victimization: A Report on the Nation's Youth*. Washington, D.C.: National Center for Missing and Exploited Children.

Hinduja, S. and Patchin, J. 2009. *Bullying Beyond the School Yard: Preventing and Responding to Cyberbullying*. Thousand Oaks, CA: SAGE.

Hinduja, S. and Patchin, J. 2010. Cyberbullying: A review of the legal issues facing education. *Preventing School Failure*, 55(2), 1–8.

Hinduja, S. and Patchin, J. 2013. Social influences on cyberbullying behaviors among middle and high school students. *Journal Youth Adolescence*, 42(3), 711–722.

Howitt, D. 1995. Pornography and the pedophile: Is it criminogenic? *British Journal of Medical Psychology*, 15(16), 68–72.

Howitt, D. and Sheldon, K. 2007. The role of cognitive distortions in pedophilic offending. *Psychology, Crime, and Law*, 13(3), 469–486.

Huang, W., Leopard, M., and Brockman, A. 2009. Internet child sexual exploitation: Offenders offenses and victims. In F. Schmalleger and M. Pittaro (eds.) *Crimes of the Internet*, pp. 43–66. Upper Saddle River, NJ: Pearson.

Interpol. 2008. Databases: Interpol Fact Sheet. COM/FS/2008-07/GI-04.

Juvonen, J. and Gross, E. 2008. Extending the school grounds? Bullying experiences in cyberspace. *Journal of School Health*, 78, 496–505.

Kowalski, R., Limber, S., Schenck, A., Redrearn, M., Allen, J., Calloway, A. et al. 2005. Electronic bullying among school-aged children and youth. Paper presented at the annual meeting of the American Psychological Association, Washington, D.C., August.

Lanning, K. 2001. *Child Molesters: A Behavioral Analysis* (4th ed.). Washington, D.C.: National Center for Missing and Exploited Children.

Madden, M., Lenhart, A., Duggan, M., Cortesi, S., and Gasser, U. 2013. *Teen and Technology*. Washington, D.C.: Pew Internet and American Life Project.

Martinez-Prather, K. and Vandiver, D. 2014. Sexting among teenagers in the United States: A retrospective analysis of identifying motivating factors, potential targets, and the role of a capable guardian. *International Journal of Cyber Criminology*, 8(1), 21–35.

McCabe, K. 2000. Child pornography and the Internet. *Social Science Computer Review*, 18(1), 73–76.

McCabe, K. 2003. *Child Abuse and the Criminal Justice System*. New York: Peter Lang.

McCabe, K. 2008. The role of Internet service providers in cases of child pornography and child prostitution. *Social Science Computer Review*, 25(2), 1–5.

McCabe, K. and Gregory, S. 1998. Recognizing the illegal activities of computer users. *Social Science Computer Review*, 16(4), 419–422.

McCabe, K. and Johnston, O. 2014. Perceptions of the legality of sexting. *Social Science Computer Review*, 32(6), 765–768.

McCabe, K. and Lee, M. 1997. Users' perceptions of Internet regulation. *Social Science Computer Review*, 15(3), 237–241.

McCabe, K. and Martin, G. 2005. *School Violence, the Media, and Criminal Justice Responses*. New York: Peter Lang.

McCabe, K. and Ore, L. 2007. Pornography. In J. Greene's *Encyclopedia of Police Science* (3rd ed.), pp. 1031–1033. New York: Taylor & Francis.

Medaris, M. and Girouard, C. 2002. Protecting children in cyberspace: The ICAC Task Force Program. *OJJDP: Juvenile Justice Bulletin*. doi:10.1037/e318172004 -001.

Middleton, D., Elliott, I., Mandeville-Norden, R., and Beech, A. 2006. An investigation into the application of the Ward and Siegert Pathways Model of child sexual abuse with Internet offenders. *Psychology, Crime, and Law*, 12(6), 589–603.

Mitchell, K., Finkelhor, D., and Wolek, J. 2003. Victimization of youths on the Internet. *Journal of Aggression, Maltreatment and Trauma*, 8(1), 1–39.

Mitchell, K., Finkelhor, D., Jones, L., and Wolek, J. 2012. Prevalence and characteristics of youth sexting: A national study. *Pediatrics*, 129(1), 13–20.

Mitchell, K. J., Ybarra, M., and Finkelhor, D. (2007). The relative importance of online victimization in understanding depression, delinquency, and substance use. *Child Maltreatment*, 12(4), 314–324.

Morrissey, S. 2006. Sinister industry. *ABA Journal*, 92, 59–61.

O'Donnell, I. and Milner, C. 2007. *Child Pornography: Crime, Computers, and Society*. Cullompton, United Kingdom: Willan Publishing.

Patchin, J. and Hinduja, S. 2011. Traditional and non-traditional bullying among youth: A test of general strain theory. *Youth and Society*, 43(2), 727–751.

Raskauskas, J. and Stoltz, A. 2007. Involvement in traditional and electronic bullying among adolescents. *Developmental Psychology*, 43(3), 564–575.

Reijnen, L., Bulten, E., and Nijman, H. 2009. Demographic and personality characteristics of internet child pornography downloaders. *Journal of Child Sexual Abuse*, 18(6), 611–625.

Sabina, C., Wolak, J., and Finkelhor, D. 2008. Rapid communication: The nature and dynamics of Internet pornography exposure for youth. *CyberPsychology and Behavior*, 11(6), 691–693.

Schell, B., Martin, M., Hung, P., and Rueda, L. 2007. Cyber child pornography: A review paper of the social and legal issues and remedies—And a proposed technological solution. *Aggression and Violent Behavior*, 12(1), 45–63.

Schmalleger, F. 2016. *Criminology* (3rd ed.). Boston: Pearson.

Seto, M. and Eke, A. 2005. The criminal histories and later offending of child pornography offenders. *Sexual Abuse: A Journal of Research and Treatment*, 17(2), 201–210.

Sheldon, K. 2011. What we know about men who download child abuse images. *The British Journal of Forensic Practice*, 13(4), 221–234.

Sheldon, K. and Howitt, D. 2007. *Sex Offenders and the Internet*. Chichester, United Kingdom: Wiley.

Sinclair, R. and Sugar, D. 2005. Internet based sexual exploitation of children and youth environmental scan. Available at http://www.rcmp-grc.gc.ca/ncecc -cncee/factsheets-fichesdocu/enviroscan-analyseenviro-eng.htm. Accessed on November 12, 2015.

Smith, P., Mahdavi, K., Carvalho, M., Fisher, S., Russell, S., and Tippett, N. 2008. Cyberbullying: Its nature and impact in secondary school pupils. *Journal of Child Psychology and Psychiatry*, 10, 1469–1476.

Sourander, A., Klomek, A., Ikonen, M., Lindroos, J., Luntamo, T., and Koskelainen, M. 2010. Psychological risk factors associated with cyber-bullying among adolescents: A population-based study. *Archives of General Psychiatry*, 10, 79–85.

Sullivan, J. 2002. The spiral of sexual abuse: A conceptual framework for understanding and illustrating the evolution of sexually abusive behavior. *Notanews*, 41, 17–21.

Strassberg, D., McKinnon, R., Sustaita, M., and Rullo, J. 2012. Sexting by high school students: An exploratory and descriptive study. *Archives of Sexual Behavior*, 10, 1007–1013.

Taylor, M. and Quayle, E. 2003. *Child Pornography: An Internet Crime*. Hove, United Kingdom: Routledge.

Ward, T. and Beech, A. 2006. An integrated theory of sexual offending. *Aggression and Violent Behavior*, 11(1), 44–63.

Ward, T. and Siegert, R. 2002. Toward a comprehensive theory of child sexual abuse: A theory of knitting perspective. *Psychology, Crime and Law*, 8(2), 319–351.

Webb, L., Craissati, J., and Keen, S. 2007. Characteristics of Internet child pornography offenders: A comparison with child molesters. *Sexual Abuse: A Journal of Research and Treatment*, 19, 449–465.

Wethal, T. 2009. The problem with porn. *Law Enforcement Technology*, 37(2), 18–20.

Willard, N. 2010. *Sexting and Youth: Achieving a Rational Response*. Eugene, OR: Center for Safe and Responsible Internet Use.

Williams, K. and Guerra, N. 2007. Prevalence and predictors of Internet bullying. *Journal of Adolescent Health*, 10, 8–18.

Wolak, J., Mitchell, K, and Finkelhor, D. 2003. *Internet Sex Crimes Against Minors: The Response of Law Enforcement*. Durham, NH: University of New Hampshire. Crimes Against Children Research Center.

Wolak, J., Finkelhor, D., and Mitchell, K. 2009. *Trends in Arrests of On-Line Predators*. Durham, NH: University of New Hampshire. Crimes Against Children Research Center.

Criminal Justice Responses
to Today's Child Abuse

The US Criminal Justice System was established to deliver justice for all individuals while protecting society members from crime and criminal victimization.

Since the late 1800s, US society has been attempting to address the problems of child abuse and neglect by establishing appropriate legislative responses for those children who have been victims of abuse. Currently, there exist over 27,000 federal and state statutes that directly or indirectly affect victims of crime (Tobolowsky et al. 2010). Many of these legislative efforts focus upon the protection of children.

The purpose of this chapter is to identify accomplishments by our society, including laws and protocols designed to address the needs of the child victims of abuse and neglect. The discussion in this chapter will also focus on the three components of the criminal justice system (police, courts, and corrections), as well as responses to child abuse and neglect by professional and nonprofit organizations outside of the criminal justice system. These efforts began in the United States with the Child Savers Movement.

The Child Savers Movement was spearheaded by upper class, white women with a need to support children and child victims.

☐ Child Savers Movement

The Child Savers Movement emerged in the 19th century as an official recognition that children formed a particular group with their own special needs (Siegel and Welsh 2008). This was a new focus for children who were laboring in sweatshops, coal mines, and factories across the United States or who were considered abandoned or orphaned (Cox et al. 2014). From society's perspective, abused and neglected children may become delinquents and eventually victimize the *good citizens* of the community; thus, society required preventative measures to help these children through the education and training of citizens.

This altruistic perspective of the 20th-century reformers continued for these children and began imitating methods to mitigate delinquency. This proactive judgment was largely responsible for the creation of the first juvenile court in the United States in 1899. The focus of these courts was the care and protection of the child. Included were corrective efforts and discipline directed toward the rehabilitation of the delinquent youths (Cavan 1969). This laid the foundation for more of a rehabilitative model for addressing delinquency.

☐ Progressive Era

The Progressive Era in the United States (1900–1920) included extensive social reforms and campaigns against child labor. The philosophy of the reformers during this period mandated that the courts would now act *in loco parentis* (in place of parents) in cases of children who violated the law or who were neglected, dependent, or in need of intervention (Cox et al. 2014).

Both the Child Savers Movement and the Progressive Era were instrumental in addressing the specific needs of children and were the first to recognize that an official response from the government was necessary to be implemented. Throughout this chapter, criminal justice system responses to the needs and necessities of children will be discussed, as well as the interactions that are still in effect today as preventive measures for juvenile delinquency.

☐ The 1974 Juvenile Justice Delinquency Prevention Act

In 1974, the US Congress enacted *The Juvenile Justice Delinquency and Prevention Act*, which was a law that separated juveniles from adults when they were incarcerated. This was the first of the legislative efforts designed to protect juveniles from potential abuse from adult offenders while incarcerated. Additionally, this law prohibited status offenders from being detained in a secure facility. (By definition, a status offense is an offense that can only be committed by a juvenile such as running away, truancy, and a curfew violation.) This legislation had a significant impact in deterring abuse, as some runaways had fled their homes to escape mistreatment.

Although the separation of adults from children can reduce potential abuse, it does not eliminate it. Annually, in the United States, approximately 9000 young people are in custody within juvenile detention centers. Of those young people, approximately 10% reported being a victim of sexual abuse; in many of these cases, the abuse is by staff members within the facility. In addition, approximately 30% of all incarcerated youths reported being a victim of rape by another adjudicated youths (Sentenced to Abuse 2010).

Although the United States is assumed by many to be a leader in the protection of children, this has not always been the case. In fact, the United States was not a pioneer for having separate systems for adults and juveniles. In fact, other countries identified the potential dangers for children and created laws of separate correctional systems years prior to the US system. Specifically, the juvenile justice system in France began in 1945 when the treatment of juveniles was removed from the adult prison setting. Within the United Kingdom, juveniles and adults were also incarcerated separately. Finally, throughout Europe, the separation of juveniles and adults had been established.

In contrast, many countries still do not separate adults and children within their criminal justice systems. For example, Saudi Arabia does not have a separate juvenile justice system (Dammer and Albanese 2011). In these systems, punishment is based upon the convicted crime, not the age of the offender. Whether a child or an adult, the punishment is consistent with the penalty of the crime. Hence, research suggests that reform and rehabilitation programs are based on religious instruction, social reorientation, education, training, and work (Gilani 2006).

The National Sex Offender Registry, coordinated by the Department of Justice, allows every citizen to search for information from all 50 states, the District of Columbia, Puerto Rico, and Guam on known sex offenders.

☐ Sex Offender Registration

Sex offender registration originated in the United States based on a sexual assault in New Jersey against a seven-year-old girl named Megan Kanka. The perpetrator was Jesse Timmendequas, a neighbor of Megan who had been convicted of two separate incidents of sexual assaults on children. On July 29, 1994, Timmendequas lured Megan into his house promising she could play with his puppies. He then proceeded to sexually assault Megan, strangle her, and dispose of her body. The public was outraged that such a horrific act could occur, especially in their community, as they were unaware that someone so dangerous was living among them. States passed new legislation commonly referred to as *Megan's Law*, requiring the notification as to the whereabouts of convicted sex offenders be available to the public. Megan Kanka was not the only child whose victimization triggered a legislative response.

Jacob Wetterling was a young boy whose name has become well-known due to his victimization. Since his abduction in Minnesota in 1989, Jacob has never been seen again. The federal government enacted their own legislation known as the *Jacob Wetterling Act*, which was based on Megan's Law, requiring states to have a sex offender registry in order to receive federal funding. This legislation was considered the national standard until the implementation of the Adam Walsh Child Protection and Safety Act of 2006.

Adam Walsh was abducted from a Sears store in 1981 and was later found murdered. This crime prompted Adam's father to become an advocate for victims' rights and assisted in the formation of the National Center for Missing and Exploited Children (Burgess et al. 2013). To this day, department stores still employ a *Code Adam* alert when a child who visited their store is missing. *The Adam Walsh Child Protection and Safety Act* strengthened the Jacob Wetterling Act by broadening the range of offenses requiring registration, to include child pornography and tracking the whereabouts of some juvenile offenders. Although there has been a net-widening of categories requiring registration, there have been amendments in the *age of consent* laws where sex offender registration is no longer compulsory under certain circumstances.

The Adam Walsh Act requires additional data be collected for those on the registry (Rogers 2007) and established three tiers of registration requirements based on the severity of the offense. However, the Adam Walsh Act includes a clause that states are not required to register statutory rape offenders if the sexual act was between peers, and the victim was at least 13 years old, and/or the offender was no more than four years senior to the victim (Mancini 2014). Tier 1 offenders must register annually for a period of 15 years. Tier 2 offenders are considered more serious criminals, and must contact law enforcement twice a year, updating their status for a period of 25 years. Tier 3 offenders are considered the most dangerous, and must update their status with law enforcement every three months for the remainder of their lives (Rogers 2007). Registered sex offenders must now provide their fingerprints, as well as a DNA sample, to law enforcement. The new provisions under the Adam Walsh Act are requiring states to alter their existing procedures as they may not match the federal three-tiered classification system and will have to revise their guidelines (Doerner and Lab 2012).

Sex offender registration in the United States requires any person convicted of a sex offense to register with their local law enforcement agency, disclosing where they reside and their place of employment, even though a substantial number of convicted sex offenders indicate they are unemployed. Registered sex offender information may also include photographs, the type of sexual offense committed, and whether the offender is considered violent. This registration provides restrictions as to where the offender can reside and be employed. Specifically, registered sex offenders cannot live within a certain distance from a school or where children will congregate (Chon 2010). Information on sex offenders can be readily available through the Internet or law enforcement agencies. Notification can also occur through the distribution of flyers, door-to-door visits, emails, and letters to the community providing information on the offender.

☐ Age of Consent

During the 19th and early 20th centuries, moral reformers embarked on an age of consent campaign designed to protect young women from the adults who preyed upon their innocence. Prior to the age of consent campaign, the legal age of consent to sex in 1885 ranged from between

10 and 12 years of age in most states, and, by 1920, all states raised the age of consent to 16 or 18 years of age (Mallicoat and Ireland 2014). Age of consent laws were created as it was believed that an underage person did not have sufficient knowledge, wisdom, or the capacity to understand and engage in a sexual encounter with an adult. Even though these adults may be sexually mature, the law suggests that they are not psychologically equipped to deal with sexual situations and could easily be manipulated by an adult (Burgess et al. 2013). By definition, children are immature, and an adult can capitalize in self-serving ways on this immaturity and exploit the child (Groth 1979). One of the many reasons to enact age of consent Laws is the undeniable fact that sexual acts can, and in some circumstances do, transmit human immunodeficiency virus (HIV), as well as other sexually transmitted diseases (STDs), which we will discuss further later in this chapter.

With the age of consent laws came a national trend toward removing some sex offenders from the registry. Despite the expansion of categories requiring sex offender registration under the Adam Walsh Protection and Safety Act, states have lowered the age of consent and, in some cases, lowered the penalty to the point of sometimes decriminalizing the acts in certain situations, specifically, if the offender's age is within a certain number of years of the victim. These laws, which are commonly referred to as *Romeo and Juliet laws* in many incidents, do not require offender registration. The question that needs to be asked is

> Are these laws being created in the best interest of the child, or are they designed to protect the offender from harsher sanctions?

Some states, such as Virginia, do not classify such an offense as a sexual assault, if the victim is between 15 and 17 years of age; instead, they refer to the occurrence as

> causing or encouraging acts rendering children delinquent, abused etc.

thus not requiring sex offender registration (Virginia code 18.2-371).

Some offenders are serving in a supervisory capacity when they abuse children in the age bracket they are responsible for. This offense may consist of a high school teacher who is sexually involved with a student. One of the most infamous cases of this type of crime was that of a high school teacher named Pamela Smart.

> In 1990, Pamela Smart, who was in a supervisory position in a high school in Hampton, New Hampshire, became involved in a sexual relationship with a 15-year-old sophomore by the name of Billy Flynn. Smart was accused of persuading Flynn to kill her husband by threatening to end

their sexual relationship if he did not comply. Billy Flynn, along with two other juveniles, murdered Smart's husband by shooting him as he entered his apartment. Pamela Smart and the juveniles were convicted in this murder, which garnered national attention including the development of a movie called "Murder in New Hampshire: The Pamela Wojas Smart Story."

☐ HIV/STD Testing

Sexual assault victimization can create significant anxiety, which can be amplified with the concern of contracting STDs or HIV. HIV destroys the body's natural immune system. The body is then no longer able to protect itself from infections and diseases. Whether someone has HIV is considered confidential information as it is a medical condition. However, several states have implemented policies that allow sex offenders to submit to HIV testing (Daigle 2012). These laws apply to those arrested, convicted, or pled guilty to crimes involving sexual penetration or exposure to bodily fluids (Wallace and Roberson 2015). If the suspect tests positive, it is not assured that the victim has contracted the virus, but the victim should be tested to ensure that the virus was not transmitted. At the federal level, sexual assault victims can request that the offender be tested for HIV if there is probable cause that the defendant committed the offense (Wallace and Roberson 2015).

The Centers for Disease Control and Prevention (2006) estimates that there is between a 0.1% and 0.2% chance of contracting HIV through intercourse and a slightly higher percent for consensual rectal sexual intercourse. Anal intercourse carries the highest risk of transmission due to the fragile tissues of the anus, which may tear during intercourse (Wallace and Roberson 2015). Children who are sexually assaulted are considered to be at higher risk of contracting HIV since many child victims are exposed to repeated assaults over a long period of time and that children are at greater risk of injury during penetration. Physical evidence may not be common in child sexual abuse cases; however, sexually transmitted diseases are considered invaluable evidence in the prosecution of offenders.

☐ Mandatory Reporting Laws

The Child Abuse Prevention and Treatment Act was passed in 1974 and required states to pass mandatory reporting laws for suspected cases of child abuse in order to receive certain federal funding (Daigle 2012).

To this date, all 50 states have enacted child abuse reporting laws (Cox et al. 2014). The standard of knowledge that triggers the duty to report may vary from state to state. Some states require reasonable suspicion, whereas others may specify a reason to believe or know or suspect (Daigle 2012). The subjectivity in some aspects of abuse may prevent the reporting of child maltreatment. Numerous authorities have attempted to define child abuse; however, there seems to be a continuous struggle as to what constitutes child abuse and neglect (Wallace and Roberson 2015). For example, what is considered physical abuse by one individual may be considered discipline or acceptable corporal punishment to another individual.

Typically, *mandated reporters* include individuals who work with children in some capacity and/or are responsible for the safety and protection on a professional basis (Quinn and Brightman 2015). Statutes require reporters to contact the appropriate authorities as soon as possible, but this arrangement may be unsatisfactory as most social service agencies conduct their business on a 9 to 5, Monday through Friday schedule (Doerner and Lab 2012). There are 24-hour hotlines available when immediate intervention is warranted. For instance, law enforcement has the authority to place a child in protective custody when they feel that the child is in imminent danger and would need to contact social services immediately for the temporary placement of the child. Social workers, law enforcement, mental health workers, medical personal, medical examiners/coroners, and school personnel are usually specifically identified as mandated reporters. The responsibility of clergy, though, varies from state to state and specifies under what circumstances they are obligated to report. Other states, however, conclude their mandated reporting laws with the phrase *any other person*, virtually stating that everyone is required to report.

Based upon state-level definitions of mandated reporters, social workers, teachers, school officials, child care providers, medical personnel, and law enforcement officers are all mandated reporters for cases of child abuse. In some states, this reporting requirement is extended to commercial photographers, substance abuse counselors, youth directors, coaches, and members of the clergy.

In 2012, approximately 60% of the calls related to speculations of child abuse or neglect were from mandated reporters (USDHHS 2013). However, counts differ by source, and reciprocity one would assume to exist among reporting agencies is not always present. Specifically, although law enforcement is required to report maltreatment to social services, social services agencies are not required to report all maltreatment cases to law enforcement since a significant amount of cases will not require police intervention. In addition, some potential reporters have been reluctant to report maltreatment as they only suspect abuse and are concerned about repercussions should their suspicions become unwarranted.

Approximately 75% of reports to social services involve children under the age of 12. The majority of those calls come from someone other than the actual victim or family members, who are important since most victimizations of younger children are caused by family members themselves (Quinn and Brightman 2015). Statutes have been written to give immunity to those who make a child maltreatment report in good faith. Even with these safeguards, many authorities believe that the number of reported cases of child abuse are only the *tip of the iceberg* (Roberson and Wallace 2016). Statutes also detail potential criminal charges for any mandated reporter who fails to report suspected child abuse.

Delvin Thompson, 47, a mathematics teacher at a local high school, had a reputation of establishing seating assignments where all the *pretty girls* would sit toward the front of the classroom. One year, Delvin made arrangements for a high-school girl (Jenna) to take a make-up test after school hours in his classroom. While taking her test, she noticed that her teacher seated behind his desk with a large briefcase open. She could see that he was positioning his body so that most of his body was concealed by the briefcase and the desk itself. Even with this partial concealment, she was aware that his arm was moving back and forth in a repeated motion consistent with masturbation. Although Jenna had not noticed him lower his pants or unzip his fly, she could clearly tell that he was adjusting his pants and observed him stand up and place some paper towels in the wastebasket. Jenna was extremely upset believing that her math teacher had masturbated in the classroom but never reported it to any school officials.

A few days later, another student (Noel), who had also made arrangements with Mr. Thompson to take a make-up test after hours in his classroom, went to take the test. Noel, like Jenna, observed this same teacher position his body behind his open briefcase and the desk, and she too saw him moving his arm in a manner consistent with masturbation. Noel then observed him stand up and throw paper towels into the classroom wastebasket. After completing her exam, she immediately contacted her parents who came to the high school to file a formal complaint. The high school administration conducted their own investigation including interviewing the math teacher who denied the allegation. The school attorneys and the administration did not report the alleged abuse to social services or law enforcement since they felt it did not meet the criteria as a mandated reporter requirement, since no physical contact occurred. It was not long before the story of the alleged incident circulated through the high school and came to the attention of Jenna. Jenna, who did not know Noel, then reported what she had experienced with the teacher. After receiving a second complaint, the school waited a few days and, upon consultation with their attorneys, notified law enforcement who then contacted social services.

Law enforcement conducted an investigation but was unable to gather any physical evidence from the briefcase or the wastebasket due to the delay in reporting. They did learn, however, that a previous complaint was made a year earlier by an additional student who alleged that this same teacher kissed her on the neck while she was in the process of taking a make-up exam. This previous allegation had also been dealt with by the high school administration alone without reporting to the police. Law enforcement brought charges against Delvin Thompson despite the lack of physical evidence knowing the case would come down to the student's word against the teacher's. Law enforcement officials were also aware that they could only bring one case forward at a time. The initial case went to trial where the judge ruled that the math teacher was *not guilty*. Knowing the outcome of the previous case, the other alleged victimized students were no longer willing to proceed with their testimony as they did not wish to be subjected to the same scrutiny and embarrassment as that of their fellow classmates.

Although this teacher was found not guilty, his reputation, as well as that of the school's, was tarnished to a degree where he was no longer able to instruct at that high school. The school was not capable of firing him since he was not convicted; therefore, they paid him $150,000 to take early retirement. Delvin Thompson then obtained a teaching assistant job at a middle school in a bordering state. He was arrested during his first year of employment on allegations by two mentally challenged students who reported that he had sexually assaulted each of them.

Statute of Limitations

Statute of limitations refers to laws designed to have specific perimeters or time spans within which a victim can report a crime. A common standard is one year for a misdemeanor and seven years for a felony. For instance, burglary is considered a felony, but, if reporting was delayed by more than seven years, the matter would not be investigated as the time constraint would not allow for a charge to be filed. Legislators and criminal justice officials realize the challenges in reporting child abuse, such as in circumstances where a victim is unwilling to address the trauma they faced. This can often be the motivation for delays in reporting the abuse. In response to this dilemma, states have been giving more latitude with the amount of time a victim can report. In some states, there are no statute of limitations allowing the victim a lifetime to seek justice for child abuse. However, even without these restrictions, some adults may choose to never report their victimization.

Statutes of limitations are designed to protect defendants. These limits are based upon the rationale that victims should pursue acts against them with diligence and that, over time, the defendants may not be able to disprove a false claim.

☐ Missing and Exploited Children

Having a missing child can instill anxiety and terror into any parent or caretaker. Simply losing sight of a small child in a public arena may generate immediate fear and panic. High-profile cases, such as that of the abduction of Adam Walsh in 1981, reinforce the reasons for such alarm. To address these concerns, the Office of Juvenile Justice Delinquency and Prevention mandated a periodic nationwide assessment on how many children went missing each year. Prior to the 1980s, there were no good indicators as to the number of children who went missing each year and how many of those children were found or had returned home (Quinn and Brightman 2015). A missing child refers to children whose whereabouts are unknown to their parent, guardian, or legal custodian. Runaways make up the majority of missing children (Burgess et al. 2013). Many worried parents will file a missing person report with law enforcement only to find their child returning home a few hours later. Other juveniles may just be defiant and decide to stay overnight at a friend's home without notifying their parents. Some children's whereabouts may be unknown as they are considered by their families and communities as throwaways. This category refers to children who have been told to leave their homes, or they have no parent or guardian who makes an effort to look for or recover the child. Children in this category are at the highest risk of exploitation by child traffickers and those interested in children for use in child pornography.

Children can also be reported missing through family and stranger abductions. Family abductions commonly occur when parents separate, and there is a custody dispute. These type of abductions are easily accomplished as the tactic can be as simple as not returning the child during a designated visitation period. In this type of scenario, the offender may be several states away before the unsuspecting parent becomes aware that their child is missing. There are also extreme cases where one parent may have dual citizenship and flees the country with his or her child to a place where there is no extradition treaty. According to US law, nonfamily abductions are defined as the coerced and unauthorized taking of a child into a building, a vehicle, or a distance more than 20 feet and/or the detention of a child for a period of more than 1 hour. Nonfamily abductions include a friend's neighbors, acquaintances, or strangers. More than 65% of nonfamily abductions are girls. Of these girls that are abducted, approximately, 50% are sexually abused, and approximately 30% are physically abused. In 75% of the cases, the perpetrators are men and that most of them target children within their own ethic group (Sedlak et al. 2002). In some circumstances, nonfamily abductions can involve more than one assailant.

> In 1991, Jaycee Dugard, age 11, was kidnapped on her way to the bus stop. She was discovered 18 years later after she had been kept in a concealed area behind the home of Phillip and Nancy Garrido in Antioch, CA. Both were charged with rape and forcible confinement. During the sentencing phase of their trial, Dugard had sent an impact statement stating that she chose not to be at the hearing as she refused to *waste another second of her life* in their presence. (Dugard 2011)

An additional concern with children is the abduction of infants from hospitals by nonfamily members. Hospitals have established significant security protocols, which include electronic security systems that are activated if the infant leaves a designated area (Burgess et al. 2013). As with most police action, this is in response to cases of infant abductions from hospitals.

The Missing Children's Act of 1982 requires law enforcement to take a report of a missing child and enter the information into the Federal Bureau of Investigation's National Crime Information Center (NCIC), sharing it with law enforcement throughout the country. The information should include a description of the child, where they were last seen, and any additional information that may help locate the child or concerns relating to the child's safety. If the circumstances reported to law enforcement indicate that the child was abducted or in danger, then they can establish an *AMBER Alert*. Through technology, AMBER Alerts are now provided to the public through television, radio, and cell phones.

☐ AMBER Alert

On January 13, 1996, Amber Hagerman (age 9) was abducted while riding her bike in Arlington, TX. A neighbor witnessed the abduction and called the police. Amber's parents contacted the media, and, their neighbors, after hearing of this abduction, began assisting with the search. Four days after the abduction, her body was found, but Amber's murderer has never been identified. The community was distraught that the police were unable to locate Amber and developed a plan whereby local radio stations and television stations could broadcast vital information so that anyone could spot a victim or abductor and notify law enforcement.

Today, all 50 states have some form of the AMBER Alert system in place (Doerner and Lab 2012). Although the criteria for implementing an AMBER Alert may vary between states, they still have strict requirements for its use. The federal government established four guidelines (USDoJ 2004) that need to be met: (1) law enforcement must confirm that a child has been abducted, (2) there must be some indication that the child is endangered, (3) there must be some information indicating a plausible recovery, and (4) the information must be entered in the NCIC. As of 2012, there have been approximately 600 successful recoveries as a result of these AMBER Alerts (NCMEC 2012).

☐ Courts

If a child is a victim of abuse or neglect, the criminal justice system can intervene both through juvenile court and criminal court as the objective is different with each jurisdiction. In the criminal court, the purpose is to hold the abuser accountable for their actions and impose sanctions that can include incarceration. In contrast, the primary objective of an abuse and/or neglect hearing in juvenile court is to ensure the child's safety and guarantee that the child is receiving the appropriate services. Based on the facts surrounding the abuse, jurisdiction will be determined on who handles the case.

Jurisdiction means the legal power or authority to hear a case. Not all allegations of abuse and/or neglect proceed to criminal court just as not all cases of abuse and or neglect are brought up in juvenile court. In some circumstances, the facts may warrant that the case be heard in both criminal and juvenile court. It is unlikely that that an abuse case that does not involve a family member or caretaker will be referred to juvenile court.

☐ Juvenile and Adult Court

In 1870, the state of Massachusetts enacted separate hearings for juveniles and New York followed with a similar law in 1877. In 1938, the federal government enacted the Juvenile Court Act, and, by 1945, every state had enacted legislation focusing on how to handle juveniles (Schmalleger 2012). Juvenile courts were now established to address an array of issues involving juveniles, including delinquent children, and those who have been abused or neglected.

In juvenile court, an abuse/neglect hearing is initiated when social services, or, in some cases, law enforcement, file a petition alleging misconduct by a caretaker. At the arraignment, the juvenile court judge will determine whether the child is still in danger and will evaluate whether placement outside the child's home is necessary pending a trial. Once a trial is scheduled, the facts of the alleged abuse case are brought forward.

Unlike a criminal trial, the focus of the juvenile court is the needs of the victim and not that of the suspect. The burden of proof in an abuse/neglect hearing is a preponderance of evidence, which means there is a likelihood that the abuse did occur, unlike a criminal proceeding, which requires proof beyond a reasonable doubt. The technical rules of evidence may not be required in abuse hearings so that someone may be able to testify on behalf of the child. The rules of testimony are a lot more stringent in criminal court.

If, at the conclusion of a trial, there is a finding that there was abuse/neglect, then there will be a dispositional hearing to determine what steps are needed to ensure what services are available to the victim and what consequences are imposed against the offender. The offender will not be incarcerated for the abuse, as he or she would be in a criminal proceeding, but can be ordered to stay away from the child. The court has the authority to give temporary custody to another relative or terminate parental rights and legal guardianship. The court may also mandate that the offender attend a rehabilitation or counseling program to avoid reoffending with the goal of reunification of the family.

☐ Criminal Court

Criminal court, unlike juvenile court, has an objective of making an offender accountable for their actions if the allegations against the offender are sustained. The prosecution must prove beyond a reasonable doubt that the allegations are true and then recommend sentencing upon conviction. The technical rules of evidence apply in a criminal proceeding where the defendant's constitutional rights must be adhered to including the right to face your accuser.

Judges presiding over child molestation cases have received significant ridicule for agreeing to and imposing what the public sees in many cases as too lenient of a sentence for such a horrific crime. Unfortunately, most of the public is not privy to the challenges of prosecuting a case of child abuse. Many victims of abuse may be absolutely terrified with the idea of testifying or even seeing the perpetrator again and are unwilling to cooperate with authorities. Others may be willing to testify but *freeze up* once they enter the courtroom. In 1990, the US Supreme Court gave tacit approval to protect child victims in court. These procedures include the use of videotaped testimony, testimony through one-way circuit television, and testimony by experts in the child abuse field (Carelli 1990). Even with these safeguards implemented, many children are unwilling to cooperate with the criminal justice system, forcing the prosecution to recommend a plea that is favorable to the defendant and that the judge may reluctantly accept. Plea bargaining is not unique to child abuse cases. Approximately 90% of all cases in the criminal justice system do not appear as a trial (Erez and Roberts 2013).

☐ Incarceration

When an offender is sentenced as a sex offender, the place of incarceration can depend on the length of the sentence. Offenders serving more than one year will be sentenced to a prison, whereas those sentenced to less than a year will serve their time in a local jail. A common management in both of these facilities is to keep the sex offenders away from the general population as they are deemed offensive to the other inmates.

Although there is a primary objective of punishment when incarcerating sex offenders, there are also services provided in hopes that they will not reoffend upon their release. In some cases, offenders serve their entire prison sentence but are still considered extremely dangerous when they are scheduled for their release. Some states allow civil commitment upon the completion of their prison sentence. Of course, these civil commitments are usually mandated through an additional court.

☐ Civil Commitment Orders

Civil commitment orders are directives that require sex offenders be confined to a mental institution after completing their prison sentence. These orders can be imposed indefinitely and are implemented in order to prevent further victimization (Doerner and Lab 2012). Approximately 20 states have civil commitment laws reserved for sex offenders (Mancini et al. 2013). These commitments have been challenged in court as being a cruel and unusual punishment or a violation of double jeopardy. The challenge of these commitments have been addressed in the US Supreme Court in Kansas v. Hendricks (1997). The Supreme Court ruled against Hendricks indicating that there was a sufficient amount of procedural checks to provide for due process. A similar ruling supporting civil commitment of sex offenders was addressed in United States v. Comstock (2010) when a federal court ruled against a sex offender prisoner that was ordered to civil commitment. In this case, the defendant argued that the federal government did not have the authority to have a civil commitment, but that argument was rejected by the US Supreme Court (Doerner and Lab 2012).

☐ Key Figures in Child Abuse

There are several professions that are dedicated to help victims of child abuse. Some of these professionals are official members of the criminal justice system, while others, through their expertise, are called upon to address the various needs in child maltreatment cases. We will discuss some of these key roles as they play an intricate part in ensuring a child's safety, provide the appropriate services, and pursue the appropriate consequences for those who offend. (For information on organizations dedicated to the protection of children across the country, see Appendix C.)

☐ Mental Health

The mental health professional is an essential component in addressing the needs of child abuse victims. In many circumstances, the mental health professional may be the first *official* contact with a child abuse victim. Many children are sent to psychiatrists, psychologists, or counselors because of behavioral issues that may be related to their victimization, although their victimization has not been disclosed. During these sessions, a child can develop a rapport with the mental health worker and feel comfortable enough to report their victimization. Although confidentiality is a significant component in these types of sessions, mental health workers are considered mandated reporters and must report the abuse even if the child has requested that abuse be kept secret. Once the report is made, the allegations will be investigated, and a determination will be made on whether to take official action.

Certain victims of abuse may face years of therapy before they are willing to disclose their victimization, which is discussed in the statute of limitations. Other victims may never develop the strength to come forward and report their abuse and live with that daunting secret, which can affect them for a lifetime. Childhood physical and sexual abuse are related to numerous problems for victims later in life, including attempted suicide (Joiner et al. 2007). The role of the mental health professional does not end after the disclosure of a child's victimization. Victims are frequently sent to mental health professionals to deal with the emotional trauma associated with abuse. These sessions also help prepare children with anxiety prepare for the possibility of facing their abuser in court.

Child abuse is a traumatic event in a child's life that may need the assistance of mental health intervention well into their adulthood. Mental health professionals also respond to the needs of adults who may also require therapy not relating to their victimization. In some of these circumstances, abusers may report their own maltreatment of these children to a mental health professional, although this is the exception and not the rule (Crosson-Tower 2010).

☐ Law Enforcement

The role of law enforcement has changed significantly over the years to address the needs of child abuse victims. In fact, a significant proportion of arrests come from proactive efforts by law enforcement (Wolak et al. 2009). Law enforcement has addressed the necessity of child abuse prevention through community relations and the specific training needed in properly investigating child abuse. Police departments, through their community relation officers, develop programs to develop a better relationship with police. This is significant as it is important that children are willing to come forward and talk to the police if needed. Many police departments provide a fingerprint program so that there is a record of your child if they become missing. Other programs such as *stranger danger* have also been addressed although abuse rarely occurs at the hands of a stranger.

In addition to these crime prevention programs, more jurisdictions require police departments to have specialized training for juvenile officers who investigate child abuse cases, although financial resources make training and specific juvenile assignments challenging. Many rural law enforcement agencies do not have officers specifically trained to address incidents involving juveniles (Cox et al. 2014). Smaller departments may request assistance from larger departments to handle certain types of juvenile abuse.

Department policies have been established where only trained individuals can handle these sensitive investigations. These individuals, commonly referred to as juvenile officers, receive specialized training within their state to handle child abuse investigations. Some of the specialized training can include interview and interrogation techniques specifically designed for child sex offenders. There is also a particular instruction on how to interview a small child as an untrained officer may ask leading questions that can be later challenged in court. Juvenile officers also need to be technically savvy as so much child abuse occurs through the exploitation of the Internet.

Law enforcement officers, when working with any victim, should address three basic needs of the victim. First, they should make the victim feel comfortable. Second, the victim should be able to express their emotions. Finally, the victim needs to know what happens next (Woods 2010). These are the three basic principles on how police should respond to victims. Of course, these principles may have to be amended based on the age of the child. In addition to the specialized training that juvenile officers have obtained within their own jurisdiction, the US Department of Justice (2014), through the Office of Justice programs, have established guidelines to assist law enforcement agencies in the proper handling of these types of investigations.

After receiving a referral, officers should always consider the possibility of child abuse and talk with children at the scene when responding to a domestic dispute, identify any personal or professional biases you may have with child abuse cases, develop the ability to desensitize yourself to those issues and remain objective, understand your department's guidelines and state statutes, know the investigative resources that are available within your department or the larger law enforcement community (e.g., medical examiner's office, child protection team personnel, forensic interviewers), know what resources are available to the victim and family in the community (e.g., therapy, victim compensation) and provide this information to them, and introduce yourself to the victim and other team members who may be present. Explain your role and the focus and objective of the investigation, ensure that the best treatment will be provided for the protection of the child, schedule a forensic interview with a trained professional, obtain information for the preliminary report, and inquire about the history of the abusive situation. An accurate timeline of events is crucial to the successful investigation and prosecution of all types of child maltreatment; obtain any elements of the crime necessary for the report, and inquire about the instrument of abuse or other items at the scene. Check the scene for potential instruments of abuse; do not discount children's statements about who is abusing them, where and how the abuse is occurring, or what types of acts occurred; save your opinions for the end of the report and provide supporting facts highlighting the atmosphere of disclosure and the mood and demeanor of participants in the complaint; preserve the crime scene; treat the scene as a crime scene (even if the abuse occurred in the past) and not as the site of a social problem; secure the instrument of abuse or other corroborative evidence that the child identifies at the scene; photograph the scene in detail from all angles of each room; photograph injuries noted on the victim; always include a scale in the photographs; and rephotograph injuries as needed to capture any changes in their appearance.

Afterwards, the follow-up is critical. Therefore, an officer should conduct a follow-up investigation, be supportive of the child and family, and arrange for a medical examination and transportation to the hospital. Collect a change of clothes for the victim, if needed, use appropriate investigative techniques, ensure that the child and family are linked to support services or therapy, provide your contact information so that the family can report further information, if necessary, and contact other agencies, such as Child Protective Services (CPS), as appropriate.

Finally, during the court phase, the officer should bring the child to court before the first hearing to familiarize him or her with the courtroom setting and atmosphere. The prosecutor or a victim/witness service provider may assume this task. Prepare courtroom exhibits (e.g., pictures, displays, sketches) to support the child's testimony, file all evidence in accordance with state and court policy, and update family members (other than those who are suspects) about the status and progress of the investigation and maintain contact with them throughout the court process. Use caution when providing information to the family because they may share it with others, provide court results and case closure information to the child and family, and follow up with the probation department to prepare the presentence report and victim impact statements.

Although some law enforcement officers have extensive training in the investigation of child abuse cases, a strategy has been formulated through the establishment of a child abuse task force. These groups have a specialist within their own discipline and work as a team as they share their expertise in child abuse investigations. The members of these task forces include, but are not limited to, police, social services, attorneys, and victim advocates. The members of the task force may intervene at different phases of the criminal justice process or work together at certain points.

Prior to the development of these task forces, victims of child abuse were subjected to multiple interviews from professionals within the criminal justice system. In the prior format, children were being asked the same questions by different officials within the criminal justice system, which was determined to be that it was not in the child's best interest to share these traumatic events over and over with different interviewers.

A common procedure now used among many professionals in the criminal justice system is to have one person conduct the interview in front of a two-way mirror where other members can listen in on the conversation and direct the primary interviewer to ask a certain question if needed. This process significantly diminishes the amount of unnecessary interviews the child is subjected to when they disclose their victimization.

☐ CPS

Child Protective Services, also commonly referred to as *Social Services*, is a governmental agency that receives complaints of child abuse/neglect from mandated reporters or any other person who suspects abuse. Upon receipt of these allegations, CPS determines the validity of these reports and determines whether the complaint warrants further investigation. They will then determine what services are needed for the family and take whatever steps are necessary in preventing further abuse. This can include having a child removed from the household or take steps to safeguard that the alleged abuser no longer has access to the child or take steps to ensure the abuser will refrain from further abuse.

It is a disheartening task when a decision has to be made on whether or not to remove a child from their home. The debate centers on whether the constancy of parents who are functioning at a barely minimum level is preferable to separating the child from their primary caretakers (Crosson-Tower 2010). Someone must decide if the danger to the child outweighs the need for constancy (Weber 1997). If the decision is to remove the child, then the social worker must prepare the child for this separation by familiarization of the foster care facility and providing information to the foster care family with pertinent information about the child they may be caring for (Crosson-Tower 2010).

Although the removal of a child from their home may be the best option, it can be a frightening experience for the child. If the allegations of abuse or neglect are confirmed, CPS can establish a plan without formal court intervention to provide services for the family. In some cases, court intervention is necessary where court proceedings are pursued to formulate a plan to provide services or treatment to both the child and their family (Sedlak et al. 2005). Child Protective Services may also be involved in cases of abuse or neglect in institutional settings and will monitor their operations in order for their facility to remain open.

Not all reports of abuse are reported to law enforcement; however, allegations reported to law enforcement must be relayed to Social Services. Cases involving abuse outside an institutional setting may not involve Social Services if the abuse is committed by a nonfamily member. Social Services may provide information to assist a victim but will not be involved in the investigation unless requested by law enforcement.

☐ Court Appointed Special Advocates

Court Appointed Special Advocates (CASA) are trained volunteers who are appointed by the court in cases of abuse or neglect and who make recommendations on what is in the best interest of the child. Once a judge decides what action is needed, CASA volunteers will continue to monitor the case to ensure that the child or family receive the services ordered by the court (Cox et al. 2014).

Guardian ad Litem

The position of *guardian ad litem* has existed for many years in child abuse cases. A *guardian ad litem* is a court-appointed attorney who is assigned to a child who has been a victim of abuse or neglect. They may also be assigned during custody battles between parents. The *guardian ad litem*, like volunteers from CASA, will gather information about the child and make a recommendation to the court on what they believe is in the best interest of the child. These individuals serve as a protector and supporter of the child. In cases of child abuse, this person is essential.

Victim Advocate

Many children are terrified about the prospect of having to testify in a criminal proceeding. One of the responsibilities of a victim advocate is to make a victim/witness as comfortable as possible as they move forward through the judicial process. The victim advocate is a friend and counselor on whom the child can depend when others in the child's life may be under too much pressure to offer support (Noel 2009). The victim advocate has many avenues to help a child through the process, including showing the child around the court when it is not in session and letting the child sit where they would later testify. This can alleviate some of the mysteries of a courtroom and will relieve some potential anxiety. The victim advocate can explain how the court system works and what is expected of the child. In some cases, the simple task of holding a child's hand during judicial proceeding can put a child's mind at ease.

Forensic Nurse

A forensic nurse, also referred to as a sexual assault nurse examiner (SANE), is a medical professional who assists with the examination and care of sexual assault victims. The SANE program was created whereby specially trained forensic nurses would provide 24-hour coverage to care for adult and adolescent sexual assault victims in emergency departments and nonhospital settings (Campbell et al. 2005). Forensic nurses are trained to deal with the emotional impact victims face and provide care for any injuries sustained from the assault.

Forensic nurses are specifically trained with the protocol in the collection and documentation of physical evidence. The evidence is placed in a container commonly referred to as a *rape kit* and is turned over to the police. It has been reported that some doctors were reluctant to collect evidence as it may require them to testify and that their qualifications in gathering evidence may also be questioned (Little 2001).

The forensic nurse is not required to release the identity of any adult sexual assault victim to law enforcement but is required as a mandated reporter to notify law enforcement if a child comes to seek medical care after being a victim of sexual assault. This special protection helps to ensure that children who are victims of abuse receive help and attention as soon as possible. Forensic nurses may be required to testify in court to explain the process of how the evidence was gathered and their interaction with the reported victim.

Foster Care

The last key figure to be discussed in this chapter is the role of foster care. Judges have the difficult decision in some cases to remove the child from their home for their own protection and place the child in foster care. Foster care is a system where a child in placed in the custody of a group or a private home that is certified by the state. The placement may be voluntary in that the parents may think they are pleasing the social worker, and the placement is short term (Crosson-Tower 2010). Other times, the placement is forced upon the parents. Either way, the separation can be traumatic for both the parents and the child. A parent giving up their children to other parents is a clear sign to them of their own failure (Berrick 2008; Grant 2004; Karson 2001).

Children who are placed in foster care have a sense of instability as they may move from one foster care facility to another. Foster care can be long term. which may include multiple facilities. or their foster care placement may be a temporary solution until they are reunited with their families. About 30% of children will return to their birth parents only to reenter care (Kaufman and Grasso 2006; Wulczyn 2004). The constant transitions can put an emotional strain on a child as they lack attachment with short-term caregivers. The opposite effect can occur with the caretaker when a bond is developed through long-term placement, and the child is forced to leave.

☐ Summary

Although thousands of laws have been passed to address the needs of victims of crimes, we have focused on some of the tragedies that have dramatically changed the way we respond to child abuse. In this chapter, the changes in the historical and philosophy and attitudes were introduced and discussed as applied to provide a background and to address the needs of children who have been abused or are in need of services. Authorities, whether legislators, criminal justice officials, or professionals with expertise in child abuse, have intervened at various stages either in an attempt to prevent further abuse or to become part of a network designed to respond to the needs of the victimized child. Even today, this process is critiqued and improved to provide child victims of abuse and neglect the best opportunity for services.

CHAPTER QUESTIONS

1. What is the importance of the Child Savers Movement?

2. What do we mean by the Age of Consent?

3. What is the role of the Forensic Nurse?

QUESTIONS FOR FURTHER THOUGHT

1. Should the laws surrounding Age of Consent be reexamined?

2. Given today's changing world, should the Criminal Justice System be revised regarding child abuse?

3. Should all sex offenders be placed on the Registry?

☐ References

Berrick, J. 2008. *Take Me Home: Protecting America's Vulnerable Children and Families.* New York: Oxford University Press.

Burgess, A., Regehr, C., and Roberts, A. 2013. *Victimology: Theories and Applications* (2nd ed.). Burlington, MA: Jones & Bartlett Learning.

Campbell, R., Townsend, S., Long, S., and Kinnison, K. 2005. Organizational characteristics of sexual assault nurse examiner programs: Results from the National Survey Project. *Journal of Forensic Nursing,* 1(2), 57–64.

Carelli, R. 1990. Court backs sparing children in abuse cases. *Peoria Journal Star,* p. A2, June 28.

Cavan, R. 1969. *Juvenile Delinquency: Development, Treatment, Control* (2nd ed.). Philadelphia: J.B. Lippincott.

Centers for Disease Control and Prevention. 2006. HIV statistics and surveillance. Atlanta, GA.

Chon, S. 2010. Carr v. United States (08-1301). Ithica, NY: Legal Information Institute, Cornell University Law School. Available at http://topics.lawcornell .edu/supct/cert/08-1301. Accessed on March 30, 2015.

Code of Virginia. n.d. Causing or encouraging acts rendering children delinquent, abused, etc. Available at http://leg1.state.va.us/cgi-bin/legp504.exe ?000+cod+18.2-371. Accessed on November 3, 2015.

Cox, S. Allen, J., Hanser, R., and Conrad, J. 2014. *Juvenile Justice: A Guide to Theory, Policy, and Practice.* Thousand Oaks, CA. SAGE.

Crosson-Tower, C. 2010. *Understanding Child Abuse and Neglect* (8th ed.). Boston: Allyn and Bacon.

Daigle, L. 2012. *Victimology.* Thousand Oaks, CA: SAGE.

Dammer, H. and Albanese, J. 2011. *Comparative Criminal Justice Systems* (4th ed.). Belmont, CA: Wadsworth Cengage Learning.

Doerner, W. and Lab, S. 2012. *Victimology* (6th ed.). Burlington, MA: Anderson Publishing.

Dugard, J. 2011. Victim impact statement. ABC News. Available at http://abcnews .go.com/GMA/jaycee-dugards-victim-impact-statement/story?id=13745897. Accessed on April 4, 2015.

Erez, R. and Roberts, J. 2013. Victim participation in the criminal justice system. In R. Davis, A. Lurigio, and S. Herman (eds.), *Victims of Crime* (4th ed.), pp. 251–270. London: Sage Publications.

Gilani, S. 2006. Juvenile justice in Saudi Arabia. In P. Friday and X. Ren (eds.) *Delinquency and Juvenile Justice Systems in the Non-Western World* (pp. 145–163). Monsey, NY: Criminal Justice Press.

Grant, L. 2004. *Breaking Up Families.* Jamaica, NY: Yacos.

Groth, A. 1979. *Men Who Rape.* New York: Plenum.

Joiner, T., Sachs-Ericsson, N., Wingate, L., Brown, J., Anestis, M., and Selby, E. 2007. Childhood physical and sexual abuse and lifetime number of suicide attempts: A persistent and theoretically important relationship. *Behavior Research and Therapy,* 45(3), 539–547.

Karson, M. 2001. *Patterns of Child Abuse.* New York: Haworth.

Kaufman, J. and Grasso, D. 2006. The Early Intervention Foster Care program. *Child Maltreatment,* 11(1), 90–91.

Little, K. 2001. *Sexual Assault Nurse Examiner (SANE) Programs: Improving the Community Response to Sexual Assault Victims.* OVC Bulletin. Washington: US Department of Justice, Office of Justice Programs, Office for Victims of Crime. NCJ 186366.

Mallicoat, S. and Ireland, C. 2014. *Women and Crime: The Essentials.* Thousand Oaks, CA: SAGE.

Mancini, C. 2014. *Sex Crime Offenders and Society.* Durham, NC: Carolina Academic Press.

Mancini, C., Barnes, J., and Mears, D. 2013. It varies from state to state: An examination of sex crime laws nationally. *Criminal Justice Policy Review,* 24(1), 166–198.

National Center for Missing and Exploited Children. 2012. AMBER Alert program. Available at http://www.ncmec.org/missingkids/servlet/PageServlet?Language Country=en_US&PageId=4319. Accessed on March 15, 2015.

Noel, J. 2009. Court services on behalf of children. In C. Crosson-Tower (ed.) *Exploring Child Welfare,* (pp. 252–274). Boston: Allyn & Bacon.

Quinn, E. and Brightman, S. 2015. *Crime Victimization: A Comprehensive Overview.* Durham, NC: Carolina Academic Press.

Roberson, C. and Wallace, H. 2016. *Principles of Criminal Law* (6th ed.). Upper Saddle River, NJ: Pearson Education Inc.

Rogers, L. 2007. United States Department of Justice: Sex Offender Sentencing, Monitoring, Apprehension, Registration and Tracking (SMART) office. Available at http://ojp.gov/smart/pdfs/so_registry_laws.pdf. Accessed on March 15, 2015.

Sedlak, A., Doueck, H., Lyons, P., and Wells, S. 2005. Child maltreatment and the justice system: Predicators of court involvement. *Research on Social Work Practice,* 15, 389–407.

Sedlak, A., Finkelhor, D., Hammer, H., and Schultz, D. 2002. National estimates of missing children: An overview. In J. Roberts Flores OJJDP Administrator (ed.) *National Incidence Studies of Missing, Abducted, Runaway, and Throwaway Children.* Washington: Office of Juvenile Justice and Delinquency Prevention, Office of Justice Programs, US Department of Justice. Washington: Government Printing.

Sentenced to Abuse. 2010. *The New York Times,* p. 26, January 15.

Schmalleger, F. 2012. *Criminal Justice: A Brief Introduction* (9th ed.). Upper Saddle River, NJ: Pearson Education Inc.

Shusta, R., Levine, D., Wong, H., and Harris, P. 2005. *Multicultural Law Enforcement: Strategies for Peacekeeping in a Diverse Society* (3rd ed.). Upper Saddle River, NJ: Prentice Hall.

Siegel, L. and Welsh, B. 2008. *Juvenile Delinquency: The Core* (3rd ed.). Belmont, CA: Wadsworth.

Tobolowsky, P., Gaboury, M., Jackson, A., and Blackburn, A. 2010. *Crime Victim Rights and Remedies* (2nd ed.). Durham, NC: Carolina Academic Press.

US Department of Health and Human Services. 2013. Child Maltreatment 2012. Available at http://www.acf.hhs.gov/programs/cb/research-data-technology /statistics-research/child-maltreatment. Accessed on April 3, 2015.

US Department of Justice. 2004. Guidelines on criteria for issuing AMBER Alerts. Washington: Office of Justice Programs. Available at http://www.amberalert .gov/guidelines.htm. Accessed on April 15, 2015.

US Department of Justice. 2014. Office of Justice programs: Law enforcement's response to child abuse. Available at http://ojjdp.gov/pubs/243907.pdf. Accessed on May 3, 2015.

US Department of Justice. n.d. Office of the Juvenile Justice Delinquency and Prevention. Available at http://www.ojjdp.gov/. Accessed on March 30, 2015.

Wallace, H. and Roberson, J. 2015. *Victimology: Legal, Psychological, and Social Perspectives* (4th ed.). Upper Saddle River, NJ: Pearson Education Inc.

Washington: Office of Juvenile Justice and Delinquency Prevention, Office of Justice Programs, US Department of Justice. Washington: Government Printing.

Weber, M. 1997. The assessment of child abuse: A primary function of Child Protective Services. In M.E. Helfer, R.S. Kempe, and R.D. Krugman (ed.) *The Battered Child*, (pp. 120–149). Chicago: Chicago University Press.

Wolak, J., Finkelhor, D., and Mitchell, K.J. 2009. Law Enforcement Responses to Online Child Sexual Exploitation Crimes: The National Online Juvenile Victimization Study, 2000 & 2006. Durham, NH: Crime Against Children Research Center.

Woods, T. 2010. *First Response to Victims of Crime*. Washington: US Department of Justice, Office of Justice Programs, Office for Victims of Crime. NCJ 231171.

Wulczyn, F. 2004. Family reunification. *The Future of Children* 14(1), 95–113.

APPENDIX A: Human Trafficking—Country Demographics as Related to Tier Classification

Many researchers have suggested that the demographic characteristics of a country are related to the prevalence of human trafficking within that country (Lulo 2013; Kendall and Funk 2011; McCabe and Manian 2001; Sheldon 2000). This report was intended to explore that suggestion.

Specifically, this report examined the demographic characteristics of unemployment, poverty, percent of the population between the ages of 0 and 14, life expectancy, percent of female literacy, and population growth as related to tier classification. For clarity, variables were operationalized as follows:

Unemployment—percent of the population unemployed within the country

Poverty—percent of the population living at or below the poverty level within the country

Percent Age 0–14—percent of the population between the ages of zero and 14 within the country

Life Expectancy—Average years of life lived within the country

Female Literacy—Percent of the female population (age 18+) literate within the country

Based upon the 2015 Trafficking in Persons (TIP) Report, produced by the Office to Monitor and Combat Trafficking, there were approximately 200 countries included in the tier classifications. Those counties, displayed in the list below, along with their demographic characteristics as displayed in the Central Intelligence Agency Fact Sheet, were utilized for this analysis of country demographics as related to tier classification.

Countries by 2015 Tier Classifications

Tier 1

Armenia, Australia, Austria, the Bahamas, Belgium, Canada, Chile, Czech Republic, Denmark, Finland, France, Germany, Iceland, Ireland, Israel, Italy, South Korea, Luxembourg, Macedonia, The Netherlands, New Zealand, Norway, Poland, Portugal, Slovakia, Spain, Sweden, Switzerland, Taiwan, United Kingdom, and United States of America

Tier 2

Afghanistan, Albania, Angola, Argentina, Aruba, Azerbaijan, Bahrain, Bangladesh, Barbados, Benin, Bhutan, Bosnia and Herzegovina, Brazil, Brunei, Caboverde, Cameroon, Chad, Colombia, Cote D'Ivoire, Croatia, Curacao, Cyprus, Dominican Republic, Ecuador, El Salvador, Estonia, Ethiopia, Fiji, Georgia, Guatemala, Greece, Honduras, Hong Kong, Hungary, India, Indonesia, Iraq, Japan, Jordan, Kazakhstan, Kenya, Kiribati, Kosovo, Kyrgyzstan, Latvia, Liberia, Lithuania, Macau, Madagascar, Malawi, Malta, Mexico, Micronesia, Moldova, Mongolia, Montenegro, Morocco, Mozambique, Nepal, Nicaragua, Niger, Nigeria, Oman, Palau, Panama, Paraguay, Peru, Philippines, Romania, Rwanda, St. Lucia, St. Maarten, Senegal, Serbia, Seychelles, Sierra Leone, Singapore, Slovenia, South Africa, Swaziland, Tajikistan, Togo, Turkey, Uganda, United Arab Emirates, Ukraine, Uruguay, Vietnam, and Zambia

Tier 2 Watch

Antigua and Barbuda, Bolivia, Botswana, Bulgaria, Burkina Faso, Burma, Cambodia, China (PRC), Democratic Republic of Congo, Republic of Congo, Costa Rica, Cuba, Djibouti, Egypt, Gabon, Ghana, Guinea, Guyana, Haiti, Jamaica, Laos, Lebanon, Lesotho, Malaysia, Maldives, Mali, Mauritania, Namibia, Pakistan, Papua New Guinea, Qatar, Saudi Arabia, Sri Lanka, St. Vincent and the Grenadines, Solomon Islands, Sudan, Tanzania, Timor-Leste, Trinidad and Tobago, Tunisia, Turkmenistan, Turkey, Ukraine, and Uzbekistan

Tier 3

Algeria, Belarus, Belize, Burundi, Central African Republic, Comoros, Equatorial Guinea, Eritrea, the Gambia, Guinea-Bissau, Iran, North Korea, Kuwait, Libya, Marshall Island, Mauritania, Russia, South Sudan, Syria, Thailand, Venezuela, Yemen, and Zimbabwe

Analysis of variance results (as displayed in Table A.1) indicated that, for each of the selected country demographic characteristics, a significant ($p < 0.05$) difference existed among tier classifications. In fact, overall, in every case (i.e., unemployment, poverty, percent population age 0–14, life expectancy, and female literacy), those countries with *better* conditions were classified Tier 1.

These results provide support for research that attempts to explain human trafficking from an economic perspective. Specifically, if children are considered property and property worthy of profit for those who exploit (traffic) them, then it stands to reason as the rational choice perspective suggests, that areas or countries with little in terms of economic development would have the highest prevalence of human trafficking cases.

TABLE A.1. ANOVA Results for Country Demographics by Tier Classification

Variable	Mean (Std)	F Statistics	P Value
Unemployment			
Tier 1	11.0 (9.4)	2.800	0.042
Tier 2	20.2 (24.2)		
Tier 2 Watch	16.6 (20.0)		
Tier 3	27.2 (31.9)		
Poverty			
Tier 1	14.3 (6.8)	5.720	0.001
Tier 2	32.9 (19.9)		
Tier 2 Watch	26.8 (15.3)		
Tier 3	28.1 (17.7)		

(Continued)

TABLE A.1. (CONTINUED) ANOVA Results for Country Demographics by Tier Classification

Variable	Mean (Std)	F Statistics	P Value
Percent Population Age 0–14			
Tier 1	18.2 (3.7)	3.354	0.020
Tier 2	29.4 (9.6)		
Tier 2 Watch	29.8 (8.8)		
Tier 3	28.8 (10.6)		
Life Expectancy			
Tier 1	78.1 (2.9)	12.810	0.000
Tier 2	67.6 (10.6)		
Tier 2 Watch	66.7 (9.3)		
Tier 3	68.1 (8.6)		
Percent Female Literacy			
Tier 1	92.9 (21.9)	6.493	0.000
Tier 2	79.6 (22.8)		
Tier 2 Watch	75.9 (22.9)		
Tier 3	74.6 (21.7)		

☐ References

Kendall, V. and Funk, T. 2011. *Child Exploitation and Trafficking: Examining the Global Challenges and US Responses*. Maryland: Rowman and Littlefield.

Lulo, S. 2013. Child exploitation and trafficking. *Criminal Justice*, 28(1), 63–65.

McCabe, K. and Manian, S. 2011. *Sex Trafficking: A Global Perspective*. Lanham, MD: Rowman and Littlefield/Lexington Books.

Sheldon, K. 2011. What we know about men who download child abuse image. *British Journal of Forensic Practice*, 13(4), 221–234.

US Department of State. 2015. Trafficking in Person Report, June 2014. Washington, D.C.: Office to Monitor and Combat Trafficking in Persons.

APPENDIX B: Internet Crimes Against Children, 2008 and 2014 (Abridged Report)

Bryce L. Coulter, B.A. and K.A. McCabe, Ph.D.

The Child Protection Act of 1984 was designed to address the production and distribution of child pornography. The Child Protection and Obscenity Enforcement Act of 1988 outlawed the distribution of child pornography over the Internet and forced producers of sexually explicit material to provide proof of age for the individuals involved. In 1996, both the Telecommunications Reform Act and the Child Pornography Protection Act were created to regulate information dispersed over the Internet including the regulation of pornography. In 2003, the Exploitation of Children Today Act (i.e., the Protection Act) was created to further strengthen laws prohibiting child pornography.

The information presented in this appendix was collected as part of a larger study on Internet crimes against children (ICAC) and is intended to be presented as a simple documentation of the change in ICAC over the years. The information displayed is cases data from 2008 and 2014. These data were provided by the Southern Virginia Internet Crimes Against Children Task Force (located within the Bedford County Sheriff's Office in Bedford, Virginia). This Task Force, established in 1998 through funding from the Department of Justice, was designed and implemented to combat the sexual exploitation of children over the Internet.

Results indicate an increase over the years in the proportion of child enticement cases. For clarity, child enticement is the use of the Internet to knowingly persuade, entice, or coerce a child younger than the age of 18 to meet for sexual acts or attempt to arrange such a meeting (Figure B.1). Also demonstrated through these data were an increase in the proportion of male victims (Figure B.2) and an increase in the use of sexting as related to ICSAC (Figure B.3).

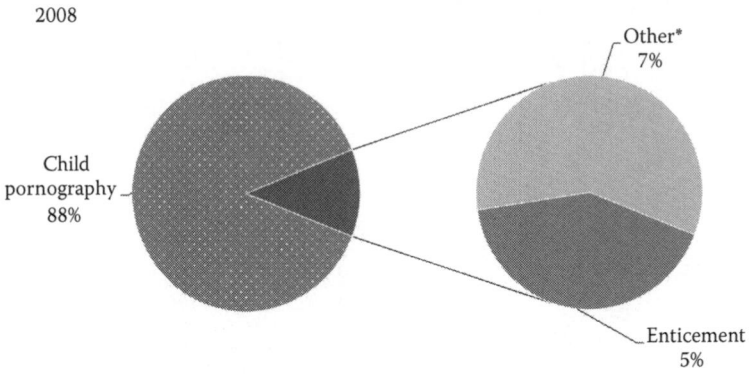

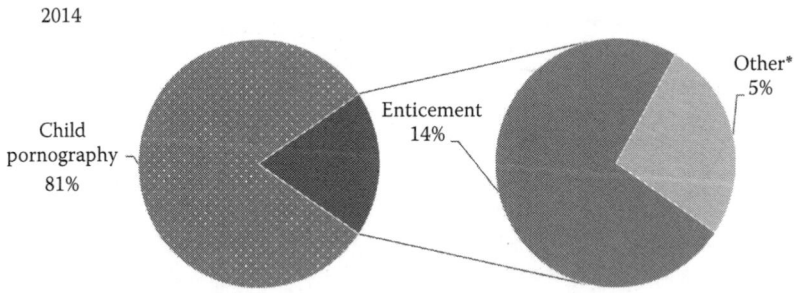

FIGURE B.1 ICAC—crime. *Other includes: child sexual molestation, obscenity, and child prostitution.

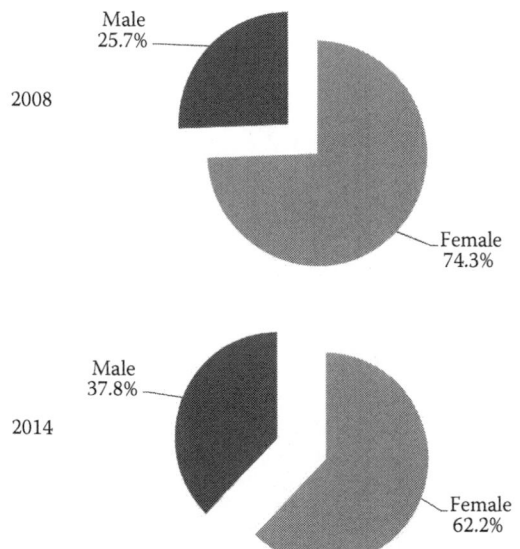

FIGURE B.2 ICAC—sex of victim.

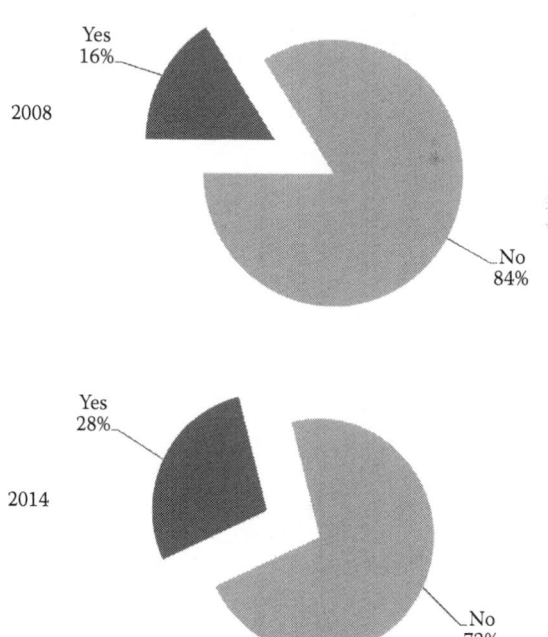

FIGURE B.3 ICAC—sexting.

APPENDIX C: Contact Information for Child Abuse Organizations

1. American Humane Association

   1400 16th Street NW, Suite 360

   Washington, D.C. 20036

   (800) 227-4645

   http://www.americanhumane.org

2. American Professional Society on the Abuse of Children

   940 N. E. 13th Street

   CHO 3B-3406

   Oklahoma City, OK 73104

   (614) 827-1321

   http://www.apsac.org

3. Association to Benefit Children

   419 East 86 Street

   New York, NY 10028

   (212) 831-1322

   http://www.a-b-c.org

4. Child Abuse Prevention Foundation

   9440 Ruffin Court, Suite 2

   San Diego, CA 92123

   (858) 278-4400

   http://www.capc-coco.org

5. Children's Bureau

   330 C. St, SW, Room 2068

   Washington, D.C. 20201

   (202) 205-8618

   http://www.acf.dhhs.gov/programs/cb/

6. Child Welfare League of America

   1726 M St NW, Suite 500

   Washington, D.C., 20036

   (202) 688-4200

   http://www.cwla.org

7. Disability, Abuse, and Personal Rights Project

   2100 Sawtelle Blvd, Suite 204

   Los Angeles, CA 90025

   (310) 473-6768

   http://www.disability-abuse.com

8. Head Start Bureau

   330 C. St, SW, Room 2018

   Washington, D.C. 20201

   (866) 763-6481

   http://www.acf.dhhs.gov/programs/hsb/

9. Kempe Children's Center

   13123 E 16th Avenue,

   Aurora, CO 80045

   (303) 864-5250

   http://www.kempecenter.org

10. National Alliance of Children's Trust and Prevention Funds'

    Alaska Children's Trust

    P.O. Box 92155

    Anchorage, AK 99509-2155

    (907) 248-7370

    http://www.ctfalliance.org/

11. National Association of Counsel for Children

    13123 E. 16th Avenue B390

    Aurora, CO 80045

    (303) 864-5320

    http://www.naccchildlaw.org

12. National Center for Missing & Exploited Children

    699 Prince Street

    Alexandria, VA 22314-3175

    (703) 224-2150

    http://www.missingkids.org

13. National Clearinghouse on Child Abuse and Neglect Information

    9300 Lee Highway,

    Fairfax, VA 22031-1207

    (703) 934-3603

    http://www.calib.com

14. National Committee to Prevent Child Abuse

    2950 Tennyson Street

    Denver, CO 80212

    (877) 224-8223

    http://www.childabuse.org

15. National Criminal Justice Reference Service

    P.O. Box 6000

    Rockville, MD 20849-6000

    (800) 851-3420

    http://www.ncjrs.org

16. National Data Archive on Child Abuse and Neglect

    College of Human Ecology

    Cornell University

    Ithaca, NY 14853

    (607) 255-7799

    http://www.ndacan.cornell.edu

17. National Exchange Club Foundation

    3050 Central Avenue

    Toledo, OH 43606

    (419) 535-3232

    http://www.nationalexchangeclub.org/foundation/

18. National Indian Child Welfare Association

    5100 S.W. Macadam Avenue, Suite 300

    Portland, OR 97239

    (503) 222-4044

    http://www.nicwa.org

19. Prevent Child Abuse America

    228 South Wabash Avenue

    10th Floor

    Chicago, IL 60604

    (312) 663-3520

    http://www.preventchildabuse.org

20. The Natural Child Project

    The Natural Child Project 3

    Gabriola Island, BC V0R 1X0

    Canada

    (866) 593-1547

    http://www.naturalchild.org

21. Internet Crimes Against Children

    10 West Edge Drive, Suite 106

    Durham, NH 03824

    (877) 798-7682

    http://www.icactaskforce.org/Pages/Home.aspx

22. National Human Trafficking Resource Center

    330 C Street, SW

    Washington, D.C. 20201

    (888) 373-7888

    http://www.traffickingresourcecenter.org/

23. Human Rights Watch

    350 Fifth Avenue, 34th Floor

    New York, NY 10118-3299

    (212) 290-4700

    http://www.hrw.org/topic/disability-rights

24. Center for Parent Information and Resources

    ℅ Statewide Parent Advocacy Network

    35 Halsey St, Fourth Floor

    Newark, NJ 07102

    http://www.parentcenterhub.org/

INDEX

A

Abductions, 159
Acting out, 106
Adam Walsh Child Protection and Safety
    Act, 152, 153
Age of consent, 42
AMBER Alert, 160–161
American Humane Association (AHA),
    61, 183
American Professional Society on the
    Abuse of Children, 183
Association to Benefit Children, 184

B

Baby talk, 20
Battered child syndrome, 4
Behavioral indicators
    cyberbullying, 141–142
    emotional abuse, 70–71
    neglect, 90–91
    physical abuse, 18–21
    sexting, 143
    sexual abuse, 38
Bilateral Border Safety Coalition, 119
Biological theory, 103
Brittle bone disease, 15
Bruises, 11–13
Burns, 13–14

C

CAPTA, see Child Abuse Prevention
    and Treatment Act
CASA, see Court Appointed Special
    Advocates

CDA, see Communications Decency Act
Center for Parent Information
    and Resources, 189
Chapter questions
    child trafficking, 128
    criminal justice responses, 171
    emotional abuse, 75
    neglect, 95
    physical abuse, 28
    sexual abuse, 55
    technology, child abuse and, 144
    theoretical explanations for child
        abuse, 111
Child abuse, introduction to, 1–8
    book purpose, 6–7
    child abuse defined, 2–3
    child fatalities, 3–5
        battered child syndrome, 4
        classification, 4
        definition, 3
        Munchausen syndrome by proxy, 4
        shaken baby syndrome, 4
        suicide, 4, 5
    history of child abuse, 5–6
Child abuse organizations, contact
    information for, 183–189
    American Humane Association, 183
    American Professional Society on the
        Abuse of Children, 183
    Association to Benefit Children, 184
    Center for Parent Information and
        Resources, 189
    Child Abuse Prevention Foundation,
        184
    Children's Bureau, 184
    Child Welfare League of America, 184

Disability, Abuse, and Personal Rights
    Project, 185
Head Start Bureau, 185
Human Rights Watch, 189
Internet Crimes Against Children, 188
Kempe Children's Center, 185
National Alliance of Children's Trust
    and Prevention Funds' Alaska
    Children's Trust, 185
National Association of Counsel
    for Children, 186
National Center for Missing & Exploited
    Children, 186
National Clearinghouse on Child
    Abuse and Neglect Information,
    186
National Committee to Prevent Child
    Abuse, 186
National Criminal Justice Reference
    Service, 187
National Data Archive on Child Abuse
    and Neglect, 187
National Exchange Club Foundation,
    187
National Human Trafficking Resource
    Center, 188
National Indian Child Welfare
    Association, 187
The Natural Child Project, 188
Prevent Child Abuse America, 188
Child Abuse Prevention and Treatment
    Act (CAPTA), 9, 136, 155
Child Abuse Prevention Foundation, 184
Child Fatality Review Boards, 84
Child pornography, 50–51
Child Pornography Act, 136
Child Pornography Protection Act, 179
Child Protection Act, 136, 179
Child Protection and Obscenity
    Enforcement Act of 1988, 179
Child Protection Enforcement Act, 136
Child Protective Services (CPS), 167,
    168–169
Children's Bureau, 184
Child Savers Movement, 150
Child trafficking, 52, 113–130
    chapter questions, 128
    convictions, 114
    damaged goods, girls viewed as, 123
    distinction between smuggling
        and trafficking, 115
    financial investment, 127
    how trafficking is facilitated, 121–122
    identification of cases, 115

labor trafficking, 118
legislative measures, 125–127
parents, 115, 122
profiling of victims, 116
questions for further thought, 128
sex trafficking, 120
why children are trafficked, 117–121
why children don't leave their captors,
    122–123
why child trafficking continues, 123–125
Child Welfare League of America, 184
Coalition Against Trafficking in Women,
    119
Code Adam alert, 152
Communications Decency Act (CDA), 133
Containment theory, 106
Corporal punishment, 9, 103
Corruption, 68–70
Court Appointed Special Advocates
    (CASA), 169–171
Courts, 161
    criminal, 162–163
    juvenile and adult, 161–162
    Supreme Court rulings, 136, 138, 163,
        164
    topic of liability in, 85
CPS, *see* Child Protective Services
Criminal justice responses, 149–174
    age of consent, 153–155
    AMBER Alert, 160–161
    chapter questions, 171
    Child Savers Movement, 150
    civil commitment orders, 163–164
    Court Appointed Special Advocates,
        169–171
        forensic nurse, 170
        foster care, 170–171
        guardian ad litem, 169
        victim advocate, 169–170
    courts, 161
    CPS, 168–169
    criminal court, 162–163
    HIV/STD testing, 155
    incarceration, 163
    juvenile and adult court, 161–162
    Juvenile Justice Delinquency
        Prevention Act (1974), 151–152
    key figures in child abuse, 164
    law enforcement, 165–168
        child abuse task force, 167
        crime prevention programs, 165
        follow-up investigation, 167
        juvenile officers, 166
        needs of the victim, 166

mandatory reporting laws, 155–158
Megan's Law, 152
mental health, 164–165
missing and exploited children,
159–160
problems for victims later in life, 165
Progressive Era, 150–151
questions for further thought, 172
rape kit, 170
sex offender registration, 152–153
statute of limitations, 158–159
Cupping, 14
Cutting, 18, 25, 71
Cyberbullying, 140–142
Cycle of violence, 103

D

Demonology, 99–100
Differential association, theory of, 105
Disability, Abuse, and Personal Rights
Project, 185
Dislocation, 15

E

Ecological theory, 106–107
Emotional abuse, 59–77
chapter questions, 75
corruption, 68–70
ignoring, 66–68
isolation, 63–64
property destruction, 70–74
abusers, 72–73
long-term consequences, 73–74
physical and behavioral indicators,
70–71
questions for further thought, 75
rejection, 61–63
terrorizing, 64–66
Explanations for child abuse,
see Theoretical explanations
for child abuse
Exploitation of Children Today Act, 179

F

Familial sexual abuse, 41–52
child pornography, 50–51
child trafficking, 52
combined families, 48
extrafamilial abuse, 48–49
father, 44–45
mother, 45–46
other family members, 47–48
pedophiles, 49–50
sex rings, 51–52
sexting, 51
sexual addicts, 49
sibling, 46–47
Family abductions, 159
Federal Bureau of Investigation's National
Crime Information Center, 160
Female genital mutilation (FGM), 37
Feminism, 109–110
Fetal alcohol syndrome, 85
Forensic nurse, 170
Foster care, 170–171
Fractures, 14–15
dislocation, 15
greenstick fracture, 15
spiral fracture, 14
subperiosteal fracture, 15

G

Greenstick fracture, 15

H

Head/internal injuries, 15–16
Head Start Bureau, 185
Human immunodeficiency virus (HIV),
154
-risky behaviors, 74
/STD testing, 155
Human Rights Watch, 189
Human trafficking (country demographics
as related to tier classification),
175–178
analysis of variance results, 177–178
female literacy, 175, 178
life expectancy, 175, 178
percent age 0–14, 175–178
poverty, 175, 177
tier classifications, 176–177
unemployment, 175, 177

I

Ignoring, 66–68
Incestuous rape, 43
Insanity defense, 102
Internet crimes against children (ICAC),
131, 179–181
Internet Crimes Against Children
(organization), 188
Isolation, 63–64

J

Jacob Wetterling Act, 152
Juvenile Court Act, 161
Juvenile Justice Delinquency Prevention
        Act (1974), 151
Juvenile officers, 166

K

Kansas v. Hendricks, 164
Kempe Children's Center, 185

L

Labor trafficking, 118
Law enforcement, 165–168
    child abuse task force, 167
    crime prevention programs, 165
    follow-up investigation, 167
    juvenile officers, 166
    needs of the victim, 166
Legislation
    Adam Walsh Child Protection
        and Safety Act, 152, 153
    Child Abuse Prevention and Treatment
        Act, 9, 136, 155
    Child Pornography Act, 136
    Child Pornography Protection Act, 179
    Child Protection Act, 136, 179
    Child Protection and Obscenity
        Enforcement Act of 1988, 179
    Child Protection Enforcement Act, 136
    Communications Decency Act, 133
    Exploitation of Children Today Act, 179
    Jacob Wetterling Act, 152
    Juvenile Court Act, 161
    Juvenile Justice Delinquency
        Prevention Act (1974), 151
    Megan's Law, 152
    Missing Children's Act of 1982, 160
    Prevention of Cruelty to Children Act
        of 1889, 6
    Prosecutorial Remedies and Other
        Tools to end the Exploitation of
        Children Today Act, 115, 126
    Romeo and Juliet laws, 154
    Sexual Exploitation of Children Act,
        136
    Telecommunications Reform Act, 133,
        179
    Trafficking Victims Protection Act, 125
    Trafficking Victims Protection
        Reauthorization Act, 116

Litigation
    Kansas v. Hendricks, 164
    United States v. Comstock, 164
    United States v. Satia and Nanji, 116

M

Medical examiners, 84
Megan's Law, 152
Mild neglect, 81
Missing Children's Act of 1982, 160
Moderate neglect, 81
Mongolian blue spots, 12
Munchausen syndrome by proxy,
        4, 23–24

N

National Alliance of Children's Trust
        and Prevention Funds' Alaska
        Children's Trust, 185
National Association of Counsel
        for Children, 186
National Center for Missing and Exploited
        Children, 136, 152, 186
National Child Abuse Prevention Week, 6
National Clearinghouse on Child Abuse
        and Neglect Information, 186
National Committee to Prevent Child
        Abuse, 186
National Crime Information Center
        (NCIC), 160
National Criminal Justice Reference
        Service, 187
National Data Archive on Child Abuse
        and Neglect, 187
National Exchange Club Foundation, 187
National Human Trafficking Resource
        Center, 188
National Indian Child Welfare
        Association, 187
The Natural Child Project, 188
Neglect, 79–97
    abusers, 91–93
    ages, 81
    behavioral indicators, 90–91
    chapter questions, 95
    Child Fatality Review Boards, 84
    consequences of, 93–94
    definition of, 79, 94
    educational neglect, 85–87
    emotional neglect, 87–88
    fetal alcohol syndrome, 85
    indicators of, 89
    legal standpoint, 86

medical examiners, 84
medical neglect, 83–85
mild neglect, 81
moderate neglect, 81
nonorganic failure to thrive syndrome, 84
physical indicators, 89–90
physical neglect, 82–83
questions for further thought, 95
severe neglect, 81
shock factor, 80
supervision neglect, 88–89
Nonorganic failure to thrive syndrome, 84
North American Man/Boy Love Association, 35
Not guilty by reason of insanity (NGRI), 103

O

Organizations, *see* Child abuse organizations, contact information for
Osteogenesis imperfecta, 15

P

Pedophiles, 49–50
Physical abuse, 9–31
  abusers, 21–26
    acquaintances, 25–26
    parents or caretakers, 21–24
    siblings, 24–25
  ages of victims, 10
  behavioral indicators, 18–21
    aggressive behaviors, 18
    baby talk, 20
    child starved for positive adult attention, 19
    destructive behaviors, 19
    extreme submission, 19
    potential for delinquency, 20
    social relationships, 20
  chapter questions, 28
  corporal punishment, 9
  definition, 28
  long-term effects, 26–27
    female survivors, 26
    insecurity, 27, 28
    male survivors, 26–27
    psychiatric disorders, 26
  Munchausen syndrome by proxy, 23–24
  other injuries, 16–18
  physical indicators, 11–18
    bruises, 11–13
    burns, 13–14

cutting, 18
fractures, 14–15
head/internal injuries, 15–16
questions for further thought, 28–29
shaken baby syndrome, 16
Physical indicators
  emotional abuse, 70–71
  neglect, 89–90
  physical abuse, 11–18
  sexual abuse, 35–38
Postpartum psychosis, 103–104
Post-traumatic stress disorder, 74, 109
Prevent Child Abuse America, 188
Prevention of Cruelty to Children Act of 1889, 6
Progressive Era, 150–151
Prosecutorial Remedies and Other Tools to end the Exploitation of Children Today (PROTECT) Act, 115, 126

Q

Questions for further thought
  child trafficking, 128
  criminal justice responses, 172
  emotional abuse, 75
  neglect, 95
  physical abuse, 28–29
  sexual abuse, 55
  technology, child abuse and, 145
  theoretical explanations for child abuse, 111

R

Rape kit, 170
Rational choice theory, 100
Rejection, 61–63
Romeo and Juliet laws, 154
Routine activities theory, 108

S

SANE, *see* Sexual assault nurse examiner
SBS, *see* Shaken baby syndrome
Severe neglect, 81
Sex rings, 51–52
Sexting, 51, 142–143, 181
Sextortion, 134
Sexual abuse, 33–58
  abusers, 41
  age of consent, 42
  behavioral indicators, 38
  bodily fluids, 36
  bruises, 36

chapter questions, 55
definition, 34
familial abuse, 41–52
    child pornography, 50–51
    child trafficking, 52
    combined families, 48
    extrafamilial abuse, 48–49
    father, 44–45
    mother, 45–46
    other family members, 47–48
    pedophiles, 49–50
    sex rings, 51–52
    sexting, 51
    sexual addicts, 49
    sibling, 46–47
fear of everyday activities, 38
female genital mutilation, 37
genital piercing, 37
incestuous rape, 43
long-term consequences, 52–54, 109
misperception, 36
physical indicators, 35–38
progression of sexual abuse, 38–40
questions for further thought, 55
statistics, 33
unreported incidents, 34
voyeurism, 37
Sexual assault nurse examiner (SANE), 170
Sexual Exploitation of Children Act, 136
Sexually transmitted diseases (STDs), 154
Shaken baby syndrome (SBS), 4, 16
Social disorganization, 107
Social Services, 168
Sociological theories, 104–109, see also
        Theoretical explanations for
        child abuse
    containment theory, 106
    differential association, 105
    ecological theory, 106–107
    routine activities theory, 108
    social disorganization, 107
Spiral fracture, 14
Splash burns, 13
STDs, see Sexually transmitted diseases
Subperiosteal fracture, 15
Suicide, 4, 5, 74

T

Technology, child abuse and, 131–148
    chapter questions, 144
    child pornography, 133–139
        behavioral indicators, 139
        home computer use, statistics on, 134

sextortion, 134
typologies, 135
voyeurism, 139
child solicitation, 139–140
cyberbullying, 140–142
dynamics, 144
offenders, 144
questions for further thought, 145
sexting, 142–143
Telecommunications Reform Act, 133, 179
Terrorizing, 64–66
Theoretical explanations for child abuse,
        99–112
    acting out, 106
    bad seed, child as, 100
    biological theory, 103
    chapter questions, 111
    Classical School, 100
    corporal punishment, 103
    crime-is-a-choice rationale, 100
    cycle of violence, 103
    demonology, 99–100
    feminism, 109–110
    intraindividual explanation, 101–104
        insanity defense, 102
        mental defect, 101
        personality, 102
        postpartum psychosis, 103–104
    lack of self-control, 106
    not guilty by reason of insanity, 103
    questions for further thought, 111
    rational choice theory, 100
    sociological theories, 104–109
        containment theory, 106
        differential association, 105
        ecological theory, 106–107
        routine activities theory, 108
        social disorganization, 107
Trafficking, see Child trafficking
Trafficking Victims Protection Act (TVPA),
        125
Trafficking Victims Protection
        Reauthorization Act (TVPRA), 116

U

United States v. Comstock, 164
United States v. Satia and Nanji, 116

V

Verbal threats, 65
Victim advocate, 169–170
Voyeurism, 37, 139

Made in the USA
Columbia, SC
24 January 2021